Approaches to Teaching Dostoevsky's *Crime and Punishment*

Approaches to Teaching Dostoevsky's *Crime and Punishment*

Edited by

Michael R. Katz

and

Alexander Burry

Modern Language Association of America

New York 2022

85 Broad Street, Suite 500, New York, New York 10004-2434
www.mla.org

To order MLA publications, visit mla.org/books. For wholesale and international orders, see mla.org/Bookstore-Orders.

The MLA office is located on the island known as Mannahatta (Manhattan) in Lenapehoking, the homeland of the Lenape people. The MLA pays respect to the original stewards of this land and to the diverse and vibrant Native communities that continue to thrive in New York City.

Approaches to Teaching World Literature 171
ISSN 1059-1133

Library of Congress Cataloging-in-Publication Data

Names: Katz, Michael R., editor. | Burry, Alexander, editor.
Title: Approaches to teaching Dostoevsky's Crime and punishment / edited by Michael R. Katz and Alexander Burry.
Description: New York : Modern Language Association of America, 2022. | Series: Approaches to teaching world literature, 1059-1133 ; 171 | Includes bibliographical references.
Identifiers: LCCN 2021050403 (print) | LCCN 2021050404 (ebook) | ISBN 9781603295772 (hardcover) | ISBN 9781603295789 (paperback) | ISBN 9781603295796 (EPUB)
Subjects: LCSH: Dostoyevsky, Fyodor, 1821–1881. Prestuplenie i nakazanie. | Dostoyevsky, Fyodor, 1821–1881—Study and teaching (Higher) | LCGFT: Essays. | Literary criticism.
Classification: LCC PG3325.P73 A67 2022 (print) | LCC PG3325.P73 (ebook) | DDC 891.73/3—dc23/eng/20211122
LC record available at https://lccn.loc.gov/2021050403
LC ebook record available at https://lccn.loc.gov/2021050404

CONTENTS

Introduction

Alexander Burry

In September 1865, Fyodor Mikhailovich Dostoevsky wrote to his publisher, M. N. Katkov,

> The idea of my story . . . is a psychological account of a crime. The action is topical, set in the current year. A young student of lower-middle-class origin, who has been expelled from the university, and who lives in dire poverty, succumbs—through thoughtlessness and lack of strong convictions—to certain strange, "incomplete" ideas that are floating in the air, and decides to get out of his misery once and for all. He resolves to kill an old woman . . . who lends out money for interest. . . .

This description of *Crime and Punishment* emphasizes one of the novel's key qualities: its sense of contemporaneity, its deep-rootedness in the fabric of its time. As a journalist, Dostoevsky had established two periodicals, *Time* and *Epoch*, in the years immediately preceding the writing of the novel. He constantly pored over newspapers and obsessively followed current events, and he felt that he understood better than anyone else the motivations for crimes like Raskolnikov's. Later in the same letter to Katkov, he reports several accounts of students committing similar crimes to justify the seeming oddity of his hero's murder. This sense of presentness invariably comes across to the reader of *Crime and Punishment*, who is absorbed in Raskolnikov's process of committing the crime, and then in its consequences. It is this quality that inspired reactions like Virginia Woolf's description of the excitement she experienced reading Dostoevsky, which seems as true today as when it was written in 1925:

> The novels of Dostoevsky are seething whirlpools, gyrating sandstorms, waterspouts which hiss and boil and suck us in. They are composed purely and wholly of the stuff of the soul. Against our wills we are drawn in, whirled round, blinded, suffocated, and at the same time filled with a giddy rapture. Out of Shakespeare there is no more exciting reading. (186)

Dostoevsky was born in Moscow on 11 November 1821, the second of seven children, to a military doctor who had earned nobility through service and a mother of merchant-class origins.[1] He read voraciously as a child and knew from his adolescence that he wanted to be a writer, but he acceded to his father's wishes that he go to St. Petersburg in 1837 to study at the Imperial Academy of Engineers. He resigned his commission shortly after graduation and began his literary career in 1843 with a translation of Honoré de Balzac's novel *Eugénie Grandet*. Two years later, he completed his own first novel, *Poor Folk*, which was lauded by the premier Russian literary critic, Vissarion Belinsky, and made

Dostoevsky an overnight literary sensation. Subsequent works such as *The Double* (1846), however, received more negative reviews, and Dostoevsky's career had lost its luster once he became involved with the Petrashevsky Circle, led by the socialist revolutionary Mikhail Butashevich-Petrashevsky, in the late 1840s. His arrest in 1849 as a conspirator in this circle occasioned a sharp break in his life that decisively impacted the rest of his career. Following a mock execution along with twenty other "Petrashevtsy," Dostoevsky served a commuted sentence of four years in prison in Omsk, Siberia, followed by exile in Semipalatinsk. Only through the intercession of his friend Baron Alexander Wrangel was Dostoevsky eventually able to return to European Russia in 1859 with his first wife, Maria Isaeva, whom he had married in Siberia.

Although the extent of Dostoevsky's spiritual transformation resulting from his Siberian experience has been exaggerated at times, there is no doubt that his years in prison and exile considerably altered his thinking and affected his creativity. His first great work following his return to Petersburg, *Notes from the House of the Dead* (1860–62), which recasts his prison experience in a thinly veiled fictional structure, contains musings on the nature of crime, the criminal, and the criminal's conscience that were to prove decisive for *Crime and Punishment*. *Notes from Underground* (1864), with its fierce polemic against the nihilist Nikolai Chernyshevsky's rational egoism, soon followed. Though the 1860s would yield some of Dostoevsky's most important work, they also brought many personal trials, including the death of his first wife and that of his favorite brother and collaborator, Mikhail; a disastrous affair with an "emancipated" woman, Apollinaria Suslova;[2] periodic epileptic seizures; and a gambling addiction that frequently rendered him penniless.

While writing *Crime and Punishment* for the journal *The Russian Messenger*, he had also promised a work to a publisher named Fyodor Stellovsky, on the condition that if it were not delivered on time, he would lose the rights to his own works for the next nine years. The help of an eighteen-year-old stenographer named Anna Snitkina enabled him to dictate his novella, *The Gambler*, in a month and meet the deadline, saving his career. Snitkina became his second wife, bore him four children (two of whom died at a very young age), and also stabilized his financial affairs. By the 1870s, Dostoevsky had once again become a celebrity, this time with connections in the court and the highest echelons of Russian society, as author of the popular *Writer's Diary* (a one-man periodical that contained fiction, literary criticism, religious and political articles, and other miscellanea) and a performer of public readings of his novel-in-progress *The Brothers Karamazov* (1878–80). He died of a pulmonary hemorrhage on 9 February 1881; his funeral was attended by tens of thousands of mourners.

Having come of age during the fierce Slavophile-Westernizer polemic of the 1840s about Russia's future course of development, Dostoevsky weighed in on intense political controversies throughout his career. His four major mature novels—*Crime and Punishment* (1866), *The Idiot* (1868), *Devils* (1871), and *The Brothers Karamazov*—each vigorously engage the political and religious currents of his era. Although he is often characterized as a Russian Orthodox conservative and monarchist who after his prison term in Siberia rejected the radical politics he had embraced in his youth, his religious beliefs and political ideas were in fact much more complex. He described his own faith as having "passed through a furnace of doubt" and often presents political radicals and atheists, including Raskolnikov, as sympathetic, conflicted characters who are still developing at the conclusions of his novels.

Crime and Punishment originated in two novels: one Dostoevsky originally titled *The Drunkards*, which focused on the Marmeladov family, and the other a first-person confessional novella of a murderer recounting his crime. The two conceptions eventually merged, and Dostoevsky replaced the first-person narrator with an omniscient narrator who often reports as though from within Raskolnikov's consciousness, hence the frequent use of interior monologue from the hero's perspective. The novel's sense of presentness comes in part from this switch of tenses from past to present, and also in large measure from the author's focus on contemporary ideologies that were sweeping through Russia. Raskolnikov's murder takes as its starting point the general philosophy of nihilism, derived from thinkers such as Chernyshevsky and Dmitry Pisarev, left-wing radicals whose conviction that the Russian autocracy needed to be destroyed and replaced with a socialist utopia strongly disturbed Dostoevsky.

Dostoevsky's focus on disaffected, obsessive outsiders living in extreme, often impoverished circumstances in *Crime and Punishment* and other works led him to create an innovative style known as fantastic realism, which contrasted with the rural settings, wealthier characters, and slow-moving time generally featured in the novels of his great realist rivals, Ivan Turgenev and Leo Tolstoy. *Crime and Punishment*, set in St. Petersburg, Peter the Great's intentionally Westernized "window to Europe," is emblematic of this type of urban realism. In engaging the latest radical beliefs and depicting their spread among Russian youth, Dostoevsky's novels also convey an unsurpassed sense of contemporaneity and prophetic understanding of the potential real-world consequences of radicalism. By an extraordinary coincidence, only days after the first installment of *Crime and Punishment* appeared, a student named A. M. Danilov committed a murder that closely resembled Raskolnikov's killing of an old pawnbroker.

A century and a half after its publication, *Crime and Punishment* continues to enjoy worldwide popularity and a unique status among Russian novels in the English-speaking world. It is one of the most frequently taught Russian works at the undergraduate level. Virtually all Russian and Slavic programs offer the novel as part of literature survey courses. Many English and world literature college courses include the novel as well. *Crime and Punishment* is also taught quite often as part of the secondary school literature curriculum. It is in high demand among book clubs, reading groups, and study circles. Lists of questions and discussion guides to assist general readers are readily available. A recent check of *Goodreads* indicates that there are almost 700,000 ratings for *Crime and Punishment* and nearly 22,000 reviews of the novel. *Google* cites over 1,700,000 hits for the title, and amazon.com yields over 3,000 results. As of July 2021, Dostoevsky has over 2.2 million "likes" on *Facebook* and the novel itself has more than 393,000 (Tolstoy's *Anna Karenina*, by comparison, has only 168,000 "likes"). Moreover, *Crime and Punishment* has a way of appearing in important contexts outside the literary world. In a curious twist of fate in the novel's reputation, when the whistleblower Edward Snowden was restricted to the transit area of Sheremetevo Airport in Moscow in 2013, his lawyer thoughtfully provided him with appropriate reading material to occupy his time and prepare him for what might turn out to be a long stay in Russia. He presented Snowden with works by three Russian writers, including only one novel: Dostoevsky's *Crime and Punishment*.

Crime and Punishment may be the most frequently taught and read work of Russian literature, but including the novel in the classroom poses several major challenges to instructors and students alike. First there is the problem of the book's length, as opposed to other writers' short stories and Turgenev's more compact, two-hundred-page novel *Fathers and Children* (a.k.a. *Fathers and Sons*). Students have grown unaccustomed to reading in general, and to reading lengthy texts in particular. But, as Dostoevsky's letter quoted above indicates, this book is fundamentally a murder mystery: the question that students will seek to answer is not "Who done it?" since the murderer is known from the very beginning. Rather, the operative question is "Why did he do it?" And that search for a motive is a powerful incentive to students to tackle a long narrative, especially since the definitive answer does not appear until Raskolnikov's conversation with Sonya in part 5, and the legal outcome of his crimes is not revealed until the epilogue.

The Russian system of names, too, with its patronymics, gendered last names, diminutives, and use of the first name and patronymic in polite conversation, creates unusual difficulties in a novel with more than forty major and minor characters, quite a few of whom are referred to by different versions of their names at various points. Moreover, Dostoevsky employs the device of "speaking names," which indicate some quality of the character. The most significant of these is the hero's surname, Raskolnikov: the Russian root is *raskol*, which means "schism," alluding to the famous split in the Russian Orthodox Church that occurred in the seventeenth century. *Raskolnik* means "schismatic," and *Raskolnikov* means "descended from the schismatics." Michael Katz provides a list of characters with the meanings of their names in "Materials."

As one of the many Russian works set in St. Petersburg, *Crime and Punishment* is striking in its numerous references to and detailed, precise descriptions of various streets, canals, buildings, parks, and other locations in the city; the novel in essence adumbrates a map of a large part of St. Petersburg. Dostoevsky uses the names of these streets, squares, rivers, canals, and so forth to locate the action of *Crime and Punishment*. The "Materials" section of this volume includes a map of the major locations mentioned as well as notes on the significance of each. Observing the difficulty of conveying the novel's St. Petersburg atmosphere to students who have never been to the city, Emily Johnson, in her essay, examines ways to use ethnographic sketches, other Petersburg works, and slides to illustrate Dostoevsky's milieu.

Dostoevsky's dense intertextuality can also pose a challenge to readers and teachers. *Crime and Punishment* contains frequent significant references to biblical texts, Russian and world literature, the writer's biography, current events, and other topics with which a well-educated Russian reader of the time would have been familiar. Many of these references, though, are unfamiliar to the average American reader. Each of them, however, no matter how seemingly tangential, plays a potentially important role in understanding key ideas and themes of the novel. Several sections are difficult to understand without knowledge of Chernyshevsky's utopian revolutionary novel *What Is to Be Done?* and other works by radical ideologists of Dostoevsky's time (more on this below). Dostoevsky makes considerable allusions to other writers, including Alexander Pushkin, Nikolai Gogol, and Balzac. Several of our contributors explore some of the subtexts Dostoevsky employs. Jamie Brummer and Karen Smith each examine the relevance of Edgar Allan Poe, whose works Dostoevsky translated, for *Crime and Punishment*. Brummer discusses the blurry relationship between inner struggles and external circumstances for Raskolnikov and the narrator of Poe's "The Tell-Tale Heart." Smith, referring to the same work, demonstrates how the dialogue Poe's first-person narrator conducts with the reader becomes internalized in Raskolnikov. Priscilla Meyer analyzes the impact of Balzac's *Père Goriot*, the Bible, and Dostoevsky's own prison memoir, *Notes from the House of the Dead*, on the novel.

Crime and Punishment, like all Dostoevsky's novels, stands out for its complex narrative. As mentioned, the narrator frequently reports from within Raskolnikov's mind, meaning that the reader experiences much of the action by way of the hero's subjective impressions. The narrative itself can be difficult to keep track of, as Raskolnikov interacts continually with other characters, many of whom reflect aspects of his personality and ideological background. Moreover, it is complicated by the subplot involving Svidrigailov, with his efforts to spy on Raskolnikov and gain access to Dunya. As Chloë Kitzinger demonstrates, students may find maps useful in thinking beyond sequential reading and making connections between the various characters Raskolnikov interacts with, enabling them to create visual representations of the narrative and develop their own paths through the novel. Vadim Shneyder focuses on the role of money in shaping the everyday experiences of all characters and linking particular characters to one another. For Robin Feuer Miller, the extreme centeredness of the narrative on Raskolnikov can obscure the significant role in it of seeming "trifles." Her essay encourages instructors to highlight the important, though often unnoticed, role that children play in this novel, and to consider what they can tell us about the larger problem of good and evil most often explored through the main plot event of murder.

Dostoevsky's style of fantastic realism blurs the boundaries between reality and the world of dreams, which can make the narrative difficult to follow at times. The sequence at the end of part 3, in which Raskolnikov, after meeting the tradesman who calls him a murderer, dreams of following that tradesman and unsuccessfully reenacting the murder, then wakes to see the ghostly Svidrigailov in his room, exemplifies the shadowy line between dream and reality. As Emma Lieber notes in her essay, Dostoevsky's dreamlike quality pertains not only to the actual dreams in *Crime and Punishment* but also to crowd scenes of waking life. This fantastic realism complicates the novel in another way as well: Dostoevsky focuses significantly more than his contemporaries on the lower strata of urban society, portraying poor tradespeople, students, alcoholics, prostitutes, and criminals, in extraordinary, desperate economic and psychological states. He not only displays this wide range of social classes but also allows characters from all of them to express unique world views. The critic and philosopher Mikhail Bakhtin thus viewed Dostoevsky's works as a series of "polyphonic novels," in which the author occupies the same position as his characters, rather than monologically imposing his own views on them. In this light, even a lowly tradesman, drunkard, or prostitute potentially carries a worldview that occupies as integral a place in the novel's structure as that of a member of the gentry. Bakhtin also interpreted the characters' views as in the process of being shaped rather than fully formed, and in continual dialogue with each other. Readers interpreting *Crime and Punishment* in this light, viewing Raskolnikov as a character who is still developing his ideas, must consider which other characters are evoked at different points in his dialogue and interior monologue. Caryl Emerson addresses Bakhtin's importance in her essay while also pointing out the limitations of his theory.

Crime and Punishment is also one of the world's great psychological novels. The narrator places the reader immediately in Raskolnikov's consciousness, and we are privy to his thinking—and, for shorter time periods, that of characters like Svidrigailov and Razumikhin—for a good portion of the novel. Character development is a key aspect of the realist novel, but in Dostoevsky's works as much of it takes place through psychological transformation as by way of outward changes and events. Several of our contributors explore this phenomenon. Gary Saul Morson notes the strangeness of the fact that Raskolnikov cannot say why he committed the murder, pointing out that students who try to decode his motivations are engaged in the same psychological quest as the hero. Yuri Corrigan claims that Raskolnikov and Svidrigailov in particular are faced with inner turmoil that constantly threatens to rise to the surface of their consciousness: these characters have a choice of accessing this deeply buried material or avoiding it. Corrigan views this as a model for students in search of a healthy inner life in what he refers to as a "postpsychoanalytic age." Emma Lieber, by contrast, proposes putting the novel in dialogue with psychoanalytic theories of Freud and Lacan. She uses classroom analysis of Raskolnikov's dreams and Porfiry Petrovich's interrogation of him to suggest that Dostoevsky encodes the process of psychoanalysis in the novel.

As a political novel, *Crime and Punishment* participates intensely in the central controversies of Dostoevsky's day. Turgenev's aforementioned *Fathers and Children* occasioned two opposing radical responses, each of which Dostoevsky addresses in *Crime and Punishment.* Turgenev's portrait of Evgeny Bazarov, a nihilist who rejects traditional art, philosophy, class relations, and government and religious authorities, divided critics; those on the left saw Bazarov (incorrectly) as a lampoon of the radical journalist and critic Nikolai Dobroliubov. Chernyshevsky, in part as a corrective to what he viewed as Turgenev's demeaning portrait of nihilists, set out to portray the new men and women with greater accuracy in his 1863 novel *What Is to Be Done?* He depicted a heroine, Vera Pavlovna, who liberates herself from the tyranny of her mother's home through marriage to one of the "new men," Dmitry Lopukhov, and, by establishing sewing cooperatives, manages to employ other seamstresses and fashion a communal life at great profit. While Chernyshevsky focused on the creation of a new, utopian society largely through mass movements toward greater class and gender equality, a more radical group of nihilists in the mid-1860s, led by Pisarev, favored a revolution led by "higher" individuals. Unlike Chernyshevsky, Pisarev interprets Bazarov more positively as an emancipated individual who is aware of his superiority to the lowly masses and is able to step beyond normal boundaries without moral qualms. Only Bazarov's personal taste, for Pisarev, prevents him from robbing and murdering for the benefit of humanity.

In *Crime and Punishment*, Dostoevsky explores both of these types of nihilism. Although *Notes from Underground* represents his most direct rebuttal to *What Is to Be Done?*, a continuing dialogue with this novel can also be found in *Crime and Punishment.* Midway through part 1, Raskolnikov is struck by a conversation between a student and an officer in which the student claims that murdering the pawnbroker Alyona Ivanovna would improve the lives of thousands of people victimized by her; this notion of justifying the loss of one life by benefits to others, which uncannily recalls Raskolnikov's own thoughts on his murder, clearly derives from Chernyshevsky's utilitarianism. Similarly, the young radical Andrei Lebezyatnikov's awkward, inarticulate expression of Chernyshevsky's concern for the "woman question," or the possibility of equal rights and roles for women, represents a parody of the real-life nihilist's ideas on gender egalitarianism. Raskolnikov's article "On Crime," discussed by him, his friend Razumikhin, the detective Porfiry Petrovich, and the police clerk Zametov in part 3, on the other hand, reflects the ominous, more recent ideas of Pisarev. Raskolnikov's contrasting of the extraordinary man to the unthinking masses, and his conviction that the former even have the right to commit murder to advance humanity, are drawn from this new and, from Dostoevsky's perspective, more dangerous political notion.

Several authors in our volume explore the ramifications of Dostoevsky's political ideas in *Crime and Punishment.* Gary Saul Morson connects Raskolnikov's deliberations and near-paralysis when deciding whether to commit murder to his attraction to three political theories: utilitarianism, moral nihilism, and the idea of the extraordinary man, all of which are in fact mutually contradictory. Helena Goscilo focuses on teaching the novel through a prism of gender, noting that while Dostoevsky was an opponent of the "woman question" propounded by Chernyshevsky and others, and seems to favor traditional male and female roles, students who carefully analyze his characters will see that in fact he undermines the binary opposition of active male and passive female throughout the novel. Rachel Stauffer explores the issue of poverty in the novel, reading *Crime and Punishment* through the lens of social justice education in order to help students consider the intersections of class, social status, cultural capital, labor, and art in Dostoevsky's time and in his characterization of Raskolnikov, and in the process to deepen their perceptions of privilege and poverty in their own society.

Throughout the novel, Dostoevsky proposes Orthodox Christianity as a moral and ethical alternative to nihilism. *Crime and Punishment* contains various scenes that focus on Christianity, such as Marmeladov's eloquent drunken rant to Raskolnikov, culminating in his conviction that Christ will forgive "unfortunates" such as himself; Porfiry Petrovich's's questions to Raskolnikov regarding his belief in God, the New Jerusalem, and the raising of Lazarus; and Sonya's reading of the Gospel account of the raising of Lazarus with Raskolnikov. The novel's various biblical references necessitate considerable discussion, especially because Dostoevsky is just as likely to put them in the mouths of secondary characters, such as the drunkard Marmeladov, as to express them through major characters such as Porfiry Petrovich or the Christ-like heroine, Sonya. In addition, many of the Christian references, such as Dostoevsky's description of Sonya and Lizaveta's holy foolishness and Sonya's final bit of advice that Raskolnikov bow at the crossroads, kiss the earth, and confess to the public, involve specifically Orthodox customs and gestures that may be unfamiliar to Westerners. Moreover, the biblical references themselves can be quite multilayered in terms of function and meaning. Olga Meerson's essay helps clarify some of Dostoevsky's Orthodox references and their significance in *Crime and Punishment*, explaining that several of Dostoevsky's quotations would have been understood by readers of his time as being liturgical as well as scriptural.

Beyond the novel's specific religious content, Dostoevsky raises broader moral and ethical issues that have provoked and engaged students and instructors for generations. Ultimately, Raskolnikov learns of alternative ways of life from characters like Sonya, Razumikhin, and Porfiry Petrovich that might serve him better than his commitment to proving himself an extraordinary man. He comes to the realization that he is not extraordinary, and that he can embrace Sonya's spiritual love, through her words and those of Porfiry Petrovich; in other words, from what Bakhtin describes as dialogic processes. For Caryl Emerson, however, despite Bakhtin's great insights, his focus on the dialogic word can have the effect of obscuring Dostoevsky's ethical hierarchy; she suggests a focus on the "human face" as well as the "human word," and offers examples of recent criticism that accomplishes this task. Ani Kokobobo discusses ways of teaching ethics in the novel, examining such topics as Raskolnikov's murder and his evaluation of the pawnbroker as a "louse" in terms of the ethics proposed in such works as Immanuel Kant's *Foundations of the Metaphysics of Morals*, Jeremy Bentham's *The Principles of Morals and Legislation*, and John Stuart Mill's "Greatest Happiness Principle." Brian Armstrong explores the ways philosophy can be used in the classroom to help make the novel more cogent, applying epistemological, metaphysical, and metaethical concepts to understand Raskolnikov's attempts to explain why he committed the murder; at the same time, he shows how the concept of conscience, so important for the novel, can in turn contribute to contemporary philosophical debates.

Remarkably, the same sense of currentness characterizing the novel has transferred to other time periods and cultures, as *Crime and Punishment* has enthralled countless non-Russian writers and artists. It has inspired a variety of reworkings in other national literatures. Perhaps no nineteenth-century writer—Russian or otherwise—has had a greater influence on twentieth- and twenty-first-century literature. Albert Camus, whose entire literary and philosophical oeuvre can be seen as a response to the Russian novelist's works, famously claimed that the real nineteenth-century prophet was Dostoevsky, not Karl Marx. The numerous works of the past century and a half that imaginatively rework *Crime and Punishment* include T. S. Eliot's "The Love Song of Alfred J. Prufrock," Joseph Conrad's *Under Western Eyes*, Richard Wright's *Native Son* and *The Outsider*, Ralph Ellison's *The Invisible Man*, and Bernard Malamud's *The Assistant*. More recently, Boris Akunin's *F. M.* testifies to the novel's ongoing relevance for contemporary writers. Two of our contributors, Susan McReynolds and Karen Smith, explore the impact of *Crime and Punishment* on later writers. McReynolds reads the Russian novel through Franz Kafka's *The Trial*, noting that in his reading of *Crime and Punishment*, Kafka focuses on one of the most disturbing aspects of the novel: the frequency with which male characters such as Raskolnikov and Svidrigailov prey on poor, vulnerable, young females. Smith discusses comparing Dostoevsky's novel with Camus's *The Stranger*, Toni Morrison's *Beloved*, and Margaret Atwood's *Alias Grace*, along with the TV shows *Dexter* and *Dead to Me*, to unify a comparative literature course around the theme of the outlaw figure.

The creative responses generated by *Crime and Punishment* also include nearly forty transpositions of the novel into cinema, beginning soon after the invention of the medium with three short films in the first decade of the twentieth century. The first two decades of the present century have seen several new reworkings. These include the Russian director Dmitry Svetozarov's TV serial and a feature film by the Kazakh director Darezhan Omirbaev. Moreover, numerous filmmakers, such as Woody Allen in *Match Point*, have incorporated the novel into their films as a key subtext. In my essay, I examine the history of film adaptation of *Crime and Punishment*, focusing on how cinematic reworkings of the novel, through the very changes and additions directors make, can help students think about what elements (in their opinion) are most crucial to the novel.

Not surprisingly, *Crime and Punishment* has continued to attract the interest of translators attempting to serve the novel's many English-speaking readers. Four new English translations have appeared in the past decade by Oliver Ready, Michael Katz, and Nicholas Pasternak Slater. Thus, despite the continuing popularity of Richard Pevear and Larissa Volokhonsky's 1992 version (generally assigned in the 1993 paperback format), American and British translators continue to search for solutions to the various challenges the novel poses, and the fact that the market can accommodate this many translations testifies to the novel's appeal for students, teachers, and scholars of literature. Two contributors to this volume focus on how these various translations can be used to enrich discussions of the novel. As Carol Apollonio points out in her essay, the choice of translation is one of crucial importance from a practical standpoint, one that must be front and center in a discussion of teaching approaches to the novel; and the existence of competing versions offers the instructor wonderful opportunities for exploring different possible interpretations of the novel as well. Cassio de Oliveira, similarly, suggests that comparing parallel translations of important passages can help students develop close readings and explore new interpretations; he also notes that translation itself becomes a theme in the novel (the Gospel Sonya reads to Raskolnikov is in Russian translation rather than Church Slavonic).

Liberal arts education has gradually been transformed, over the past three to four decades, from lectures accompanied by notes on a chalkboard to a much more interactive, discussion-oriented, and technologically sophisticated approach to teaching and learning. Our volume offers a variety of ways in which instructors can apply these new developments to classroom teaching of *Crime and Punishment*. Benjamin Rifkin provides a series of discussion activity frameworks that could be productively used to teach the novel. These include "think-pair-square-share," in which students share their impressions of the novel first in a pair and then in a group of four students, and "role play," in which students can act out different roles from *Crime and Punishment* in a talk show, trial, or publicity campaign. José Vergara suggests asking students to perform the various moments of pregnant silence in *Crime and Punishment*, such as the silences between Raskolnikov and Zametov in their exchange at the Crystal Palace tavern, in order to open up discussions about the function of silence in the novel, and how it relates to Dostoevsky's particular conception of realism.

The early twenty-first century has witnessed an explosion of various digital media available to students and instructors, and this has revolutionized the classroom. Katherine Bowers demonstrates how digital media can be useful in enabling students both to engage with the text and to develop their technology skills, offering examples of projects involving research into Dostoevsky's life, the Petersburg setting, and mapping the novel's narrative. Kate Holland explores the possible uses of *Twitter* for the classroom, describing how she introduces her students to the project @RodionTweets, which features scholars tweeting from Raskolnikov's point of view over a period of two years, and then assigns them to write tweets by other characters in the novel. This allows students to understand the novel in relation to the media of its time, and to build knowledge and perspectives on the way to writing a traditional paper. Chloë Kitzinger's aforementioned essay, with her description of the use of the program *Gephi* to map characters, also introduces an innovative digital project that can be used in the classroom. Moreover, the possible environments that can serve as classrooms have changed, as Meyer demonstrates in her discussion of teaching inmates at a prison near her home institution of Wesleyan University.

Like other volumes in this series, *Approaches to Teaching Dostoevsky's* Crime and Punishment is divided into two parts: "Materials" and "Approaches." The "Materials" section, which aims to make students and instructors aware of the vast resources available on the novel, includes information about Russian editions and English translations of the novel, a map of St. Petersburg that includes all locations mentioned in the novel, a list of character names and an explanation of the Russian naming system, analysis of key scenes of the novel, and a select list of criticism on the novel. Part 2, "Approaches," consists of twenty-four essays, written by leading and emerging scholars and teachers of *Crime and Punishment*.

Each of the sections of essays offers ways in which instructors at all levels can addresses the various challenges *Crime and Punishment* provides and find new ways to explore its ongoing relevance. We recognize that there have been many approaches to interpreting the novel in the first century and a half of its existence and that new pedagogical techniques of our time provide yet newer, fresher ways to study the work. We have endeavored to provide a selection of essays that both encompass a variety of teaching tools and address many of Dostoevsky's key themes.

Since *Crime and Punishment* is regularly taught at different levels and in diverse contexts, our essays attempt to provide a variety of instructor perspectives. Some essays (on teaching the novel to high school students, or on teaching it along with other works, for example) will be particularly useful for those who teach at a specific level or want to use a particular approach. However, all the essays in the volume can be mutually useful as well: for instance, college teachers may be interested in the challenges that face high school students who read the work before arriving in their classroom; a teacher looking to include the novel in a comparative literature course may wonder how the novel interrelates with other Russian writings. The volume ranges very far in content, too, from fresh close readings of the novel to comparative discussions of the novel in relation to other literature and essays that explore the novel in the light of other disciplines.

We begin with a section entitled "Major Themes" that encourages instructors to challenge the received ways of understanding the novel. This part includes Miller's essay on the frequently unnoticed role of children in the novel, Morson's exploration of Dostoevsky's extraordinarily original depiction of Raskolnikov's state of mind, and Corrigan's discussion of Raskolnikov's struggle with his inner, repressed self. The section concludes with Emerson's critical examination of Bakhtinian theory, which has been an invaluable tool for teachers, and recent alternative approaches to the novel.

Students and instructors need to appreciate the different socioeconomic, political, and cultural contexts in which Dostoevsky wrote, and the second section, "Understanding the Novel's Contexts," explores some of these circumstances. It includes the aforementioned essays by Goscilo on gender in the novel, Johnson on teaching students about Petersburg, Shneyder on the economic circumstances of Raskolnikov and other characters, and Stauffer's examination of the novel through the prism of social justice education. The section closes with Meerson's discussion of Orthodox liturgical subtexts.

Given the combination of Dostoevsky's own aforementioned intertextuality and the stunning number of writers, styles, and movements influenced by him, our third section, "Genre and Comparison with Other Fiction," will offer teachers ways to approach *Crime and Punishment* through other literary works. The section includes McReynolds's reading of *Crime and Punishment* through Kafka's *The Trial*, Brummer's essay on Dostoevsky and Poe, Smith's analysis of Raskolnikov as part of the outlaw archetype, and Meyer's discussion of the roles of Balzac, the Bible, and Dostoevsky's own *Notes from the House of the Dead* in the novel. Dostoevsky's works stretch the boundaries of discipline as well, and thus the section also includes approaches to teaching the novel through other relevant fields: philosophy (Armstrong), ethics (Kokobobo), and psychoanalysis (Lieber).

Our fourth section, "Classroom Contexts," focuses on new communicative and technological approaches to teaching. It includes the essays on digital media by Bowers and Holland, Kitzinger's discussion of the program *Gephi*, and Rifkin's examination of discussion-based learning frameworks. The fifth and final section, "Translations and Adaptations," explores the transformation of *Crime and Punishment* into other forms, with the contributions by Apollonio and de Oliveira on translation, my essay on film adaptations, and Vergara's examination of reading dramatic scenes from the novel.

The editors feel that all readers should survey "Materials" after reading this introduction. After that, readers should feel free to pick and choose from among the many essays in whatever order they prefer. Some of the essays deal specifically with classroom techniques (e.g., discussion-based learning; performing scenes); others share the experience of teaching *Crime and Punishment* to different audiences (such as students in high school or in maximum-security prisons). Readers will have divergent interests and should use the volume as they see fit. We hope that our selection of essays will offer something of interest to everyone.

Rather than insisting on citing one translation of the novel, the editors decided to allow contributors to use whichever translation they preferred. We follow the BGN/PCGN 1947 system of transliteration from Cyrillic, with the exception of common proper and geographic names, for which we follow convention and render them in a form that is likely to be most familiar to English-speaking readers. Thus we refer to Fёdor Dostoevskiy as Fyodor Dostoevsky and to Moskva as Moscow.

NOTES

1. I have used New Style dates for Dostoevsky's birth and death in this introduction. Russia used the Julian (Old Style) calendar until 1918, when it switched to the Gregorian (New Style) calendar. The Old Style is still often used to describe dates in Dostoevsky scholarship.

2. The term "emancipated" was commonly used in Russia at the time to refer to a woman who, influenced by the works of Chernyshevsky and others, demanded equal rights with men.

Part One

MATERIALS

Editions and Translations

There are two recommended Russian editions of Fyodor Dostoevsky's *Crime and Punishment*, one published in the outstanding series Literary Monuments (Литературные памятники; Literaturnye pamyatniki) in Moscow in 1970, and the other in volume 6 of the *Complete Collected Works in Thirty Volumes* (Полное собрание сочинений в тридцати томах; *Polnoe sobranie sochinenii v tridtsati tomakh*), published along with volume 7, which includes the many manuscript versions of the novel, in 1973. Both editions are copiously annotated and contain valuable information for readers of Russian.

Crime and Punishment was the author's second work to be translated into English after his prison memoir, *Notes from the House of the Dead*, which appeared the year of his death (1881). Today, editions in English translated by Michael Katz (2019, 2018), Nicholas Pasternak Slater (2017), Oliver Ready (2015), Constance Garnett (2001 [first published 1914]), Richard Pevear and Larissa Volokhonsky (1993), David McDuff (1991), Sidney Monas (1968), Jessie Coulson (1953), and David Magarshack (1951) are in print and available for purchase.[1]

Although one of the editors of this MLA volume is among the translators listed here, we do not endorse any one particular version for teaching, and the contributors to this volume cite a variety of editions. Below we include a list of names and places mentioned in the novel to assist the reader with what can be a baffling assortment at first. Spellings may differ from those used in the volume's essays.

Names and Places

The Russian system of names can be somewhat forbidding to a reader of English. Russian names seem long, and each one typically consists of three parts: the first name, which can appear in numerous forms, diminutive, affectionate, and even pejorative; the patronymic, derived from the father's first name and equivalent to "son of . . ." or "daughter of . . ." according to the sex of the child; and the last name or surname, which is also gender-marked by its ending. Thus, the hero of *Crime and Punishment* is called Rodion (Rodya) Romanovich Raskolnikov, while his sister is Avdotya (Dunya) Romanovna Raskolnikova. A list of characters, including the various forms of their names, is included at the end of part 1.

Literary characters are often given "speaking names"—names that themselves convey meaning. Thus, the hero's surname, Raskolnikov, is derived from the root *raskol*, meaning "split" or "dissent," and was the word used to describe the great schism in the Russian Orthodox Church when a group of so-called Old Believers persisted in maintaining the liturgical and ritual practices of the Church as they existed prior to the reforms of Patriarch Nikon of Moscow between 1652 and 1666. The word *raskolnik* means "schismatic" or "dissenter"; hence *raskolnikov* would mean someone descended from the schismatics. A list of the meanings of Dostoevsky's "speaking names" is also included at the end of part 1. Both of these lists can be copied and distributed to students as an aid to reading the novel.

Crime and Punishment is the most topographical of Dostoevsky's works. The capital of St. Petersburg is evident throughout the action. The city was founded in 1703 by Peter the Great on the Gulf of Finland in a marshy region around the river Neva, which flows westward into the Baltic Sea. Petersburg is crisscrossed by smaller rivers and canals with many bridges. The names of streets, squares, and bridges occur frequently in the novel. One need only cite the very first sentence to see an example of this sense of locale: "In the beginning of July, during an extremely hot spell, towards evening, a young man left his tiny room, which he sublet from some tenants who lived in Stolyarnyi Lane, stepped out onto the street, and slowly, as if indecisively, set off towards the Kokushkin Bridge" 'В начале июля, в чрезвычайно жаркое время, под вечер, один молодой человек вышел из своей каморки, которую нанимал от жильцов в С—м переулке, на улицу и медленно, как бы в нерешимости, отправился к К—ну мосту' (*Crime* 3; *Prestuplenie* 5).[2] A map has been provided which indicates important places in the novel and in Petersburg.

It is important to keep in mind that *Crime and Punishment* was first published in monthly installments in the journal *The Russian Herald* in 1866. A chart of the serialization of the novel that indicates the plot event that concludes each installment can be found in the Norton Critical Edition of the novel, edited and translated by Michael Katz (2019).

Recommended Reading

The sources listed below are limited to works in English and are divided into several categories.

Russia and Russian Literature

A useful general reference is S. V. Utechin's *Concise Encyclopedia of Russia*, covering many aspects of Russia and Russian life. The entries are condensed and easily accessible and can provide a good introduction to many topics. *The Cambridge Encyclopedia of Russia and the Soviet Union* is another collection of more detailed articles on a wide range of subjects (Brown et al.). An invaluable reference work for Russian literature is Victor Terras's *Handbook of Russian Literature*, an encyclopedia covering authors, genres, movements, and periodicals, with a useful bibliography for each entry. Ronald Hingley's *Russian Writers and Society 1825–1904* supplies the background for understanding the works of great writers of the period.

Dostoevsky

The most comprehensive source on Dostoevsky's life and work is undoubtedly Joseph Frank's magisterial five-volume literary biography cum intellectual history entitled *Dostoevsky*. Volume 4 of Frank's work, *The Miraculous Years, 1865–71*, contains several chapters devoted to the sources and a close reading of *Crime and Punishment*. A one-volume, condensed version of the 2,500-page biography was published in 2012 under the title *Dostoevsky: A Writer in His Time*. An older but established classic is the biography by a Russian critic, Konstantin Mochulsky, *Dostoevsky: His Life and Work*.

As one wag put it, "Who has not written a book about Dostoevsky?" There are numerous works to choose from for a general introduction to the writer and his oeuvre. Among those worthy of special mention are M. M. Bakhtin's *Problems of Dostoevsky's Poetics*, edited and translated by Caryl Emerson, a classic work and one that has had considerable impact on critical theory in recent years; Joseph Frank and David Goldstein's edition of *The Selected Letters of Fyodor Dostoevsky*, with 150 letters newly translated by Andrew MacAndrew; Richard Chapple's *A Dostoevsky Dictionary*, which contains a list of Dostoevsky's characters and literary allusions arranged alphabetically by work; Kenneth Lantz's *The Dostoevsky Encyclopedia*, whose more than two hundred alphabetically arranged entries detail the author's life and career; *Dostoevsky in Context*, edited by Deborah Martinsen and Olga Maiorova, with short essays on aspects of the social, historical, and cultural contexts, as well as the literature, journalism, and languages, of the period; and *A Dostoevskii Companion: Texts and Contexts*, edited by Katherine Bowers, Connor Doak, and Kate Holland, a collection of documents from the author's own time, and extracts from major critical studies.

Dostoevsky Studies: The Journal of the International Dostoevsky Society has been published since 1980 and contains a rich assortment of articles and features on the author's life and works, most of which are available online (see dostoevsky-studies.dlls.univr.it/index).

Crime and Punishment

Edward Wasiolek has edited and translated Dostoevsky's *Notebooks for* Crime and Punishment, a collection of source material on nearly every aspect of the conception, planning, and writing of the novel. It contains schematic plans, long variant of scenes, divergent characterizations, omitted scenes, and numerous reflections.

The recent Norton Critical Edition of Michael Katz's new translation of *Crime and Punishment* contains twenty-eight scholarly essays on the novel by Russian, European, and American critics, as well as a useful selected bibliography of general works on the author and specific works (book chapters and articles) on the novel.

Map of St. Petersburg

St. Petersburg was founded in 1703 by Peter the Great, close to the Gulf of Finland, in a marshy region around the Neva River, which flows westward into the Baltic Sea. The city is crisscrossed by smaller rivers and canals with many bridges. The area around the Haymarket where Raskolnikov and Sonya lived was a squalid section of the city. It is possible to trace Raskolnikov's various walks on the map, as well as Sonya's route from Raskolnikov's room to her own, and Svidrigailov's last journey before his suicide.

Important Places in *Crime and Punishment*	**Important Petersburg Locations**
❶ Raskolnikov's room	A St. Isaac's Cathedral
❷ The pawnbroker's apartment	B The Admiralty Building
❸ Sonya's room	C The Winter Palace and the Hermitage
❹ Haymarket Square	D The Stock Exchange
❺ Location of Svidrigaylov's suicide	E The Academy of Sciences
❻ Tuchkov Bridge	F St. Petersburg University
❼ Yusupov Gardens	G Falconnet's monument to Peter the Great
	H The Senate

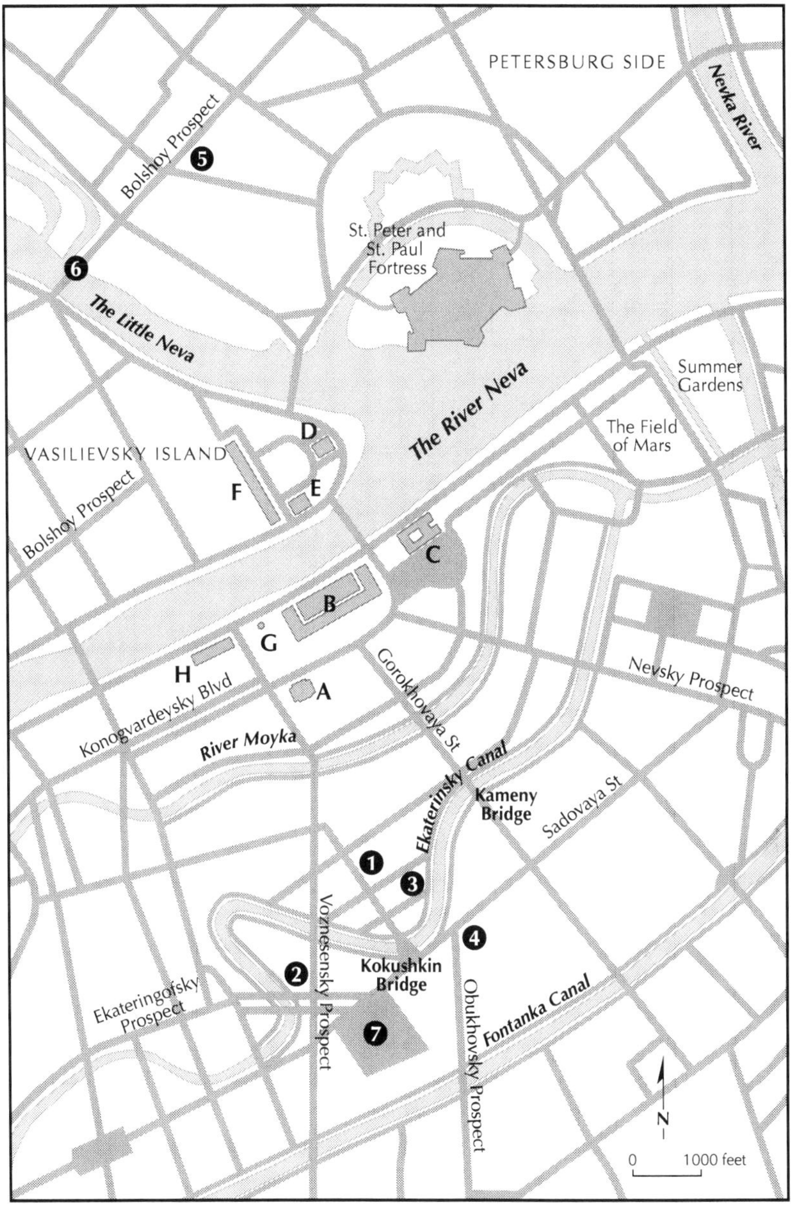

Map by Lohnes + Wright.

Names of Principal Characters

Raskólnikov, Rodión Románovich or Románych (Ródya, Ródenka, Ródka)[3]
Pulkhériya Aleksándrovna—his mother
Avdótya Románovna (Dúnya, Dúnechka)—his sister

Razumíkhin or Vrazumíkhin, Dmítry Prokófich—his friend

Alyóna Ivánovna—the pawnbroker

Lizavéta Ivánovna—her sister

Marmeládov, Semyón Zakhárovich or Zakhárych—former civil servant
Katerína Ivánovna—his wife
Sófiya Semyónovna (Sónya, Sónechka)—his daughter
Three other children: Polína (Pólya, Pólenka, Pólechka)
Lénya (Lída, Lídochka)
Kólya (Kólka)

Svidrigáylov, Arkády Ivánovich—landlord; Dunya's former employer
Márfa Petróvna—his wife

Lúzhin, Pétr Petróvich—Dunya's fiancé

Lebezyátnikov, Andréy Semyónovich or Semyónych—his friend

Porfíry Petróvich—examining magistrate; distant relative of Razumikhin's

Lippevékhsel, Amáliya Ivánovna—Marmeladovs' landlady

Zosímov—a doctor

Zamyótov, Aleksándr Grigórevich—chief police clerk

Ilyá Petróvich—nicknamed "Pórokh" (gunpowder)—police lieutenant

Note on the Characters' Names

Raskolnikov	*raskól* = schism; *raskólniki* = schismatic or dissenter
Razumikhin	*rázum* = reason, good sense
Marmeladov	*marmelád* = jam, jelly
Sofiya	"wisdom" (Greek)
Luzhin	*lúzha* = puddle, pool
Lebezyatnikov	*lebezít'* = to fawn, cringe

NOTES

1. See Burnett, who also provides a comparison of the early translations of *Crime and Punishment*.
2. The cited translation is by Michael R. Katz (2018).
3. Accents are provided to aid the reader in pronunciation; they are not part of written Russian.

Part Two

APPROACHES

Contexts: Analysis of Specific Scenes

Alexander Burry and Michael R. Katz

There are many scenes in Fyodor Dostoevsky's *Crime and Punishment* that merit close attention from the reader. We include brief remarks about several of them, intending to provoke discussion rather than to provide definitive interpretations of each.

Opening Lines

The lengthy, complex sentence that begins the novel[1] introduces the protagonist (a young man), locates the action (Petersburg), describes his circumstances (poverty), and establishes his frame of mind (indecision). Raskolnikov is contemplating a crime and undertaking a rehearsal of the deed. One Russian critic, Vadim Kozhinov, has written an entire article on this sentence, arguing that "it represents the embryo of the whole huge novel" (417).

Kozhinov's interpretation of this passage serves as an excellent example of Dostoevsky's use of details. It emphasizes precision and authenticity in its description of the time, the place, the weather, and the hero's mood. Every detail is linked in some important way with the entire novel. For example, the adverb "indecisively" (нерешительно), which is derived from the Russian root for *decision*, characterizes the hero from the beginning of the action until his confession in the last lines of part 6.

Raskolnikov's "tiny room" ("каморка"), which is later compared to a small closet and even a coffin, can be contrasted with Sonya's capacious room as described in part 4, chapter 4.

The fact that Raskolnikov and Sonya both "sublet" their rooms from tenants ("нанимал у жильцов") emphasizes the instability and rootlessness of the two protagonists in the society of Petersburg.

Dreams

Raskolnikov has five dreams during the course of the novel, from the horrific dream of the beaten mare in part 1, chapter 5, to his allegorical dream-vision in the second part of the epilogue.[2] Dostoevsky uses literary dreams in a variety of ways, including to reveal his characters' subconscious motivations, their wishes and their fears. Critics have written extensively about these dreams (see, for example, Katz 95–104; Rahv), and students enjoy the process of dream interpretation. In addition to the hero's dreams, Svidrigailov has an extraordinary series of nightmares in part 6, chapter 6.

All these passages open many avenues into the characters' psychology and the novel's major themes. For example, Raskolnikov understands his dream of the beaten horse to foreshadow the murder he is planning: "'Oh, God!' he exclaimed.

'Will I really do it, will I really take an axe, hit her over the head with it, crush her skull?'" '«Боже!» воскликнул он, «да неужели же я в самом деле возьму топор, стану бить по голове, размозжу ей череп . . . »' (Dostoevsky, *Crime* 43; *Prestuplenie* 50). But readers may doubt the hero's interpretation of his own dream. Does the innocent, tormented, exhausted nag really represent Alyona Ivanovna, who, far from innocent, victimizes numerous impoverished Petersburg residents through usury? Does the horse perhaps more closely parallel Lizaveta Ivanovna, the holy foolish half-sister of the pawnbroker, who by chance becomes the second murder victim? Or could it stand for the downtrodden, suffering Russian people themselves? If so, what does it mean that the lower-class onlookers cheer Mikolka on as he savagely beats his horse? One should also note the poignancy of the dream, in which Raskolnikov recalls his innocent enjoyment of religious ritual (the *kutya*, or dish of rice, raisins, and sugar) in childhood. Instructors and students can ask what it means that it is the boy Raskolnikov, not the present-day adult, who witnesses the horrific beating; note the differences between the two Raskolnikovs; but also ask whether the child's demand for justice can be related to Raskolnikov's motivation for committing murder.

Marmeladov's Sermon

After "rehearsing" his crime, Raskolnikov stops in a tavern to recover his equanimity. There he encounters the retired civil servant Marmeladov, who has been drinking heavily and is in an expansive mood. He senses in Raskolnikov a receptive audience and relates his painful life story, ending in an inspired monologue that contains a summary of some of the principal religious themes of the novel: forgiveness of sin, the value of even the lowest members of society, and the importance of pity.

The original title of Dostoevsky's novel was *The Drunkards*, and the Marmeladov family is the primary example of the impact of alcoholism on the lives of civil servants and their families, especially the young children. Marmeladov's life also illustrates the importance of money in the novel, as well as the conditions under which impoverished civil servants lived.

The style of this passage is particularly noteworthy: as Marmeladov's words become more inspired, he rewrites Christ's Sermon on the Mount, substituting his own words: his rhetoric approaches the biblical as he recites the categories of sinners who will be forgiven. In his request for crucifixion, he provides a poignant example of the sincere imitatio Christi, the practice of following the example of Jesus.

Raskolnikov's Confessions

Soon after committing the crime, the hero feels an overwhelming impulse to confess. He makes several attempts, going so far as to describe to the police clerk

Zametov what he would have done with the loot from the pawnbroker if he had committed the murder, leading Zametov to wonder briefly if Raskolnikov could actually be the murderer before dismissing the thought.

These incidents build suspense throughout the novel as the reader wonders if Raskolnikov will ever finally do what he seems to be contemplating. Dostoevsky's use of italics for his final confession, "*It was I who killed the old civil servant's widow and her sister Lizaveta with an axe and robbed them*" '*Это я убил тогда старуху-чиновницу и сестру ее Лизавету топором и ограбил*,' emphasizes the fact that we have finally arrived at a point we have been waiting for throughout the narrative (*Crime* 368; *Prestuplenie* 410).

But beyond the fact of Raskolnikov's numerous impulses and attempts to confess, the manner in which these episodes take place is remarkable. In particular, Raskolnikov conveys the truth twice through a silent gaze. In part 4 he gazes at Razumikhin in the stairwell of his apartment building, and his friend shudders as he apprehends a horrifying idea (*Crime* 345; *Prestuplenie* 240). This silent confession, it should be noted, does not completely come across, as Razumikhin does not believe that his friend is a murderer until the very end, and searches for other explanations, wondering early in part 6 whether Raskolnikov is some sort of political conspirator (*Crime* 487; *Prestuplenie* 338).

The second silent confession, however, delivered to Sonya Marmeladova, achieves its goal. Raskolnikov, having promised to tell her who murdered Lizaveta, tells her to "take a good look" 'погляди-ка хорошенько' (*Crime* 452; *Prestuplenie* 315) and gazes at her until she, horrified, divines the truth. These silent attempts at confession raise the question of why Raskolnikov finds it so difficult to state his crime in words.

The Epilogue

Critics have long argued over the ending of the novel: some maintain that it is an unexpected and artificial attempt to wrap up loose ends and bring some resolution to the hero's spiritual quest. Others see it as totally appropriate, foreshadowed in the hero's dreams and his transcendent moments, in Marmeladov's sermon, and in the influence of Sonya Marmeladova's love and faith. Whatever the reader's view of its superfluity or importance, the epilogue is richly evocative, further developing Raskolnikov yet simultaneously leaving his future tantalizingly unpredictable. Although Raskolnikov's epiphany on the banks of the Irtysh River certainly involves a resurrection into love, much else is left unresolved: he has still not repented of his murders and has not renounced his theory of the extraordinary man. Why does Dostoevsky leave these seemingly essential acts undone? And what will Raskolnikov's future be?

> But that is the beginning of a new story, the story of the gradual renewal of a person, the story of his gradual rebirth, and gradual transition from

> one world into another, of his getting to know a new, hitherto completely unknown reality. This could become the theme of a new narrative—but our present one is ended. (*Crime* 380)

> Но тут уж начинается новая история, история постепенного обновления человека, история постепенного перерождения его, постепенного перехода из одного мира в другой, знакомства с новою, доселе совершенно неведомою действительностью. Это могло бы составить тему нового рассказа, – но теперешний рассказ наш окончен. (*Prestuplenie* 422)

Will the "new story" tell the tale of a conversion to Christianity? of revolutionary activity? Will Raskolnikov enter into a relatively conventional marriage with Sonya, or will their relationship remain entirely spiritual?

NOTES

1. In the translation by Michael R. Katz (2018) quoted in this essay, see page 3.
2. The others occur in part 1, chapter 6; part 2, chapter 2; and part 3, chapter 6.

MAJOR THEMES

The Lives of the Children in *Crime and Punishment*

Robin Feuer Miller

Children form the bedrock of Fyodor Dostoevsky's oeuvre and are as essential as his dialogic worldview. His work not only portrays children's suffering, sexuality, and moral complexity but also reflects his awareness of children's usefulness in keeping readerly interest alive. Like Dickens and Tolstoy, for whom children were unceasingly important, Dostoevsky had a fraught relationship with his father and was, perhaps, not an ideal father himself.

The challenges of teaching novels like *Crime and Punishment* are many. Not least is encouraging students to observe within the work's broad canvas—its plot of murder, detection, punishment, and repentance—the way this novel, set in the steamy atmosphere of summertime St. Petersburg, starkly represents the streets and the poor who inhabit them. What can the many children of *Crime and Punishment* tell us about childhood, the family, and the perilous border between good and evil? This essay centers on children whom readers may fail to notice, or who, if noticed, nevertheless hover at the novel's periphery, to be glanced at fleetingly from the corner of one's eye. What happens if students train a steadier gaze upon them?

Teaching any big novel means entering a labyrinth with numerous passages through its mazes. With each reading, the experience is new. In the classroom's air the novel's words and ideas come into play, become a performance whose script results in as many interpretations as there are students in the room. Northrop Frye's observation, decades ago, that a novel is a picnic to which the author brings the words and the reader the meaning (427), rings resoundingly true in the classroom, resulting in moments of genuine polyphony among students. Dostoevsky's novel interrogates how ideas travel through the air, how they mutate like viruses; it is appropriate, therefore, to consider the air of the classroom and how conversation about the novel can impact students.

In *Plots*, Robert L. Belknap suggests that "a great book is a fearsome thing, and always tempts a reader to talk about something else" (80). Among this novel's most fearsome aspects are its many children. Is it significant that readers engrossed in the plot may fail to notice some of them or that the most elaborately described child is a nightmare, a hallucination? Why might Dostoevsky have eliminated from his final version some of the children who appear in the novel's notes?

More than Dostoevsky's other novels, we read *Crime and Punishment* as having a single center: Raskolnikov. As compelling and multidimensional as the other primary characters are, they are also foils or alternatives to Raskolnikov. The novel, a metaphysical thriller with questions of motivation, punishment, confession, and repentance at its core, is also about the air and the streets (see Klioutchkine). Raskolnikov struggles between his commitment to theory and his unconscious relief at its constant unraveling into the unexpected through the unforeseen intrusion of events, memories, or emotions. We enter Raskolnikov's mind from the first page, where he worries about encountering his landlady and having to chat: "To think that I can contemplate such a terrible act and yet be afraid of [such] trifles"[1] 'На какое дело хочу покуситься и в то же время каких пустяков боюсь!' (Dostoevsky, *Crime* 1; *Prestuplenie* 6). It is just such trifles that virtually immediately begin to undermine Raskolnikov—whether leaving the door open as he commits murder or dropping a pair of earrings behind the door of the flat below. He has even, astonishingly, forgotten to discard his distinctive German hat, although he had warned himself that the hat, "an insignificant trifle, might wreck the whole affair. . . . Trifles are important! . . . Trifles like this can bring disaster" 'Мелочи, мелочи главное! . . . Вот эти-то мелочи и губят всегда и все' (*Crime* 3; *Prestuplenie* 7; ellipses in source). Students quickly receive the narrator's signals that trifles may form the crux of the matter, that the proverbial devil (or is it God?) lurks in the details of any theory, but this awareness does not guarantee that readers will not overlook essential trifles. I urge students to reread, to scout out trifles they might have missed. Perpetually on the alert, we, like Raskolnikov, are nevertheless moths drawn to the flame.

The novel teems with children—on the streets, in the taverns and dark apartments, as subjects of dreams and fantasies. Dostoevsky's unwritten novel, *The Drunkards*, which evolved into *Crime and Punishment*, was to be a novel about families and children, the education of children, and the ramifications of drunkenness (*Fyodor Dostoevsky* 63). Despite the ubiquity of children in the novel, however, it is possible to overlook some of them. They thus figure as *trifles*—trifles at the heart of the matter, as are those irruptions of real life that invalidate attractive theories.

Nevertheless, some of the novel's most memorable moments feature children: all readers remember the evocation of Raskolnikov's seven-year-old self in his dream of the beating of the horse; the life-affirming exchange between Polyechka and Raskolnikov when she kisses him on the stairwell; the terrible scene where the dying Katerina Ivanovna and her children take to the streets to sing and dance; the seven quiet Kaupernaumov children; Svidrigailov's passionate, inquisitive young child-fiancée, struggling to maintain her dignity while sitting on his lap; the wet-haired corpse of a girl festooned with flowers conjured up by Svidrigailov; and the seductive, flushed, lascivious little girl who materializes in his final dream before his suicide. These children enhance the main plot and are central to the world of the novel.

But beyond these marked children, there are others who are, perhaps, the tale's authentic trifles, as easily overlooked by characters and readers as an awkward hat or an open door. According to the logic the novel instigates from its outset, these unmarked children may constitute the heart of the matter; they figure as part of the urban backdrop against which the crimes and good deeds of the adults are enacted. If we can persuade our busy students to cast a slow, sideward, squinting glance at this populous world of anonymous children in the novel—if we deliberately foreground them—these youngsters begin to overtake and change the perspective of the novel's center, although they possess no dominant plotline. Characters, readers, critics, and Dostoevsky agree that a person's response to the suffering of a child is an important moral test. Students realize that this same question is at the center of political debate today, for example, in regard to the immigration crisis and the suffering of children along the United States' southern border.

Students learn in psychology courses that children model their responses on those of the adults they know best. When Marmeladov tells his extraordinary story, Raskolnikov is not the only listener. There are also present the barman and several customers, as well as a "lad of about fourteen behind the bar and another, younger, who waited on the customers" 'За застойкой находился мальчишка лет четырнадцати, и был другой мальчишка моложе, который подавал' (*Crime* 8; *Prestuplenie* 12). These children are the first to laugh ("snigger" 'хихикать') at Marmeladov's heartrending tale (*Crime* 10; *Prestuplenie* 13), seeming to validate his next remark; paraphrasing Lebezyatnikov, himself a comically inaccurate paraphraser of John Stuart Mill, Marmeladov explains how "in this age the sentiment of compassion is actually prohibited by science, and that that is how they order things in England, where they have political economy" 'сострадание в наше время даже наукой воспрещено и что так уже делается в Англии, где политическая экономия.' He relates how his daughter, battered by the mocking words of her stepmother and the cries of her little stepsiblings, went to the streets as a prostitute. At this point, "the two lads at the bar burst out laughing" 'фыркнули оба мальчишки за стойкой' (*Crime* 11; *Prestuplenie* 14). It is against this eerie backdrop of the laughter of children that Marmeladov cites the words of Christ to the children, "Suffer them, suffer them!" and those of Pontius Pilate about Jesus, "Behold the man." Marmeladov tells not only the mythic story of Sonya and Katerina Ivanovna, but also that of the children, "small, smaller and smallest," whom Katerina Ivanovna is "scrubbing, washing and bathing from morning until night" 'с утра до ночи, скребет и моет, и детей обмывает' (*Crime* 13; *Prestuplenie* 16). The laughter of these two boys rings even more loudly through the tavern. What do students make of this laughter in the face of a tragic narrative?

Marmeladov's account—he is simultaneously narrator, cause of the problem, and silent semiconscious witness to the tragic scene while lying on the floor drunk—is suddenly interrupted by the arrival of rowdy merrymakers, "by the sound of a barrel-organ and the cracked voice of a seven-year-old singing 'The Little Hut'" 'звуки нанятой шарманки и детский, треснутый семилетний голосок, певший «Хуторок»,' the same popular street song that, after Marmeladov's death, his stepchildren are almost forced to sing in the streets while their mother is dying (*Crime* 16; *Prestuplenie* 17). But this seven-year-old singer is barely noticeable; Raskolnikov's attention and ours is elsewhere. Marmeladov ends his searing account by imagining God asking, "Where is the daughter who gave herself for a harsh and consumptive stepmother and the little children of another? Where is the daughter who showed compassion to that filthy drunkard, her earthly father?" 'Где дщерь, что мачехе злой и чахоточной, что детям чужим н малолетним себя предала? Где дщерь, что отца своего земного пьяницу непотребного, не ужасаясь зверства его, пожалела?' (*Crime* 19; *Prestuplenie* 21). But neither he nor Raskolnikov, nor, most likely, student readers, pay heed to the seven-year-old's voice singing right there at hand; the child is an unremarked trifle, swallowed up by Marmeladov's terrible tale of other children. This child dissolves into the background scenery and noise. The shocking family drama diverts readers from the three children actually present in the tavern during Marmeladov's narration, themselves at dire points in their lives but unremarked by character or reader or student. Mere trifles.

Marmeladov's evocation and reduction of Mill's theories quickly echoes in Raskolnikov. Departing Marmeladov's squalid quarters, he absentmindedly leaves money on the windowsill and thinks of Sonya, "[W]]hat a little gold-mine they've managed to get hold of there!—and profit from! Oh yes, they draw their profits from it!" 'Какой колодезь, однако ж, сумели выкопать! и пользуются! Вот ведь пользуются же!' (*Crime* 22; *Prestuplenie* 25). The next day, when asked why he no longer teaches children and just lies in his room like an old sack, he replies, "Teaching children is very badly paid. What can you do with a few kopecks?" 'За детей медью платят. Что на копейки сделаешь!' (*Crime* 24; *Prestuplenie* 27). Children are not economically worth the effort of educating them.

Hours later, Raskolnikov's initial efforts to help a drunken girl who has just been violated suddenly collapse into a failure of compassion rationalized through economic theory:

> Let it go! They say it must be so. Such and such a percentage, they say, must go every year . . . somewhere or other . . . to the devil, I suppose, so that the rest may be left in peace and quiet. A percentage! They have some

> capital words: they are so soothing and scientific. Once you've said "a percentage" there is no need to worry any more. If you used a different word, why then perhaps . . . it might be disturbing . . . And what if Dunyechka is included in the percentage? (*Crime* 43; ellipses in source)

> А пусть! Это, говорят, так и следует . . . Такой процент, говорят, должен уходить каждый год . . . куда-то . . . к черту, должно быть, чтоб остальных освещать и им не мешать. Процент! Славные, право, у них эти словечки: они такие успокоительные, научные. Сказано: процент, стало быть, и тревожиться нечего. Вот если бы другое слово, ну тогда . . . было бы, может быть, беспокойнее . . . А что, коль и Дунечка как-нибудь в процент попадет! (*Prestuplenie* 43; ellipses in source)

The careful student-reader dutifully makes analogies between Sonya, Dunya, and this child on the streets, but even so, compassion fatigue is sadly inevitable. The narrative moves on, but a classroom discussion about compassion fatigue elicits difficult questions: Does this experience induce shame, despair, indifference? Is there any remedy?

Raskolnikov has given money to the Marmeladovs and to the policeman for the abused girl on the street, and he is given twenty kopecks by a mother and child. Like dust, bits of loose change given in charity pass through the stifling air of the city as a poetic counterpoint to the spreading virus of economic and political theory. A donor one moment may be a recipient the next; this change carries no financial value, its currency is of a different order.

Shortly before entering the Crystal Palace tavern Raskolnikov wanders, by habit, to the Haymarket. He encounters a youth with a barrel organ accompanying a fifteen-year-old girl who is singing and wearing a flame-colored feather. Raskolnikov abruptly tells a stranger that he likes street singing. Why does Raskolnikov like this activity, usually performed by children and emblematic of poverty, corruption, illness, and despair? Is his numbness temporarily dissipated by the pleasurable pain this grim merriment provokes? This sticky sentimentality borders on the perverse—its emptiness highlighted—when, moments later, he witnesses an attempted suicide-by-drowning. Will students notice that this drunken woman, who had already attempted hanging, was being cared for by a little girl? Another trifle: a child caretaker who figures as a mere sidebar in a passing incident that is itself a sidebar.

The streets brim with abused, neglected children; conversation does too: Zosimov mentions to Razumikhin "the case of a hypochondriac . . . who could not endure an eight-year-old boy's merry chatter at table, day after day, and killed him!" 'Я один случай знаю, как один ипохондрик . . . не в состоянии будучи переносить ежедневных насмешек за столом восьмилетнего мальчишки, зарезал его!' (*Crime* 180; *Prestuplenie* 163). Later, Razumikhin rails against the Socialists' view that explains crime by the deleterious influence of the environment: "A man of forty assaults a ten-year-old girl—was it his environment that made him do it?" 'сорокалетний бесчестит десятилетнюю девочку, – среда, что ль, его на это понудила?' (*Crime* 216; *Prestuplenie* 196). Agreeing "with astonishing authority" 'с удивительной важностью,' Porfiry replies that "a crime against a little girl may very well be explained by 'environment'" 'преступление над девочкой очень и очень даже можно «средой» объяснить' (*Crime* 217; *Prestuplenie* 197). This is Porfiry's strategic preamble to confronting Raskolnikov: "Apropos of all these questions—crime, environments, little girls—I have just remembered . . . an article of yours: 'Concerning Crime'" 'По поводу всех этих вопросов, преступлений, среды, девочек мне вспомнилась теперь . . . одна ваша статейка. «О преступлении»' (*Crime* 218; *Prestuplenie* 198). Shortly afterward comes Luzhin's accusation: that Mme Resslich's niece of "about fifteen, or perhaps only fourteen" 'девочка лет пятнадцати и даже четырнадцати,' hanged herself after having been abused by Svidrigailov (*Crime* 252; *Prestuplenie* 228). These lurid anecdotes about middle-aged men killing children or driving them to suicide approach ever closer to the main plot: even Raskolnikov's account of his affection for his landlady's daughter, a strange girl of limited intelligence who dies of natural causes, has an unsavory quality.

Lebezyatnikov, in a ridiculous application of political theory, attempts solving "the problem of children" by eliminating the idea of them altogether: "Children are a social question, and one of the first importance, I agree; but the problem of the children is solved in another way. Some people even reject children altogether" 'Дети – вопрос социальный и вопрос первой важности, я согласен; но вопрос о детях разрешится иначе. Некоторые даже совершенно отрицают детей' (*Crime* 318; *Prestuplenie* 289). Students laugh at Lebezyatnikov but are thoughtful when it comes to discussing issues about family and children today.

Raskolnikov's last encounter with Svidrigailov occurs in a tavern, in a small room with a door that could be locked, where two street children, a boy with a barrel organ and a girl of eighteen with her skirts tucked up, are performing. They exit like other anonymous, youthful minstrels before them, not to reappear, and are likely forgotten, although the tragic street scene with three other reluctant minstrels, Polyechka, Kolya, and Lyonya, has just occurred. As Raskolnikov makes his final journey through the Haymarket to confess at the police station, his interior monologue bears surprising textural, textual intimations of Anna Karenina's shortly before her suicide:

> "'There is a peasant-woman with a baby, begging; odd that she should consider me more fortunate than herself. I must give her something just for the joke of it! Bah, there's a five-kopeck piece still left in my pocket; where did it come from? Ha, ha, here you are . . . take it, little mother!"
>
> "God bless you!" whined the beggar woman.
>
> (*Crime* 444; ellipsis in source)

> Баба с ребенком просит милостыню, любопытно, что она считает меня счастливее себя. А что, вот бы и подать для курьезу. Ба, пятак уцелел

> в кармане, откуда? На, на . . . возьми, матушка! – Сохрани тебя бог! – послышался плачевный голос нищей.
>
> (*Prestuplenie* 405; ellipsis in source)

This mother and baby, the final recipients of Raskolnikov's charity, likely pass unnoticed by readers; for Raskolnikov, his gift to them is a mere joke. His instinct to offer money to beggars and children is so automatic that he indulges it even at this pivotal moment.

The more-or-less forgotten children who figure more in the novel's scenery than in its plot may seem removed from the intensity of the drama being enacted at the center, but they constitute the work's elemental fabric. Perhaps the most important of these unnoticed children, these forgotten ones, is the child that Lizaveta may have been carrying. Having overheard Lizaveta in the Haymarket, Raskolnikov recalls another overheard conversation between two students six weeks earlier, just after his first visit to the pawnbroker. Vividly recalling this previous conversation, he forgets a crucial detail: that Lizaveta is "constantly pregnant" 'поминутно была беременна' (*Crime* 55; *Prestuplenie* 54). Has Raskolnikov murdered a pregnant woman? What is the impact of this? Does he ever realize this possibility? Such trifles and blind spots are the crux of the matter.

Neither the narrator nor Raskolnikov ever returns to the subject of Lizaveta's possible pregnancy, but perhaps it will remain activated in the minds of students if they notice it. I quiz my students every year; they rarely recall this detail, but they enjoy learning about the novel's notes, where Dostoevsky explores the question more fully. He even suggests that she has a child. "He caresses Sassya, and she came to him . . . It was clear that she . . . was glad to have a pretext for coming. She said that she is the daughter of Lizaveta . . . When he admitted his guilt to her, then suddenly, no Sassya" (*Notebooks* 87). Sassya then appears at the Marmeladovs'. A few paragraphs later, we read, "Child. Oh you lovable creature; (this is Lizaveta's). About Lizaveta." And then: "The baby. Who will forbid me to love this baby?" (90–93). Equally interesting is the suggestion that a prototype for Zosimov may have been among Lizaveta's lovers and made her pregnant:

> "She was a girl who tried to please. ~~It's not that she herself had to.~~ She did it by her own will, but she sort of bore it out of humility. ~~She didn't know how to say no~~. Every mischief-maker had fun with her. But the infant they found was his (the doctor's)."
>
> "What baby?"
>
> "But don't you know? They performed a cesarean on her. She was six months pregnant. A boy. Born dead." (96–97)

Sonya says he still owes Lizaveta ten kopecks for mending:

> (and she was murdered pregnant; they used to beat her for nothing, and whoever wanted could outrage her). ~~I knew her and she mended my linen.~~

> ~~She's an idiot. The old woman beat her when she was pregnant. I saw it myself. Pregnant, pregnant, sixth~~ (165)

Not only does Dostoevsky remove this disturbing material about Lizaveta—about her being a mother and having another stillborn child, and about her closer connection to Raskolnikov and Zosimov—he condenses it into a single, powerful, minute particle of charged matter, the trifle of a phrase "constantly pregnant." Ask students, "Why?" This trifle, this blind spot, becomes a trompe l'oeil: once noticed by the reader, Raskolnikov's unnerving failure to remember it becomes emblematic of the alarming trifles and blind spots that render this novel a metaphysical thriller as well as a proto-detective novel (see Miller 64–67).

Why might Dostoevsky have kept Lizaveta's possible children out of the novel? To preserve the focus and immediacy of his narration? For fear of censorship? From an awareness of compassion fatigue? Students are eager to mull these questions. Keeping in mind these largely voiceless children from the novel and the many unrealized ones in the notes, I inevitably turn to the theme of parents and children. Students then consider broad questions of forgiveness; who has the right to forgive, who does not?

The primary children of *Crime and Punishment* evoke a range of emotions, whether compassion, joy, sorrow, love, or fearsome surprise tinged with horror; yet the unmarked children convey the darker, more restless meanings of the novel. Katerina Ivanovna's children are provided for; Svidrigailov's child fiancée will inherit money; but the streets will still teem with unobserved children, sent by drunken, dying, or desperate parents into prostitution or to beg, sing, and thieve. These children are essential trifles too easily overlooked as we gaze upon and admire the grand canvas of this novel. Perhaps Dostoevsky hoped we would suddenly recall them at a needed moment and foreground their suffering.

NOTE

1. This essay cites the translation by Jessie Coulson (1975).

Why and When Does Raskolnikov Decide on Murder?

Gary Saul Morson

Many have regarded Fyodor Dostoevsky as the greatest psychologist, and one of the greatest novelists of ideas, who ever lived. Students will appreciate *Crime and Punishment* if they understand why so many have praised it.

Students easily recognize that many of Raskolnikov's motives for committing the murder are philosophical. To be sure, he claims at his trial that he committed the crime for money, but it is clear that this explanation is just what Porfiry Petrovich has advised him to say in order to get a lighter sentence. If he committed the murder for money, why does he never go near it and almost forget where it is? He worries about his mother's and sister's welfare, but he does not try to earn money, the way his friend Razumikhin does. He seems more concerned with the philosophical question, "Why is there suffering in the world?" than with alleviating his family's present suffering. He holds people at a distance, while ideas haunt him.

Have students consider the scene where the servant Nastasya, out of the goodness of her heart and at her own expense, brings him food and urges him to work. He replies that he *is* working: "I am thinking" 'Думаю' (Dostoevsky, *Crime* 30; *Prestuplenie* 26).[1] Nastasya laughs and asks him how much he earns that way, but Raskolnikov considers thinking without reward as the only work worth doing. His ideas are more real to him than his bodily needs.

Raskolnikov does get up to do one dramatic thing: commit the murder. Why? He has trouble answering this question when Sonya asks it. The reason is that he isn't sure himself why he did it. He keeps trying to say that he was putting a theory into practice, as if, unlike other people, he has the courage to act on ideas. He thinks of himself as a sort of hero in that way. But what idea was he acting on? He can't say.

First, encourage students to reflect on how counterintuitive this is: a person does something life-changing like murder for an idea but cannot say what the idea is! Then ask students to reflect on the possibilities—Which idea was it?—and point out that they are doing just what the hero is doing: trying to figure out his motives. They are engaged in the very same quest. Another way to say this is that Raskolnikov is interpreting himself from the outside, as if he were a character in a novel.

Students might easily understand why it is hard for a reader to guess someone else's motives, but Raskolnikov is analyzing not another person but himself. Is it possible that we do not understand our own motives, even when we make decisions on which our whole life depends? Dostoevsky's answer is yes.

Raskolnikov could have acted on one of at least three theories. The first is what is often called utilitarianism. This is the idea he overhears two people discussing in a tavern, just when he is thinking the very same thoughts. That apparent coincidence is Dostoevsky's way of saying that the idea was "in the air." Raskolnikov is living out the moral problems of the day.

Utilitarian reasoning is still very much with us. The idea is that a moral action is one that does "the greatest good for the greatest number." Suppose one person has five coats and another has none. The fifth coat does less good to the first person than one coat would do for the second, so at least one coat should be transferred to the person who would derive more benefit from owning it. Economists no longer like this sort of "interpersonal comparison" because it so often misleads. For example, the five hundredth book in an avid reader's collection may be valued more than the eleventh book belonging to someone who never reads at all.

But that is the least of the problems with utilitarianism: it actually sanctions murder. In the discussion Raskolnikov overhears, one person explains:

> [O]n one side we have a stupid, senseless, worthless, spiteful, ailing, horrid old woman, not simply useless but doing actual mischief, who has not an idea what she is living for herself, and who will die in a day or two in any case. . . . On the other side, fresh young lives thrown away for want of help and by thousands . . . Kill her, take her money and with the help of it devote oneself to the service of humanity and the good of all. . . . One death, and a hundred lives in exchange—it's simple arithmetic!
>
> (*Crime* 66–67)

> [С] одной стороны, глупая, бессмысленная, ничтожная, злая, больная старушонка, никому не нужная и, напротив, всем вредная, которая сама не знает, для чего живет, и которая завтра же сама собой умрет. . . . С другой стороны, молодые, свежие силы, пропадающие даром без поддержки, и это тысячами, и это всюду! . . . Убей ее и возьми ее деньги, с тем чтобы с их помощию посвятить потом себя на служение всему человечеству и общему делу. . . . Одна смерть и сто жизней взамен – да ведь тут арифметика! (*Prestuplenie* 54)

"It's simple arithmetic!" For this speaker there is no more doubt that the conclusion is right than that twice two is four. Even today, people have an irrational faith in anything written as an equation.

Students who follow Raskolnikov's logic will see that it means murder is not only morally excusable but morally obligatory: if we have an obligation to do the greatest good for the greatest number, it would be immoral *not* to kill the old woman. The instructor might also point out that the novel is set at the time when the Russian revolutionary movement was beginning—thus the allusions to the fires believed to be set by radicals who had been issuing proclamations calling for revolutionary violence. The application of utilitarianism to create a better social order demands not just one murder but millions. Fifty years later precisely, that was to happen in Russia, and it happened again in China, Cambodia, and other places. The instructor might point out that here, and in his novel *The Demons*, Dostoevsky explicitly predicted where this sort of reasoning would lead.

A second idea that obsesses Raskolnikov might be called moral nihilism. According to it, traditional moral standards come from belief in God and so are not binding on an atheist who regards them as mere superstition. Today we would say that such standards are mere social constructs. After his visit to the Marmeladovs in part 1, chapter 2, Raskolnikov's heart is torn with sympathy for their suffering, so he leaves them the little money he has. Then he does an abrupt about-face:

> "And what if I'm wrong," he cried suddenly after a moment's thought. "What if man is not really a scoundrel, man in general, I mean, the whole race of mankind—then all the rest is prejudice, simply artificial terrors, and there are no barriers and it's all as it should be." (*Crime* 28)

> Ну, а коли я соврал, – воскликнул он вдруг невольно, – коли действительно не подлец человек, весь вообще, весь род, то есть человеческий, то значит, что остальное все – предрассудки, одни только страхи напущенные, и нет никаких преград, и так тому и следует быть! (*Prestuplenie* 25)

This passage needs to be elucidated for students phrase by phrase. When he calls "man in general" a scoundrel, Raskolnikov has in mind all the awful suffering people inflict on one another. The experience of the twentieth century—the Holocaust, the millions killed in Stalin's labor camps, the execution by the Khmer Rouge of a quarter of the Cambodian population—has forced this conclusion on many and accounts for the way Dostoevsky came to be considered a prophet. But having passed this terrible judgment on humanity, Raskolnikov decides it is incorrect. If morality is mere superstition, then the very idea of evil or being a "scoundrel" is just so much religious nonsense, mere "prejudice." In nature, nothing is moral or immoral; things just are. To illustrate this point to students, I sometimes drop a coin, remind them that it falls at 9.8 meters per second squared, and ask them if that is moral or immoral. The question is absurd, but if we are nothing but so many chemicals governed by natural laws, all moral judgments are absurd in the same way.

By "artificial terrors" Raskolnikov means both the threat of hell for crimes and the psychological punishment of guilt, experienced by people who mistakenly believe in right and wrong. For a materialist and atheist everything is governed by natural laws and could not be otherwise. A few years before Dostoevsky wrote this novel, a Russian neurophysiologist, Ivan Sechenov, formulated an idea we think of as very recent, that our brains are governed by physical laws no less than anything else. Since people do what our brains make us do, choice is an illusion. Because we could no nothing else, "it's all as it should be."

There's an odd thing about Raskolnikov's attraction to this theory: he keeps turning to it just when his heart is torn by someone else's suffering. That is, he is so pained by injustice that he can't stand it and so adopts a theory that relieves his pain by telling him that justice does not exist anyway. What appears to be unjust suffering is just the laws of nature at work. Thus Raskolnikov denies morality for moral reasons!

Like utilitarianism, this theory also justifies murder, or anything else, since according to it morality is mere prejudice. It is important to point out that this sort of moral nihilism flatly contradicts the utilitarian theory because utilitarianism is based precisely on a moral argument. For utilitarians, right and wrong are not mere prejudice. People are obliged to do the right thing and can know what it is by simple calculation.

Later in the book, Porfiry Petrovich taunts Raskolnikov with the third theory. Raskolnikov has written an article in which he expresses, in extreme form, an idea that has obsessed intellectuals ever since. According to this theory, humanity is divided into two groups, the overwhelming majority of ordinary, limited people and the few extraordinary people capable of formulating, or at least grasping, big, new ideas. Common people are conservative; they cling to old values and persecute the great thinkers whom society will celebrate in future ages. By contrast, extraordinary people—Raskolnikov names political figures like Napoleon as well as philosophers and scientists—are the ones progress depends on. If one of those people needs to kill or steal in order to develop and promote great ideas, such action is not only permissible but morally obligatory. To the few geniuses, common people are "mere material" to be used, shaped, or destroyed as needed.

According to this theory, there are also people a step below Napoleon. They too are extraordinary compared to common people. These are the people on whom the Napoleons rely. Some day, Raskolnikov speculates, humanity will discover the law that determines how many such people there are: a true believer that science can explain everything, Raskolnikov states that "that law, of course, is unknown at present, but I am convinced that it exists" 'Закон этот, разумеется, теперь неизвестен, но я верю, что он существует' (*Crime* 258; *Prestuplenie* 202). What Raskolnikov has in mind is the intelligentsia as a group, and he is staking a claim common to the Russian radical intelligentsia and to many intelligentsias since: if the smart, well-educated people were given power, and if the uneducated people simply had to submit to them, the smart people could build a superior world. Of course, such a group did seize power in 1917 with disastrous results—as Dostoevsky foresaw.

This theory contradicts both of the others. Unlike utilitarianism, it regards some people as much more valuable than others. Also in contrast to utilitarianism, the Napoleonic theory holds that it is not human happiness that matters but the development and implementation of great ideas. Unlike the second, nihilist theory of ethics, the Napoleonic theory does contain a moral imperative. So

Raskolnikov's three theories justifying murder are at odds with one another. No wonder he has so much trouble figuring out which one led to the murder!

Having established this, the instructor can explain that Dostoevsky is advancing an argument about how people decide to take actions. We usually imagine—and the law usually assumes—that after a process of deliberation we formulate an intention and then act on it. If nothing intervenes, we carry it out. We assume that to act at all we must first intend to act, and that intention can in principle be located at a given moment in time. If this is true, the question, "*When* did you decide to do something?" makes sense. The more important the decision, the more momentous—in both senses—it must be.

But in Raskolnikov's case, this theory does not work. Leo Tolstoy illuminates this point when he argues that Raskolnikov's murder of the old woman became possible when he was just lying on his sofa, not thinking of any of his theories or even of the old woman at all; it became possible not at any one moment, but over a long period as "tiny, tiny alterations" were taking place in his mind (81–82).

In other words, the reason Raskolnikov cannot locate the moment he made the decision is that there was no such moment. Ask students to look at the murder scene and notice Raskolnikov's state of mind. Far from what we would expect, he is not concentrating on what he is doing; mentally, he is barely present at all. Have the students contemplate the passage where the author says that Raskolnikov behaved not at all as if he were making important choices but as if he were being dragged along by an external force, like a piece of clothing caught in a machine.

On his way to the murder the key passage occurs, and it pays to read it aloud:

> We may note in passing, one peculiarity in regard to all the final resolutions taken by him in the matter; they had one strange characteristic; the more final they were, the more hideous and the more absurd they at once became in his eyes. In spite of all his agonizing inward struggle, he never for a single instant all that time could believe in the carrying out of his plans. And, indeed, if it had ever happened that everything to the least point could have been considered and finally settled, and no uncertainty of any kind had remained, he would, it seems, have renounced it all as something absurd, monstrous and impossible. But a whole mass of unsettled points and uncertainties remained. (Dostoevsky, *Crime* 71)

> Заметим кстати одну особенность по поводу всех окончательных решений, уже принятых им в этом деле. Они имели одно странное свойство: чем окончательнее они становились, тем безобразнее, нелепее тотчас же становились и в его глазах. Несмотря на всю мучительную внутреннюю борьбу свою, он никогда, ни на одно мгновение не мог уверовать в исполнимость своих замыслов, во все это время.

> И если бы даже случилось когда-нибудь так, что уже все до последней точки было бы им разобрано и решено окончательно и сомнений не оставалось бы уже более никаких, – то тут-то бы, кажется, он и отказался от всего, как от нелепости, чудовищности и невозможности. Но неразрешенных пунктов и сомнений оставалась еще целая бездна. (*Prestuplenie* 57)

Raskolnikov does not for a single instant believe he will do it! He lives in a special kind of time that might be called "hypothetical." He is fascinated not so much by crime as by the possibility of crime, which is why he never works out the specific details of how he will commit a real one. A man dreams of committing "the perfect crime"—rational, perfectly planned, undetectable—and has not even figured out how he will get the murder weapon!

Raskolnikov lives in the territory between deciding to commit the crime and deciding not to commit it, and as soon as he is close to one extreme, he veers away toward the other. Ask students to find the moments when he does this. He wants to stay in that in-between territory, where he might (or might not) commit the crime.

Ask students to speculate on what is so attractive about that hypothetical territory. Do they ever visit it themselves? We all do; it is part of the human condition. We think of it as innocent, but Dostoevsky shows it has its dangers.

Raskolnikov could have remained in the in-between territory indefinitely if he had not by chance overheard that the old woman's sister would be away precisely at seven o'clock, so he could find the old woman alone. He could never have obtained such information deliberately without leaving traces, so if he does not act now it means he has in effect renounced the crime, which he does not want to do any more than he wants to decide on it firmly. So he keeps doing the bare minimum to keep the option open, which he is why he oversleeps and almost arrives late to his rendezvous with murder. The territory between deciding on the crime and renouncing it keeps narrowing until it is only a point. He stands there, axe in hand, but even then he is irresolute. At the last possible moment, when "he had not a minute to lose," he pulls out the axe and "almost without effort, almost mechanically, he brought the blunt side down on her head. He seemed not to use his own strength in this" 'почти без усилия, почти машинально, опустил на голову обухом. Силы его тут как бы не было' (*Crime* 78; *Prestuplenie* 63). He uses the blunt side because it doesn't require any presence of mind to aim; in fact, this is probably why he chooses an axe rather than a knife, which would be easier to conceal, in the first place. It's as if the murder happens by itself—almost without effort, mechanically—without his *doing* it.

Raskolnikov is so abstracted that he has forgotten to close the door behind him. Lizaveta comes in and Raskolnikov by sheer inertia kills her too. "The blow landed directly on the skull" 'Удар пришелся прямо по черепу' (*Prestuplenie* 65; my trans.): here Dostoevsky makes the subject of the sentence "the blow," as if it, not Raskolnikov, were the agent here.

Now get the students to appreciate how amazing this all is. A person commits a bloody murder, an action so important that, one would think, no one would take it without a firm decision—and he has never decided at all! When students realize they have never seen a murder described this way, they will recognize how brilliant a psychologist Dostoevsky is. Then ask them to think of instances from life, short of murder, resembling this. Sometimes people do bad things when drunk. What if they get themselves drunk *so that* they can do things they would never decide upon when sober? We say that we "lose our temper," lose control of ourselves when angry: could it be that we sometimes work ourselves up to anger so that we can excuse ourselves for doing bad things? What states of mind resemble Raskolnikov's hypothetical territory? They are not at all uncommon!

Raskolnikov is guided not by any one theory but by the theoretical mindset itself, which he inhabits the way other people inhabit a world with flesh-and-blood people. It is not any particular theory but the theoretical mindset itself that leads to murder, and not by dictating a decision but by allowing Raskolnikov to live in a world of hypotheticals and what-ifs.

Students come to appreciate literature when they can regard it as something more than an intellectual exercise. If a teacher can show them how their own minds, lives, and most pressing moral questions can be illuminated by great writers, they will understand why it is worth the effort to read masterpieces.

The sign of the teacher's success comes when students, after the grades are in, ask what they should read next.

NOTE

1. This essay cites the edition of Constance Garnett's translation published in 1950.

Dostoevsky's Guide to the Inner Life

Yuri Corrigan

When asked by administrators to detail the "learning outcomes" of our courses, as instructors of literature we tend to focus on the critical tools that make our students better writers and more discerning thinkers. But we are often reticent about the larger-scale foundational tools that our classes and texts inherently cultivate—the resources, that is, that help careful readers build moral and intellectual infrastructures for their daily lives. Here we may be missing an opportunity to articulate just how crucial our classroom work can be in the personal sense for our students, many of whom, in my experience, come to our classes in a state of alarmed agnosticism: technologically overstimulated, isolated, lacking traditional religious or community resources, and, most of all, eager for some constructive way to make sense of themselves. To these students, the Russian nineteenth century can feel unexpectedly like home, a bewildered age of cultural polarization and ideological inflammation that had lost its traditional answers to the questions, "How should we live?" and "What are we?" and that—perhaps less familiarly—turned to the novel as a resource for personal guidance and stabilization. In this essay, I propose a way of teaching Fyodor Dostoevsky's *Crime and Punishment* in the foundational mode, as a handbook for students on how to become more resilient and robust human beings, and, more specifically, on how to encounter and integrate the unknown, often avoided, and therefore menacing terrain of the inner life.

In approaching the problem of the "inner" for Dostoevsky, we can begin as a class by reflecting more generally on the problem of self-knowledge. Does the project of introspection, I ask students, lead to genuine discovery or simply to narcissistic self-absorption? Students tend to be divided on this; they want to live examined lives, they often say, but sitting around thinking about themselves doesn't seem productive. Dostoevsky, who was similarly ambivalent on this question, posited a roughly antonymous relationship between self-consciousness and self-knowledge. In his novels, morbid self-consciousness—obsessive preoccupation with one's own thoughts and feelings, and with one's embodied status in the eyes of others—generally appears in direct opposition to a more revelatory form of inward searching. Here Raskolnikov, hyperactively self-absorbed but squeamishly in flight from the deeper contents of his psyche, is exemplary. Like the underground man before him, who spends his prodigious mental energies trying to suppress the mysterious "something" that "refuses to die" within him and that keeps "rising up in [his] soul continually, painfully" (Dostoevsky, *Notes* 76), Raskolnikov begins the novel suffering from an unspecified source of inward torment and seeking desperately "to forget everything" 'всё забыть' (*Crime* 54; *Prestuplenie* 43): "the feeling of infinite revulsion that had begun to oppress and torment his heart . . . was so palpable that he didn't know where to hide from his anguish" 'Чувство бесконечного отвращения, начинавшее давить и мутить его сердце . . . достигло теперь такого размера и так ярко выяснилось, что он не знал, куда деться от тоски своей' (*Crime* 10; *Prestuplenie* 10).[1] Though readers have sometimes interpreted this initial sense of inward oppression as brought on by the idea of the murder, we should note that Raskolnikov in fact forces himself to think about the murder constantly, and to rehearse it in detail, as a way of distracting himself from the more mysterious "something else" 'что-то другое' (*Crime* 509; *Prestuplenie* 353) that he seeks to evade at all costs.[2] The novel, therefore, begins with one form of inwardness (self-directed, hyperactive mental activity) operating as a diversion from a deeper, unexplored source of inward anguish.

In thinking about a deeper "inwardness," some historical context can be helpful. Beginning with Pyotr Chaadaev's description in his "First Letter" of the modern Russian as an amnesiac, severed from history, we consider the nineteenth-century culture war of Slavophiles and Westernizers (with short readings from Nikolai Gogol, Ivan Kireevsky, Vissarion Belinsky, and Alexander Herzen) as a disagreement over whether to reclaim or discard Russia's own cultural memories. This, in turn, helps us make sense of Dostoevsky's view of modern educated Russians and their nation as willful amnesiacs, psychic fugitives, at war with their own depths. Raskolnikov's dream shortly after the murder offers one illustration of this condition. Secluded in his elevated but cramped room at the top of his building (a "tiny closet" 'клетушка' with a low ceiling [*Crime* 30; *Prestuplenie* 25]),. Raskolnikov is oppressed by a violent commotion on the staircase below, where he dreams his landlady is being savagely beaten as screams make their way up the staircase to his room. Paralyzed by terror, Raskolnikov attempts to lock the door, but fails. The building and its inhabitants concisely describe the inward geography of the psychic fugitive—a lofty and remote conscious mind imperfectly sealed off from and tormented by deeper, mysterious faculties that impinge themselves threateningly from below.[3]

In following this theme, we may consider the novel as an expansive exploration of the strategies and consequences of the flight from inwardness; of the protagonist's attempts, that is, to lock the door of the mind against the "howling, wailing, gnashing, weeping, beating, and cursing" 'такого воя, вопля, скрежета, слез, побой и ругательств' (*Crime* 127; *Prestuplenie* 90) that keeps surging painfully from the unconscious depths. Thus, we follow Raskolnikov's attempts to keep himself in the shallower waters of consciousness by means of three principal strategies: first, circumscriptive ideology: by exchanging the burdensome activities of thought and introspection for the ready-made instructions of political doctrine; second, collectivism: by placing himself temporarily under the guidance and administration of others (especially Razumikhin and Sonya) so as to rest from the demands of self-governance; and, third, violence: by searching out an all-encompassing external distraction, in this case, by doing something so forcefully horrific that it shifts his attention away from his prior anguish to an urgent problem in the outside world. On this last point, we examine the murder as a highly efficient means of escape from an inwardly insurgent "something." We pay close attention, for example, to the acute relief the murderer experiences, however temporarily, in cutting himself off from his "entire former past" 'все это прежнее прошлое' and from "himself, and everything else" 'и он сам, и всё, всё,' all of which now, after the murder, seems to reside in the welcomely inaccessible "depths" 'в какой-то глубине' of the Neva (*Crime* 127; *Prestuplenie* 90).

These strategies of self-medication, I should note, are readily comprehensible to today's undergraduates, who, statistically speaking, are both significantly more anxious and more thoroughly medicated than those of previous generations (see Goodwin). But, if the novel was conceived, as has often been noted, as a murder mystery posing the question of *why*dunit rather than *who*, the theme of violent escape rom "something" within should serve not so much to solve the mystery as to expand it. For now, not only are we parsing the many possible motives for the crime, but we are also dealing with the larger mystery of what this "something" might be that haunts Raskolnikov from within. As I'll suggest below, the novel offers an extremely satisfying answer to this question, but one that evokes numerous further complications for students as they attempt to apply it to their own experience.

If the novel can be read as exploring the dilemma of whether to reject or reclaim that which lies deeply within, Svidrigailov can be seen as an instructive foil to Raskolnikov—not so much as the devil on his left shoulder (across from Sonya's angel on his right, as has sometimes been suggested), but rather as a psychic fugitive par excellence, a more weathered veteran of the art of escaping the depths. Like many other inwardly tormented characters in Dostoevsky's works, Svidrigailov, in evading the ghosts that haunt his solitary state, has medicated his fear of inwardness by binding himself insistently and perversely to others. Above all, he has made sure to place himself under the strict control of a Grand Inquisitor figure, someone capable of annexing his conscience and executive mind, allowing him to live in a form of carefree but degraded innocence; in Svidrigailov's case, this figure is his wife, Marfa Petrovna. As a novelist, Dostoevsky was drawn to the dramatic crisis that occurs when his psychic fugitives become dislocated from their parental figures and are suddenly forced to confront the latent elements of their newly insurgent inner lives. (We may think of Stepan Trofimovich's hysterical attempt to escape his "benefactress" in *Demons*, or Mitya's frantic bid for independence from Katerina Ivanovna's benevolent tyranny in *The Brothers Karamazov*.) For his part, Svidrigailov enters the novel in a state of barely disguised panic. Marfa Petrovna is dead, and there is no one to shield him from the growing threat of his own interior landscape, which takes the form of certain mnemonic "apparitions." (I should note that perhaps no one is more prepared to appreciate this point, or more curious to watch its consequences play out, than those first-year students who have recently been separated geographically from a helicopter parent.) As with Mitya or Stepan Trofimovich, Svidrigailov's plan is simply to find another host, and he has identified an ideal candidate in Dunya. Therefore, upon being decisively rejected by

Dunya, he falls into an acute state of emergency. With no administrator to take control of him and to shield him from his own depths, he feels the surging of "something" from within. The waters around him are, quite literally, rising menacingly:

> "The water's rising," he thought. "By morning . . . water will pour into the streets, flooding basements and cellars; the sewer rats will emerge, and amidst the rain, people, soaking wet and cursing, will begin hauling their stuff [*sor*, "garbage"] up to the higher floors."
>
> (Dostoevsky, *Crime* 558; ellipsis in source)

> Вода прибывает, – подумал он, – к утру хлынет, там, где пониже место, на улицы, зальет подвалы и погреба, всплывут подвальные крысы, и среди дождя и ветра люди начнут, ругаясь, мокрые, перетаскивать свой сор в верхние этажи . . . (*Prestuplenie* 392; ellipsis in source)

The image is informative. What Svidrigailov fears is not simply the rising of the unconscious waters, but the repulsive elements of himself that were formerly medicated into abeyance, the "garbage" and "rats" that inhabit the avoided life of the soul.

The uncannily rising Neva points us to another trait of Dostoevsky's psychic fugitives: their tendency to turn the external world into a projective allegory for their own suppressed inward geographies. Like Raskolnikov, Svidrigailov, in the midst of his inner emergency, evades the deeper waters (whether literally or figuratively) by shutting himself into a "tiny closet" 'клетушка' (*Crime* 553; *Prestuplenie* 388) that is rendered in terms almost identical to those describing Raskolnikov's closet (*Crime* 30; *Prestuplenie* 25). But here Svidrigailov, unlike Raskolnikov, finds himself venturing out, in his dream, into the uncharted darkness, walking "for a long time through the long, narrow corridor," until "in a dark corner" he discerns "some strange object, something that seemed alive": "it was a child — a little girl aged five, not more . . . shivering and crying" 'долго ходил по всему длинному и узкому коридору . . . как вдруг в темном углу . . . разглядел какой-то странный предмет, что-то будто бы живое . . . – девочку лет пяти, не более . . . дрожавшую и плакавшую' (*Crime* 559; *Prestuplenie* 392). The "something" that Svidrigailov finds in the darkness, then, is both an "object" and a living being; and to his relief, he succeeds in sending it back into unconsciousness (into a "sound and peaceful" sleep 'крепким и блаженным сном' [*Crime* 559–60; *Prestuplenie* 393]). Like the "something" on the rise in Svidrigailov, however, it refuses to remain dormant; the child's "eyelashes" begin "fluttering and winking . . . as if the little girl were not asleep, and only pretending" 'ресницы ее как будто вздрагивают и мигают . . . точно девочка не спит и притворяется' (*Crime* 560; *Prestuplenie* 393). Here we have a focused image of the awakening principle of soul that terrifies the conscious mind and that, in Svidrigailov's case, directly motivates his suicide—regardless of how the action becomes ultimately confabulated (i.e., in Svidrigailov's case, a superhuman "overcoming" of a fear of death 'одолел же Свидригайлов' (*Crime* 598; *Prestuplenie* 418).

In reading the novel as a forceful appeal to integrate the dynamic unconscious, or "soul," we as readers should be careful, I think, not to conflate Dostoevsky's psychological project with the psychoanalytic edifice that it would later inform and inspire. A definite resonance can be discerned between Dostoevsky and Freud on the unconscious, especially in Dostoevsky's depiction of wounded fugitives reenacting their traumas in the world so as to experience them as present rather than past. Dostoevsky's concept of the unconscious, however, is different in kind from that of Freud, and perhaps nowhere is this difference more apparent than in the author's portrayal of Sonya, yet another instructive foil to Raskolnikov, but this time as a bastion of reclaimed interiority. Having abdicated his own inwardness, Raskolnikov is fascinated by the evident residence of mysterious resources within Sonya. "How could she have stayed in her present situation for so long and not lost her mind?" he asks himself. "What had supported her?" 'почему она так слишком уже долго могла оставаться в таком положении и не сошла с ума? . . . Что же поддерживало ее?' (*Crime* 354–55; *Prestuplenie* 247). As Sonya reads the Lazarus story aloud from the New Testament, Raskolnikov peers into the secret space of her personality and observes the phenomenon (so rare in Dostoevsky's world of morbidly avoided interiors) of a personality drawing sustenance from within:

> He understood all too well how painful it was for her to expose and betray all that was *her own*. He realized that these feelings seemed perhaps to constitute her genuine and cherished secret, perhaps from her own girlhood, . . . with her unfortunate father and her stepmother, demented by grief, among hungry children, hideous cries, and reproaches.
> (*Crime* 358)

> Он слишком хорошо понимал, как тяжело было ей теперь выдавать и обличать все свое. Он понял, что чувства эти действительно как бы составляли настоящую и уже давнишнюю, может быть, тайну ее, может быть, еще с самого отрочества, . . . подле несчастного отца и сумасшедшей от горя мачехи, среди голодных детей, безобразных криков и попреков. (*Prestuplenie* 250)

Generative inwardness for Dostoevsky, as suggested here, has a hybrid quality to it, being both internal and external to the psyche. Raskolnikov is looking into a space that both belongs to Sonya (a "genuine and cherished secret . . . that was *her own*") and extends beyond her. Raskolnikov notes that "these feelings"—Sonya's devotion to the text—began with her own childhood wounds (amid "hideous cries, and reproaches"), but the substance of her meditation is not the wounding experiences themselves but the text toward which her wounds direct her: namely, the story of a corpse rotting in a cave and being brought back miraculously to life. In this sense, Dostoevsky, anticipating psychoanalysis but seeking to preserve the spiritual resources of Eastern Christianity, describes the wounds of the mind as opening the self toward a deeper, transcendent form of inwardness.

Dostoevsky, therefore, with his gallery of wounded and self-medicating characters, is ultimately interested in the wound as a kind of inward aperture that expands the personality beyond itself. The goal of the introspective journey for Dostoevsky is not to become absorbed with one's wounds, but to find a way through memory to a deeper, stabilizing and nourishing form of interiority. One goes into the cave, in other words, to find the dead and rotting body of Lazarus, not to behold it but to bring it to life. The landscape of the novel, therefore, offers three kinds of characters that will define the moral spectrum of Dostoevsky's world: first, the *un*wounded: those "neither cold nor hot" (*Bible* [New International Version], Revelation 3:16), lacking any inward aperture and therefore without recourse to a deeper inwardness, a category embodied in the figure of Luzhin; second, the *excessively* wounded: those for whom the inward presence of the divine is overpowering and utterly debilitating (this being Svidrigailov's role); and, third, the *sufficiently* wounded: characters who are capable of encountering and channeling the divine terrors within. Here we think of Sonya, and eventually Raskolnikov too, since the latter, with Sonya's help, ultimately endures a confrontation with the insurgent "something." What Dostoevsky depicts at the end of the novel is not a repentant sinner in the traditional sense but an exhausted fugitive who can no longer defend himself from within. As he awaits his capture, he longs for his former distractions ("no, some sort of struggle would be better than this! Better to see Porfiry again" 'Нет, уж лучше бы какая борьба! Лучше бы опять Порфирий' [*Crime* 486; *Prestuplenie* 337]) so as to shield himself from the rising agency that "burn[s] in his soul like a spark and suddenly envelop[s] him completely, like fire" 'загорелось в душе одною искрой и вдруг, как огонь, охватило всего' (*Crime* 577; *Prestuplenie* 405), "pierc[ing] his heart" 'пронзило . . . его сердце' (*Crime* 601–02; *Prestuplenie* 420), "seiz[ing] hold of him, and . . . cast[ing] him down at [Sonya's] feet" 'вдруг что-то как бы подхватило его и как бы бросило к ее ногам' (*Crime* 603; *Prestuplenie* 421).

The task of personal formation, therefore, if we follow Raskolnikov's progress, is perhaps counterintuitive: not to build and reinforce a self, but to relinquish the project of selfhood so that a more substantial, grounded, and open-ended personality can be established in its ruins. The formation of a robust personality, for Dostoevsky, culminates in its annihilation from within. This "within" is depicted as an arena of feeling, thought, and memory, which, in its deepest reaches (most terrifyingly for the conscious mind), opens onto the transcendent energies of the living God. Students will emphasize different aspects of this inwardly insurgent "something"—as alternately a life principle, a sacred text, a memory, a transcendent agency, the Holy Spirit—depending on critical inclination. For Dostoevsky, the howling from within was both personal and part of a wider cultural experience; for modern Russia as a whole, it was the memory of the Christian ideal, as well as that of Christ's violent crucifixion, that was lodged painfully in the collective psyche. In depicting the various forms of emotional and intellectual addiction that offer escape and distraction from the project of deep inwardness (whether pathological forms of intimacy, compulsive acts of violence and cruelty, or the various philosophical narcotics, the nihilisms and dogmatic ideologies that anesthetize the mind from the anguish of expansion), the novel alerts its readers to the grave dangers of self-avoidance. In order to benefit from Dostoevsky's meditation on the inner life, our students need not embrace his religious belief in the divine sources that underlie the self. The novel, rather, offers its readers a richly suggestive symbolic geography of the unconscious, a series of models against which students can ponder their own uncharted inwardness. The violent howling on the staircase, the child awakening in the corridor, the corpse of Lazarus rotting in the cave—these images (among many others) speak to a postpsychoanalytic age, a readership eager for a new topography of the inner life, a way of explaining the anguish of inward development, the dangers of self-medication and distraction, and the possibility of the turn inward as a form of expansion.

NOTES

1. All quotations from *Crime and Punishment* in English are reproduced from the translation by Michael R. Katz (2018).
2. I have presented this argument in greater detail in Corrigan, "Dostoevsky on Evil" 232–36.
3. For a more detailed discussion of this image, see Corrigan, *Dostoevsky* 47–48.

Polyphony and Its Discontents

Caryl Emerson

How much literary theory can a great nineteenth-century novel tolerate, and at what point should students be introduced to it? Every humanities classroom develops its own priorities. Some teachers prefer first to situate the novelist in time and place; others, to contextualize the specific work. But many insist that students start (and even remain) with the world that the author created. After all, novels are neither formulas nor period photographs. A novel is designed as a translatable, talking, self-sufficient world that provides everything necessary to pull its readers in. Whatever readers aren't told or shown, they don't need. And if told or shown too much too soon by outside experts, students can be anesthetized against feeling this world on its own terms.

This essay uses Fyodor Dostoevsky's most influential twentieth-century theoretician, Mikhail Bakhtin, as a test case for this pedagogical challenge. Bakhtin deserves his global fame. He opened up unparalleled potentials in the reading of Dostoevsky. But famous critics can colonize famous novelists, and in this literary equivalent of gunboat diplomacy, teachers can be unwitting accomplices. Given the high status of theory among literary professionals, the temptation is always present to organize classroom discussion through a charismatic critic or paradigmatic shorthand. Bakhtin's *Problems of Dostoevsky's Poetics* provides a convenient toolkit of analytic concepts—polyphony, the double-voiced word, the "word with a sideways glance," the loophole, the threshold chronotope—often supplemented by categories (dialogism, heteroglossia) that apply to all novels. A Bakhtinian lens is attractive because it combines two seeming opposites. It is scientific-sounding and ideologically neutral (Bakhtin prudently introduced his book to the Soviet public as a technical study of the way words work in Dostoevsky, not a discussion of the novelist's psychological, political, or religious worldviews). But Bakhtin also insists that each word, as a unit of analysis, is an individualized voice with its own history, intentions, and consciousness. His is a thoroughly intersubjective formalism, unembarrassed by the human face. (By "face" is meant an identity and inner unity to the subject made possible by an author's grasp of the person as a unique, animated, unfinalized whole.) Unfinalized wholes are free as human persons—or as free as persons can ever be. This commitment to organicism and personality is sensed in all Bakhtin's writings. It makes his categories very appealing to undergraduates, who, left to their own devices, would probably experience Dostoevsky's novels as evolving populated worlds rather than as formal artistic structures. As reading strategies, polyphony and dialogism manage to satisfy both criteria. But there is a cost.

An Open-Ended World

What is polyphony, and what does it reveal and obscure? Bakhtin borrowed the term from German literary and music criticism—he had in mind, of course, non-imitative polyphony, not the strictly sequenced polyphony of the European musical tradition—but he endowed the term with many values, ethical and personalistic, that music can ignore. Spatially, a polyphonic novel does not have a finalized authorial center: utterances are equally weighted. Temporally, it does not have a predetermined plan. If authorities do seem to exist in the text, or if flashbacks occur from some fixed point in the future, the narrative voice relaying the information is usually unreliable. A novel thus designed is peopled with characters ("heroes") for whom the future is open, filled with others' words, and who know, at any given moment, as much about their own lives as their authors know. What moves these fictive characters forward, Bakhtin claims, is not a specific sequence of events—that is, not the external plot. Plot events in Dostoevsky are big, simple, sensational, and blunt like the blow of an axe: murder, child abuse, poverty, prison camp, epilepsy. What drives a polyphonic novel are the ideas, or proliferating sequences of ideas, released by an explosive event. An idea uses a hero as its carrier in order to realize its potential in the world. These *idea-heroes* create a fantastically energetic and complex fabric of talk and scandal around their deeds, in which the reader is invited to participate, also as an equal. (This invitation to readers is the primary difference between the epic and the novel, according to Bakhtin: epics do not invite you inside.) Dostoevsky's notebooks testify to his continual surprise at the turns his plots were obliged to take to accommodate the growth of ideas being carried by his heroes.

Because Dostoevsky's characters are structurally so free, and because their words are events in their own right, they exist vibrantly in the here and now. Polyphonic heroes have little personal history and little need of it. What matters is not the evolution of an individual biography but "coexistence and interaction"—or, as Bakhtin rapturously overstates the case, "there is no causality in Dostoevsky's novels, no genesis, no explanations based on the past, on the influences of the environment or of upbringing . . . Every act a character commits is in the present tense" (28–29). An all-inclusive present coextensive with all that exists also defines eternity, a realm without time. Although Bakhtin could not have developed such analogies in the atheist Bolshevik state, surely he had in mind the example of medieval polyphony, in which the "melody line" (in novels, the dynamic forward movement of utterances in the heroes' dialogues) is subordinate to the overall harmony of the composition (the novelist's "orchestration" of figural meaning). Sacred polyphony is the musical equivalent not of profane melody but of allegory: the mystical simultaneity of all things.

Polyphonic multiplicity exists not only on the level of plot, idea-hero, or a hierarchy of times that privileges the present. Bakhtin was careful to stress a less idealist aspect of his model, in keeping with the materialistic and militarized rhetoric of his time. Inside every emerging thought or uttered word is a struggle for meaning. Each word I utter now has had earlier lives elsewhere; thus every speaking voice is a battlefield. Authors and heroes (and presumably narrators, although Bakhtin largely ignores them) can choose to muffle this struggle, thereby deploying the word monologically. Or they can emphasize the word's double-voicedness, its ability to subvert and parody itself and others. Dostoevsky was very skilled at exploiting the slippery, confounding double-voiced word, which can flourish inside the mind—consider the Underground Man—as well as outside it. We must be careful not to confuse this sort of dialogue with interpersonal communication. Drawing on an early scene in *Crime and Punishment* (from pt. 1, ch. 4), Bakhtin provides a riveting analysis of what he calls "microdialogue" inside a "dialogized interior monologue": those ironic, indignant, proliferating, and generalizing voices that assault Raskolnikov after he reads his mother's letter (74–75). In that famous passage, we witness "how Raskolnikov tortured and teased himself" 'так мучил он себя и поддразнивал' (Dostoevsky, *Crime* 33; *Prestuplenie* 39), turning family love into resentment and hatred, further isolating himself in his own solipsistic world.[1] At this point, the self-loathing hero is pleasured by such solitary verbal torment. Only much later in the novel does a different sort of inner microdialogue become possible for Raskolnikov, after real-life exchanges that he will alternately seek out and flee: on the secular plane with the wise and shrewd Porfiry Petrovich, and on the spiritual plane with the wisdom-bearing Sonya.

What Is Obscured

The dynamics of polyphony and dialogue are breathtaking. But, importantly, polyphony is not a moral system. Bad, dead ideas exist, of course, but what matters for Bakhtin is not which ideas win, but simply that a mass of ideas is being discussed. Since polyphonic readings feature the word, which is immortal, rather than the body, which emphatically is not, they tend to make Dostoevsky seem rosier and more affirmative than the actual texture of his novels suggests.

Critics routinely point out other problems with Bakhtin's analytical frameworks. Aside from the commonsensical objection that created characters in a novel are not alive, not free, and do what their authors want them to do, we must also consider hierarchies of value. For it is not true that all words matter equally in a novel. All words might be equally weighted—that is, have an equal right to exist as ideas—but Luzhin's words are not the moral equivalent of Sonya's or Razumikhin's. Bakhtin does not provide interpretations of whole novels, preferring to make his points through close readings of select verbal scenes. But deeds in a novel add up, chapter by chapter. Ends might interact with beginnings but do not coexist with them. Unsurprisingly, Bakhtin is weak on ends. He did not care for the epilogue of *Crime and Punishment*, with its suddenly spacious new metric (still a prison, but in sun-flooded Siberia rather than a cramped Petersburg garret), and considered it monologic. Perhaps the epilogue didn't interest Bakhtin because a large salvational role is played in it by silence. And just as

Bakhtin is slow to condemn the fibs and lies that issue forth from Dostoevsky's pathological chatterers—he tends to see their talk as a sort of inspired creativity, because words always create *something* by way of ideas—so is he slow to see the absolute dialogic virtue of saying nothing at all. When the convict Raskolnikov meets Sonya on the riverbank and flings himself down, weeping and embracing her knees, they "wanted to speak, but could not" 'хотели было говорить, но не могли' (*Crime* 379; *Prestuplenie* 421). Merely pictorial or iconic communication does not put new, redeployable words into circulation, however, and thus in Bakhtin's world cannot stave off death. Students too often dislike the epilogue and are confused by it. After the tough love of Sonya's Gospel, the brutal suicide of Svidrigailov, and the infinite sadness of Raskolnikov's mother, the final scene can indeed seem unmotivated and sentimental. Fairer to Bakhtin, however, is to take our cue from his study on François Rabelais—a provocative, inspirational, transnational meditation on laughing cultures, the grotesque body, and the carnival impulse that does not pretend to prioritize that Renaissance author's own literary goals. Bakhtin is a powerful thinker who used literature to illustrate his beloved philosophical ideas. He did not trim his ideas to elucidate a literary text.

Building on Bakhtin

Bakhtin's polyphony has long been part of the Dostoevsky scholar's interpretive arsenal. It insists on looking first at how words work. More productive for discussion in the undergraduate classroom, however, might be to begin not with the Bakhtinian word but with the human face and the accomplished deed. To that end, this final section mentions three recent representative approaches (out of a large rich pool) that acknowledge Bakhtin's insight into a "polyphonic Dostoevsky" but offer adjustments to it, or even outright correctives. Each intuits what an untutored reader would probably notice first and care about the most. And thus each "teaches honestly"—by which I mean, each begins inside the zone of Dostoevsky himself, to the extent that we can recuperate it, rather than the comfort zone of his later critics or handlers. That's where our students should begin too.

The first corrective is Yuri Corrigan's 2017 monograph, *Dostoevsky and the Riddle of the Self.* Corrigan sees that riddle buried, for most of Dostoevsky's characters, in their traumatized past. Beginning with the smaller pre-exile texts, he highlights the fragile psyche of the child and its easy wounding. Grown-ups inflict a wound, either carelessly or with deliberate cruelty, and the humiliated child reacts with self-protective amnesia (31). The wounded ego is so vulnerable that it will go to any length to avoid confronting its buried private self. Thus Corrigan takes issue with the idea, beloved by Bakhtin, that Dostoevsky's heroes have no biographical past. On the contrary, the past matters enormously; it hurts and is hidden. But those with the strength to turn inward and face this buried dread have a good chance of reclaiming themselves on a higher plane. They cannot move forward simply by moving outward into a world of I-Thou dialogues or multivoiced polyphony. Corrigan intimates that Bakhtin's "outsideness," which always roots us first in others' worlds, is a dodge (17). Applying this thesis to *Crime and Punishment*, he argues that Raskolnikov is not only a murderer for ideological reasons, but also a "psychic fugitive"—who uses nihilism and external violence to distract himself from the inner work that some deep, terrible wound, the product of unconscious energies and agencies, calls on him to engage ("Nihilism" 3). Underlying this hypothesis is the assumption that Dostoevsky's fictive personalities "are not merely allegorical vehicles, disembodied voices, or representatives of ideas, but also implied human beings" (*Dostoevsky* 7). Our undergraduate students, who love bodies and seek guidance in the great Russian novel on what in themselves to confront and what to flee, would intuitively agree with this verdict.

The second corrective is by Anna A. Berman, whose 2015 monograph *Siblings in Tolstoy and Dostoevsky* includes an extended treatment of the horizontal (brother-sister) bond in *Crime and Punishment*. She reads it as a family novel, one in which Raskolnikov's immediate family—mother and sister—are crucial to the hero's pathology. Both women burden him with excessive love. But she notes that their role has been underappreciated by most feminist scholarship, which prefers to focus on more sexualized themes: woman as prostitute, rape victim, emancipated rebel, or absent mother. Examining the novel through a sibling lens and in the context of Russia's powerful kinship systems, Berman proposes a different, more load-bearing triangle than the usual "Dunya between Razumikhin and Svidrigailov" (65). Crucial for the novel's structure, she argues, is Raskolnikov between Dunya and Sonya, the two self-sacrificing sisters in maimed or dysfunctional families. Dunya's powerful love for her brother creates the original mold; Sonya, desperate to save her step-siblings, is the later stand-in (66). Both these sisters have been tested in the body and can be stern. Eros is not necessarily excluded from their lives, but sexual appetite as such does not play a happy role in their experience (Sonya because of her status as prostitute, Dunya because of Svidrigailov's unwelcome advances). What matters to both these women is what matters in healthy sibling relations: protection, healing, and self-respect, not the more selfish commodity of sexual desire or its consummation. Berman notes that Razumikhin, who is welcomed into the family as a brother, moves to the role of lover only after all the important work of the novel has been done. Although Berman mentions Bakhtin's insight into Dostoevsky's universe of simultaneously existing antinomies (54), in setting up her sibling lens she does not (as Corrigan does) take Bakhtin to task. This is because Bakhtin is not much interested in gender issues or in biological kinship. For him, the uttered word does the work of family.

The final approach is the religious dimension to Dostoevsky's writings that Bakhtin was not free to address in the USSR—although he wished he could have done so. In discussions with his younger colleague Sergey Bocharov in 1972, Bakhtin remarked ruefully that his book on Dostoevsky was morally flawed:

"I severed form from the main thing . . . what Dostoevsky agonized about all his life—the existence of God" (Bocharov 1012). True, theologically inflected interpretations are often marginalized in the modern classroom (teachers are not routinely prepared in this area). But such readings need not be done piously; nor need they presume faith of any sort. Proselytizing is out of the question. A religious grid simply has the advantage of reflecting what Dostoevsky himself believed and felt, as opposed to the interests and values of his later readerships. It contributes to the literacy that we need as participants in his world and thus is a sensible place for students to begin.

In February 1975, the Dostoevsky scholar Robert Louis Jackson visited Bakhtin at his rest home in Moscow to inform him that Yale University was conferring on him an honorary doctorate. But honorees were obliged to receive the degree in person, and by then Bakhtin (disabled his entire life and an amputee since 1938) was too ill to travel. Bakhtin died three weeks later. Subsequently, Jackson became one of the first in English to argue for a Christian subtext to Bakhtin's Dostoevsky book, emphasizing the centrality of artistic visualization—the higher value of the image of Christ—over abstract and verbally based cognition (286–89). Since that time, *Crime and Punishment*, the most perfectly structured of Dostoevsky's long novels, has received close attention from many scholars qualified to identify Biblical "harmonies" as part of its polyphony. I mention only two with unusual pedagogical potential.

In her 2008 monograph *Profane Challenge and Orthodox Response*, Janet Tucker treats the novel as one large "lesson"—with St. Petersburg as the classroom. In Tucker's view, Dostoevsky was targeting an audience of young nihilists and utopian socialists in the capital. Although rebels and atheists now, they had been raised literate in their country's spiritual vocabulary. Working with familiar devices of Russian Orthodoxy embedded deep in oral folk tradition—icons, icon-ladders, sacred architecture and clothing, and Biblical parables, such as the stories of Lazarus and the Prodigal Son—Dostoevsky aimed to woo back Russia's youth from imported Western doctrine with an irresistible detective story that would morph at the end into the miracle of resurrection. This lesson could only be taught emotionally and thus required not a logical treatise but a novel. In her chapter 6, Tucker considers the much-maligned epilogue and Bakhtin's judgment of it as "monophonic." She dismisses his verdict as misguided (218). In fact the epilogue, with its "rational" and "non-rational" parts, fits the novelistic whole perfectly, recapitulating its progressive emancipation from "Western philosophies based on what [Dostoevsky] regarded as a misuse of empirical evidence in the domain of the human personality" (208). Reinforcing Corrigan and Berman, Tucker reads the final scene as one that heals Raskolnikov from the wound of his childhood nightmare: the fatal beating of the mare and his father's helplessness. The epilogue reintegrates Raskolnikov into a new family and allows him to become again "God's Child" (217).

While Tucker pleads Dostoevsky's case through folk-religious allegories, the last exemplar offered here works through one radiant personality permeated by a sacred text. In her discussion of Sonya Marmeladova and the Christian concept of "radical hospitality," Valentina Izmirlieva investigates the vexed act of welcoming in strangers, the homeless, the poor and sick. Such acts are risky because they cannot be repaid, and they subvert the "we-them" dichotomy that underlies most official social orders. Sonya finds Raskolnikov homeless and helpless. He is drawn to her, even as he denounces to her face all she lives by. She is a "harlot with a 'radically hospitable' body, but her promiscuity is sublimated into a pure symbol of spiritual generosity" (Izmirlieva 280). To be a symbol, however, does not mean to be "unproblematic and monolithic," as is often assumed (281). Sonya is fallible, constantly tested, and never more cruelly than in her reading of the raising of Lazarus. Izmirlieva emphasizes that this is a kenotic and sacramental "*interpersonal* encounter—reading for another" (283). Once uttered, the Lazarus story enters the novel with agency of its own.

One senses that Bakhtin would have rejoiced in this interpretation. Izmirlieva believes so. Sonya personifies "the perfect ministry of radical hospitality" (284), more a Marian figure who nurses the Word than a Christ figure who is himself the sacrificial word. Sonya is a radically hospitable *reader*—a word-laden, deeply dialogic Bakhtinian act. Or, as Izmirlieva exquisitely argues, Sonya "*lends* her body and voice to the Word, without imposing her own ego" (284). She has an ego that can be wounded, to be sure. But by reading her precious text to a hostile, skeptical Raskolnikov, she takes on his burden and agrees to answer for him. Sonya, then, is not quite a girlfriend to Raskolnikov. Arguably, she is also more than Anna Berman's potent concept of a sister. After the Lazarus scene, the longest interpolation of Holy Writ in modern Russian literature, Raskolnikov's feverish grip on the narration loosens and change becomes possible. There are no violations of narrative logic; Dostoevsky is a "Christian realist" (285), not a preacher from a pulpit. There is only complexity and human courage.

Where does this leave Bakhtin's polyphony? His canonized ideas are still very much in play. Increasingly we can contextualize them, find loopholes in them, understand the subtexts beneath them, and grasp why Bakhtin needed Dostoevsky to formulate truths dear to his own philosophy. But the cost of remaining exclusively within a polyphony of the word is high, and probably felt as a constraint to most readers. Polyphonic reading also overlooks much of what matters in Dostoevsky. This essay has entertained a larger sense of polyphony, one broadened from words to relationships in general—sisterly, divine, or wounded. If students are urged to hear and visualize these novels from the bottom up, in dialogue with their own deepest anxieties, Bakhtin will begin to speak.

NOTE

1. This essay uses the translation of *Crime and Punishment* by Michael R. Katz (2019).

Syncretizing Gender: Binarism, Agency, and Sexuality

Helena Goscilo

> *Men Are from Mars, Women Are from Venus*
> —John Gray

Fyodor Dostoevsky's *Crime and Punishment* (1866) appeared during a decade that witnessed Russia's impassioned debates across multiple cultural genres about the nature of women, their conjugal and legal rights, and their social status. Nikolai Chernyshevsky's highly controversial novel *What Is to Be Done?* (*Chto delat'?*; 1863) propounded a pragmatic feminism within a utopian framework,[1] Nikolai Nekrasov's poems lamented women's sorry circumstances and celebrated their stoicism,[2] and progressive "thick" Petersburg journals such as *The Contemporary* (*Sovremennik*; 1836–66) and *The Cause* (*Delo*; 1866–88) served as platforms for heated disputes about "the woman question" (*zhenskii vopros*). Mikhail Mikhailov's article in *The Contemporary*, "Women, Their Upbringing, and Their Significance in Society" ("Zhenshchiny, ikh vospitanie i znachenie v obshchestve"; 1860), which explicitly agitated for women's equality in education and marriage, had the effect of an ideological explosion and provoked instant responses.[3] So did his translation of an article by the liberal English philosopher-economist John Stuart Mill and his future wife, Harriet Taylor, titled "The Enfranchisement of Women" (1851), which appeared in *The Contemporary* later in 1860 and sparked enthusiasm among forward-looking segments of educated society.[4] Conservatives such as Nikolai Strakhov and Leo Tolstoy countered this accelerating trend by insisting that woman's "natural" function was domestic—

her gendered predestination was to breed, feed, raise children, and oversee the household. An avid reader of newspapers and journals, Dostoevsky typically integrated contemporary sociopolitical issues into his fiction, and *Crime and Punishment* briefly alludes to these polemics, if only tangentially, when Razumikhin offers Raskolnikov a German article for translation that solemnly asks, "Are Women Human?" That ontological question and the circumstances of the novel's female characters beg for an analysis of the novel in terms of gender identity and gender relations.[5]

Any classroom discussion of *Crime and Punishment* from the standpoint of gender necessitates posing, minimally, four weighty questions (which generate a host of subsidiary issues): To what extent and how consistently is Dostoevsky's treatment of gender essentialist? How does Dostoevsky's relationship to Russian Orthodoxy influence his representation of gender in the novel, and with what consequences? Does the novel credit women with agency, both in their individual behavior and in the dynamics of plot development? Is sexuality treated evenhandedly or marked as gender-specific, and therefore, in the context of the relevant period, does it privilege males?

Essentialism rests on the immemorial argument of "Adam's rib": the unexamined assumption that men are the primary human category or the norm, possessing irreducible qualities such as activity, dominance, logic, and intellect, which define masculinity. Accordingly, since gender identity pivots on hierarchical complementarity, the constitutive traits of women as the purportedly secondary category are the antithesis—passivity, submissiveness, irrationality, and emotion. The inequitable ascription of these dichotomous traits to men and women received its most eloquent formulation in 1975, with the vastly influential *La jeune née* (*The Newly Born Woman*) by the French theorist Hélène Cixous. Her study mapped a paradigm of what she denounced as universal misogynistic concepts governing sociocultural conventions enforcing putatively inherent gender distinctions. If this essentialism, cemented into Western thought for centuries, posits manhood as synonymous with subject, speech, and reason, she contended, then by definition womanhood must equate with the subordinate categories of object, silence, and intuition (Cixous and Clément).

To an extent, one may detect this reductive binary model in Dostoevsky's major novels, insofar as both *siuzhet* (structural organization) and *fabula* (chronological plot) situate the male protagonist at the center of the fictional world, with secondary characters and especially women conceived as lunar satellites drawing energy from his solar identity—a schema explicitly articulated by Pyotr Verkhovensky in *The Devils* (*Besy*; 1872), which also satirizes the "woman question" in its radical register. Masculinity, Cixous argues, is perceived as the energy-generating sun, palely reflected in the timid, waxing and waning (i.e., inconstant) "feminine" moon. It is no accident that menstruation traditionally has carried associations with abjection, volatility, and hysteria. In fact, the highly influential historian Jules Michelet, whose ideas Mikhailov debunked, lamented in his *L'amour* (*Love*) the biological inferiority of women, their "physical fatalism" and weakness cause by "the great malady of maternity" and "the eternal wound of menstruation," which occasion their state of sickness and frailty (32–33). His compatriot, the politician Pierre-Joseph Proudhon, equating the purported smallness of the female brain with women's intellectual inferiority, stated outright, "Genius is virility of spirit, its power of abstraction, of generalization, of creation, of conception; these gifts were lacking to an equal extent in the child, the eunuch and the woman" (Proudhon 197). Precisely such ideas prompted not only Mikhailov's rebuttal as he verbally agitated for gender parity, but also twentieth-century feminists' rejoinders in an avalanche of scholarship.

Discussion Questions. On what basis do Michelet and Proudhon seem to formulate their opinions and what is the legitimacy of their argument? Do Cixous's generalizations overstate or simplify gender disposition? What counterexamples, if any, exist in Western societies? How does the trope of solar vs. lunar operate in *Crime and Punishment*—is Raskolnikov the sun around whom other characters orbit?

Social and physical power as well as intellectual capacities in the novel unambiguously belong to men, illustrated by such characters as Lebezyatnikov, Luzhin, Porfiry Petrovich, Razumikhin, Raskolnikov, Svidrigailov, and Zosimov. A "rather stupid man" 'глуповат,' though "nice" 'добренький,' (Dostoevsky, *Crime* 401; *Prestuplenie* 279),[6] Lebezyatnikov espouses radicals' utilitarianism and notion of a commune (*Crime* 404–08); Luzhin's financial security, his portentous mediocrity notwithstanding, not only can lead to possible marriage with a much younger honorable beauty but also enables him to tyrannize Dunya and her mother, Pulkheriya Aleksandrovna (*Crime* 334–36); Porfiry Petrovich's cerebral (deductive) skills are reflected in his important professional position of examining magistrate; the good-natured student Razumikhin's stoicism, contacts, and command of foreign languages enable him to support himself, if on a marginal level (55–56, 124–25); Svidrigailov appreciates hypotheses, ruminates on such phenomena as eternity and ghosts (315–18), and, as an affluent, landowning widower, for better and worse, possesses the funds for whatever satisfies his sensual appetites; and Zosimov's profession of doctor automatically lends him authority. No woman in the novel enjoys a comparable standing, for philosophizing is alien to Dostoevsky's women, many of whom financially rely on men or, as in Sonya's case, belong to society's "dregs" and therefore are disempowered. Yet intelligent, strong-willed Dunya unwittingly exercises enormous psychosexual power over Razumikhin and Svidrigailov; Katerina Ivanovna not only holds the Marmeladov family together but psychologically terrorizes her weak drunkard-husband;[7] and Raskolnikov desperately needs the emotional support of the significantly named Sonya (a version of the Greek Σοφία/Sophia, meaning "wisdom"), who lacks education and social legitimacy but points the way to his redemption. Moreover, several secondary female characters support themselves through moneylending, renting apartments, and owning a brothel—hardly impressive professions but sources of income that vouchsafe economic independence.

Whereas Western thought since the Enlightenment has enshrined reason as the supreme value, *Crime and Punishment*, like *The Brothers Karamazov* (*Brat'ia Karamazovy*), repeatedly emphasizes its destructive potential, as illustrated in the conversation about justifiable murder overheard by Raskolnikov (71–73), his two homicides (85–89), his published article (284–87), and Luzhin's crude, rationalized pragmatism. Indeed, Raskolnikov thinks himself into murder, his coffinlike garret indexing the perilous limitations of relentless, unleavened thought. Instinct and emotion guide Razumikhin, his name (разум, meaning "reason") notwithstanding, while appetite, not reason, drives Svidrigailov. Porfiry Petrovich may provide rational explanations, but his investigative strategies rest on an intuitive sense of Raskolnikov's guilt (he "had seen right through him" 'человек, насквозь его раскусивший' [*Crime* 500; *Prestuplenie* 347). For Dostoevsky, in other words, reason—immemorially identified as quintessentially masculine—is a faculty to be overcome or at least tempered by other capacities.

Discussion Questions. Does the absence of philosophizing by Dostoevsky's female characters diminish their stature? What is the role of social rank and money in the novel? How does the status of rationality in the work affect readers' perception of gender? Is psychological insight gendered in the novel?

One mitigating capacity is psychological acumen—Dostoevsky's own talent writ large and in his works related to religion. By definition religious belief, as Blaise Pascal and Immanuel Kant acknowledged, exists independently of reason. At its best, it has in common with psychological insight an inexplicable penetration into the human psyche, as exemplified in Tikhon and Zosima—the two saintly elders in Dostoevsky's later novels, *The Devils* and *The Brothers Karamazov* respectively. Without question, the foremost representative of religion in *Crime and Punishment* is Sonya/Sofiya, an incarnated version of the Eternal Wisdom of Vladimir Solov'ev's imaginings and simultaneously a childlike urban prostitute.[8] And, logic to the contrary, she is the meek, religious individual who ventriloquizes the optimistic philosophy of salvation that conveys Dostoevsky's own hopes and acquires meaning for Raskolnikov in the closing section of the novel. Tellingly, Dostoevsky has Sonya share Orthodox meekness with the "fool in Christ" (*iurodivaia*) Lizaveta,[9] who gives her a cross and a Bible that they read together.[10] Moreover, he parallels Sonya's humility with the sectarian Nikolai Dementiev's Christian sense of his sinfulness (*Crime* 385–87). As elsewhere, he endows the "insulted and injured"—the socially disenfranchised—with spiritual righteousness. In other words, Dostoevsky's sui generis reliance on the ostensibly oxymoronic blend of psychological insight and Orthodox belief complicates what initially may appear as a patently retrograde treatment of gender.

Discussion Questions. Who possesses religious belief in the novel, and how does belief color that person's image? Raskolnikov commits murder yet professes to believe in God—how can one reconcile such a paradox? Is it analogous to that of a saintly prostitute? What is the effect of endowing women and men with parallel traits?

Agency resides with the male characters in the novel, but their exercise of it repeatedly takes the form of violence, much of it against women.[11] Raskolnikov viciously kills not only the old moneylender but also her innocent younger sister; Svidrigailov may be responsible for two murders and almost rapes Dunya (*Crime* 541–47); in Raskolnikov's prophetic dream Mikolka the peasant brutally slays the mare (60–65), an act that is analogized not only with Alyona Ivanovna's murder, but also by Katerina Ivanovna on her deathbed with her own broken life (478); an unknown male rapes the girl drunkenly staggering along the street, about to be assaulted by yet another man; Luzhin psychologically violates Dunya and Sonya; and Ilya Petrovich, the insolent lieutenant at the police station, verbally abuses Luiza Ivanovna, whose establishment services men (107–11). Women appear as victims of uncontrolled male violence—a configuration that drives the plot but hardly presents agency in an unambiguously desirable light.

Discussion Questions. Which personae in the novel exercise agency in productive or admirable ways? Given the Orthodox underpinnings of the novel, is agency a desideratum (think Boris and Gleb—martyred sons of Prince Vladimir, Russia's christianizer, who gained sainthood by passively accepting their deaths instead of resisting evil with violence)?

Throughout, sexuality is strongly marked as male, as exemplified most thoroughly in the figure of Svidrigailov and, secondarily, in the unnamed opportunist who stalks the intoxicated girl who clearly has been raped (*Crime* 49–53). Dunya may inspire sexual desire in several men, but she manifests none herself. And Sonya is probably literature's most asexual prostitute, for her so-called profession merely tropes her loving self-sacrifice. Prostitution as a social and moral problem receives relatively short shrift, though Luzhin's accusation of Sonya's supposed theft indicates the association of prostitutes with criminality. Lebezyatnikov, who tries to "educate" Sonya by propounding to her the need for women's emancipation, views prostitution as "the most normal condition of a woman" 'самое нормальное состояние женщины' (*Crime* 405; *Prestuplenie* 282) and Sonya's profession as "a vigorous and personal protest against the social order" 'энергический и олицетворенный протест против устройства общества' even though forced upon her (*Crime* 406; *Prestuplenie* 283) under prevailing conditions. Once the requisite sociopolitical changes are in place, he maintains, she will be at liberty to choose prostitution freely. Intriguingly, that argument has been made by several contemporary American feminists, such as Annie Sprinkle and Audacia Ray, self-proclaimed "sex workers" who consider their profession empowering. Whereas Luzhin's sniggering, prurient innuendos suggest that Lebezyatnikov's admiration for Sonya is lascivious ("And, of course, you're educating her . . . he-he!" 'И вы, разумеется, развиваете . . . хе-хе! доказываете ей'; *Crime* 407; *Prestuplenie* 284; ellipses in source) and that she derives satisfaction from prostitution, Raskolnikov's view that her profession is a crime against her very self is closer to Dostoevsky's stance, for he refers indirectly to "her dishonorable and shameful predicament" 'о бесчестном и позорном ее положении'

(*Crime* 354; *Prestuplenie* 247). In any event, the novel's women seem utterly devoid of erotic stirrings—a lack, however, shared by Raskolnikov.

Discussion Questions. Why do the novel's women seem to lack sexuality? Or does their sexuality manifest itself differently from men's? If so, how? Does denying women sexuality accord with the immemorial stereotypes of women as either saints or whores? Is Dunya's contemplated marriage to Luzhin a type of prostitution? And is the motivation behind Raskolnikov's earlier intention to marry his landlady's daughter comparable to Sonya's prostitution?

A striking but understudied aspect of *Crime and Punishment* well worth examining is its humor and those characters at whom Dostoevsky directs his considerable satirical skill. A rich means of influencing readers' responses to fictional personae, humor tends to endear to readers characters who manifest wit. When they serve as the butt of the narrator's irony, however, the effect is at best ambiguous and at worst derogatory. Few writers match Dostoevsky's daring in introducing humor in the midst of tragedy, and *Crime and Punishment* particularly showcases his ability to carry off such a mix of registers in the personae of Marmeladov and above all Katerina Ivanovna—during a funeral "feast," no less (420–30). More pertinent to the question of gender, however, is the novel's humorous treatment of five middle-aged women: Pulkheriya Aleksandrovna, Praskovya Pavlovna, and the three united by their patronymic of Ivanovna—Katerina Ivanovna, Amaliya Ivanovna, and Luiza Ivanovna.[12] Raskolnikov's mother, depicted as a still-beautiful, gentle, and loving woman, clearly subordinates herself to her self-assured daughter and feels helpless vis-à-vis her son. Unable to cope with his sullen uncommunicativeness, she resorts to the sort of empty chatter that satirists normally reproduce to convey the superficiality of specific social relations, as when she babbles about the late Marfa Petrovna, Svidrigailov's dead wife. Dostoevsky treats her with measured humor and after her death ascribes greater understanding to her than was apparent during her exchanges with her offspring. A somewhat less sympathetic humor inflects the character of Praskovya Pavlovna, Raskolnikov's bashful landlady, as described by Razumikhin. Urging Zosimov to take over his role of her friendly interlocuter after he becomes enamored of Dunya, Razumikhin disparagingly reassures him, "[A]fter a few sighs she'll melt like wax. . . . Talk whatever nonsense you want, but sit next to her and talk. . . . it's absolutely all the same to her whether it's you or me, as long as someone's sitting next to her and sighing" '[П]ри всем этом – вздохи, и тает, как воск, так и тает! . . . ей решительно все равно будет. . . . она будет на тебя смотреть и вздыхать, и так целый год сряду' (*Crime* 229–30; *Prestuplenie* 160).

Two Ivanovnas who bear the brunt of Dostoevsky's outright ridicule are Amaliya Ivanovna, the Marmeladovs' landlady, and Luiza Ivanovna, the brothel-owning madam whom Raskolnikov encounters at the police station. Again, Dostoevsky relies chiefly on comments by another character to belittle Amaliya Ivanovna, whom Katerina Ivanovna calls a "cuckoo" 'кукушка' (*Crime* 421; *Prestuplenie* 294), "screech owl" 'сычиха' (*Crime* 422, 426; *Prestuplenie* 294, 297), "German sausage-maker" 'колбасница' (*Crime* 435; *Prestuplenie* 303), and "revolting Prussian chicken leg dressed up in crinoline" 'подлая прусская куриная нога в кринолине' (*Crime* 435; *Prestuplenie* 303, impugning her intelligence, her command of Russian, and the authenticity of her patronymic, which, Katerina Ivanovna insists, is really Ludvigovna (*Crime* 200). The author also casts the landlady's Germanized Russian in hilarious terms intended to alienate her from Russian readers (428–29).[13] An unsympathetic figure who instantly believes Luzhin's accusation of Sonya's theft, Amaliya Ivanovna shares with Luiza Ivanovna her German identity, though the plump, well-dressed, sycophantic madam is in many ways a more likable, though no less comic, figure, satirized through her physical attributes. As a so-called "elegant lady" 'пышная дама' (*Crime* 109; *Prestuplenie* 78), wearing a dress that "spread out around her chair like a balloon" 'точно воздушный шар, распростанилось вокруг стула' (*Crime* 6; *Prestuplenie* 76), "a brooch the size of a saucer on her bosom" 'с брошкой на груди, величиной в чайное блюдечко' (*Crime* 106; *Prestuplenie* 75, and "a very foolish smile" 'с преглупейшею улыбкой' (*Crime* 109; *Prestuplenie* 78), she is erroneously addressed as "Laviza Ivanovna" and spouts a torrent of Teutonic Russian before hurrying out, "her rear end collid[ing]" with the superintendent 'наскочила задом на одного видного офицера' (*Crime* 111; *Prestuplenie* 79). The humor in all these instances cannot but distance the novel's middle-aged women from its readers.

Discussion Questions. Does the satirical treatment of Katerina Ivanovna modify the tragedy of her situation? If so, how? Which male characters are the object of humor, and does Dostoevsky handle that humor differently? Why does Dostoevsky not subject any young female characters to satire?

In 1873 Dostoevsky noted in his *Writer's Diary*:

> One sees more and more prominently in our women the qualities of sincerity, perseverance, seriousness and honesty, a longing for truth and sacrifice. Indeed, all these qualities were always stronger in Russian women than in men. Women are more persistent and patient in work; they are *more serious* than men, and want to work in order to do something, not merely *to seem* to do something. (278; trans. adjusted)

Do his words accord with what he depicted in the 1866 novel? An analysis of dichotc nies, agency, Orthodoxy, sexuality, and humor within the narrative reveals productive paradoxes and subtleties in the author's representation of gender that contemporary readers would benefit from incorporating into discussions of the work's overall plan.

NOTES

1. Chernyshevsky's unfinished later novel, *Prologue* (*Prolog*, published in part in 1877 and more fully in 1906), further expounded the same ideas.

2. See his "What does the old woman think . . ." ("Chto dumaet starukha"; nekrasov-lit.ru/nekrasov/stihi/271.htm), "Katerina" (nekrasov-lit.ru/nekrasov/stihi/291.htm), "Mother" ("Mat'"; *Izbrannye proizvedeniia* 91), and "Russian Women" ("Russkie zhenshchiny"; 148–94). Nekrasov was also one of the very few poets to compose lyrics with a sympathetic portrayal of female prostitutes: "When out of the dark . . ." ("Kogda iz mraka . . ."; 8), from which Dostoevsky cited in an epigraph to the second part of *Notes from the Underground*, and "Whenever I drive at night . . ." ("Edu li noch'iu"; 18).

3. In two June 1876 entries in *Diary of a Writer* (*Dnevnik pisatelia*) Dostoevsky voiced profound admiration for George Sand and called higher education for women "a most urgent necessity" in Russia (507–14, 534).

4. See Stites, "M. L. Mikhailov." The most comprehensive study of politicized gender activities in Russia remains Stites's *The Women's Liberation Movement in Russia*.

5. It is worth noting that not all progressive thinkers addressed the issue of gender in the novel. In his lengthy review of *Crime and Punishment* in 1867 ("A Struggle for Life" ["Борьба за жизнь"; "Bor'ba za zhizn'"]), the radical Dmitry Pisarev ignored the question and discussed the text in terms of class poverty, which he adduced as Raskolnikov's sole motivation for murder.

6. Here and throughout, references to relevant passages in the novel rely on the translation by Katz (2018) and are identified by pages cited within the text.

7. Marmeladov confesses that he drinks because he genuinely wants to suffer (*Crime* 17; *Prestuplenie* 15), a masochistic desire typically gendered feminine.

8. Drawing on a range of Greek philosophers, Solov'ev transformed the Eastern Orthodox notion of Holy Wisdom (Αγία Σοφία; Hagía Sophia) as a female being, supposedly encountering her hypostasis in a vision in the British Library.

9. Raskolnikov privately calls Sonya a "holy fool" 'юродивая' (*Crime* 356; *Prestuplenie* 248).

10. In a prophetic moment, Sonya says about Lizaveta, "She will see God" 'она бога узрит' (*Crime* 357; *Prestuplenie* 249).

11. On male violence in the novel, see Straus 21–36.

12. Two other Ivanovnas are the moneylender, Alyona, and her perennially pregnant, religious younger sister, Lizaveta the *iurodivaia*.

13. As readers of Dostoevsky's works cannot fail to notice, he dislikes the French, Germans, Poles, Catholics, and especially Jews. A sweeping anti-Semitic remark referring to a watchman in the novel reads, "On his face was written that age-old querulous grief so sourly imprinted on the face of all members of the Jewish tribe, without exception" 'на лице его виднелась та вековечная брюзгливая скорбь, которая как кисло отпечаталась на всех без исключения лицах еврейското племени' (*Crime* 561; *Prestuplenie* 394).

The Urban Context of *Crime and Punishment*

Emily D. Johnson

Fyodor Dostoevsky's *Crime and Punishment* is a consummate realist novel that illustrates real problems associated with Russia's mid-nineteenth-century capital: poor sanitation, crushing poverty, despair, violence, and the radical political ideas that emerged partly in response to deplorable living conditions. The novel's protagonist, Raskolnikov, moves through streets and squares that seem so easily recognizable to anyone well acquainted with St. Petersburg that even before scholars of the novel had mapped its topography, readers sometimes felt inspired to retrace the footsteps of the protagonist and see the urban blight and despair firsthand (Konechnyi and Kumpan 17). And yet, for all the social and topographical detail that is provided, *Crime and Punishment*'s urban setting can be one of the most challenging aspects of the novel to teach to English-speaking undergraduates. If students do not understand how nineteenth-century Russian apartment houses looked and functioned, many of the details surrounding the murder of the pawnbroker may make little sense; if they have little exposure to earlier works of Petersburg description, they will not understand how ideologically charged Dostoevsky's urban descriptions often are. Many students may also need help understanding even more basic aspects of Dostoevsky's urban descriptions, such as his references to closed visual perspectives (streets that end or appear to end in a brick wall), particularly if they do not have firsthand exposure to big cities as a sensory environment.

This essay considers ways in which instructors can help students who have never been to Petersburg and know little of the city's history, literary heritage, or myth understand the role that the city plays in Dostoevsky's *Crime and Punishment*. Here I suggest approaches to organizing discussions as well as supplemental materials that can help instructors draw out the Petersburg theme in the novel in discussions. I also show ways in which references to both nineteenth- and twenty-first-century political rhetoric concerning urban centers can be used to help students gain additional perspective on some of the major issues that emerge from Dostoevsky's novel, including the question of how cities as built and social environments shape the lives of their inhabitants.

Because providing students with at least some information about nineteenth-century Petersburg is so important, when I read *Crime and Punishment* with students, on the first day that I allot to discussion of the novel, I generally devote a fair amount of time to exploring the novel's setting. As part of a larger discussion of the motives for the murder of the pawnbroker, I make sure that students have understood Raskolnikov's living conditions and surroundings as they are described in the very first pages of the novel: the closet-like apartment, the crush of people on the streets, the heat, the taverns and fetid canals. How, I ask the students, does the district around Raskolnikov's apartment building smell? What sounds does Raskolnikov hear as he moves through the city on his way to and from the pawnbroker's apartment? What kind of food is for sale in the taverns where he stops during the walks he takes while rehearsing for and contemplating the crime? What economic enterprises surround him?

Often, as we discuss the Petersburg landscape of part 1 of Dostoevsky's novel, students will note exactly how contemporary this portrait of urban blight feels. Raskolnikov might fairly be described as living in a food desert: taverns, the raucous Haymarket, and the nineteenth-century equivalent of convenience marts represent the chief sources of provisions in his neighborhood. At the bar where Raskolnikov first meets the drunken former civil servant Marmeladov, the greasy-faced owner and his underage assistants offer patrons "sliced pickles, black rusks, and pieces of fish; it all smelled" 'крошеные огурцы, черные сухари и резанная кусочками рыба; всё это очень дурно пахло' (*Crime* 12; *Prestuplenie* 12).[1] As he passes through Haymarket Square, Dostoevsky's description highlights "the eating houses on the filthy, stinking lower floors of the buildings" 'харчевен в нижних этажах, на грязных и вонючих дворах домов' and the taverns where the craftsmen and ragpickers gathered (*Crime* 66; *Prestuplenie* 51). Signs of substance abuse and despair are everywhere; educational and employment opportunities are rare. The Marmeladov children receive minimal instruction at home. Their mother fantasizes about opening a school for young ladies in the provinces—seemingly unable to conceive of such an establishment in her current neighborhood even in her dreams. Open-air recreational space is so inadequate that, while on his way to commit the murders, Raskolnikov fantasizes about adding fountains to the Yusupov Gardens, the only expanse of green in the neighborhood (*Crime* 80). It had opened to the public three years before Dostoevsky wrote *Crime and Punishment* and was by most accounts poorly maintained. Heavily used by single male laborers and tradesmen, it featured "dusty paths, sickly vegetation, and heaps of [shells from] sunflower seeds" 'пыль ные дороги, чахлая зелень, вороха семечек,' a favorite snack of lower-class Russians (Antsiferov 247; my trans.).[2] Nonetheless, the park's two ponds and paths offered at least some escape from the crowding of the Haymarket district, where many streets ended in visual dead ends, including the bar- and whorehouse-lined Tairov lane, where Raskolnikov returns when he wants "to make himself even queasier" 'чтоб еще тошней было' (*Crime* 173; *Prestuplenie* 122). How, it can be helpful to ask students, might the absence of air and light have affected residents of the area? References to "court[yard]s reeking with poisonous and malodorous gases from accumulations of sewage," "filthy passages swarming with vermin," and crowded "rookeries" in which almost every house features a bar or whorehouse figure prominently in the writing of late nineteenth-century journalists and social reformers about the slums of London, Paris, New York, and St. Petersburg (Mearns 4–7). I encourage students to consider how Dostoevsky uses such well-known features of nineteenth-century slum life to add to the oppressive atmosphere of the novel.

When I teach *Crime and Punishment* as part of a class on St. Petersburg in Russian culture, I prepare students for Dostoevsky's descriptions of the city by assigning nineteenth-century sketches. Excerpts from *Petersburg: The Physiology of a City*, the sketch collection that is most readily available in English, can be particularly helpful (Nekrasov). Vladimir Dal's "Petersburg Yardkeeper" can help students understand exactly where Raskolnikov obtains the axe and also the ways in which the courtyards and staircases of Petersburg apartment buildings were organized and used. "The Petersburg Organ-Grinders," by Dmitry Grigorovich, gives students a closer view of the kinds of street entertainers who figure prominently in so many scenes in Dostoevsky's novel. Nikolai Nekrasov's "The Petersburg Corners" provides an exposé of slum living conditions, drunkenness, and domestic violence that sets the stage for the dysfunctional Marmeladov family. Most important, all three sketches can help students think about the ethics of urban description. From whose perspective do we see these members of the lower classes and spaces? What are the ethical implications of using generalized types to represent members of lower-class professions and minority ethnicities? Doesn't this practice potentially dehumanize the poor by casting them as ethnographic subjects for the educated to study and observe? Seth Koven's *Slumming: Sexual and Social Politics in Victorian London* and material from *Slum Tourism: Poverty, Power, and Ethics*, a volume edited by Fabian Frenzel and colleagues, can help inform a discussion of the ways in which nineteenth-century journalistic investigations of urban poverty led to successful efforts to address social problems and yet also can seem voyeuristic and exploitative.

When he first emerged as a writer in the 1840s, Dostoevsky was associated with the Russian Natural School, which produced the key collections of physiological sketches about St. Petersburg, building on earlier French and English efforts. Authors of physiological sketches aimed to study large cities "scientifically" as a kind of giant organism with a circulatory system (roads and rivers, its carriage drivers and omnibuses), a belly (its slaughterhouses and markets), an excretory system (ragpickers), and many distinctive types of inhabitants, each of which might perhaps be equated with a kind of limb, organ, or cell. In many ways, *Crime and Punishment* can be seen as a reaction by a much more mature artist to this literary and journalistic trend. Representatives of lower-class professions that would have been familiar to Russian readers from sketches, such as street musicians, carriage drivers, housepainters, and laborers, people the novel's pages, but here the act of looking at the poor and the division of the population by class and income are continually problematized. Although educated enough to write philosophical treatises for journals and translate foreign literature, Raskolnikov enters the novel in clothes so frayed and faded that they stand out even in the world of the slums (Dostoevsky, *Crime* 5). One might argue that this costume not only serves as a mark of his real poverty; it also reads as a reference to the strategies that nineteenth-century sketch-writers and later novelists employed in their efforts to gather material on lower-class life: they dressed and spoke in ways that were meant to mask their class status and help them blend in, but their behavior often struck contemporaries as theatrical. For example, the novelist Vsevolod Krestovsky, whose sensational, fifteen-hundred-page adventure novel *The Slums of Petersburg* (*Peterburgskie trushchoby*) was appearing in the "thick journal" *Notes of the Fatherland* (*Otechestvennye zapiski*) just as Dostoevsky was working on *Crime and Punishment*, claimed to have spent several years investigating the city's slums (Krestovsky 1: 31). Contemporaries remembered how the author had showed up unexpectedly for breakfast at a friend's house dressed in a crumpled, dusty frock coat with uncombed hair and dirty boots, straight from a night in the lockup after being caught in a raid on a local tavern. Stories circulated about his visits to criminal dens and the periods he spent roaming through the streets of Petersburg, costumed to fit in with the populations he was studying (Elets x–xiii).

Although Raskolnikov is penniless at the start of the novel, he clearly, like Krestovsky and the writers of the Natural School, sees himself as an outsider in the world of the slums as opposed to an ordinary inhabitant. He gives alms even when, logically, he has nothing to spare; he wades in and tries to play the role of prince and rescuer to drunk girls; he imagines himself a social reformer building fountains; he wants to play the part of noble savior as opposed to fellow sufferer in many scenes. Raskolnikov's charitable impulses are not just important as a sign that he retains an essential core of goodness, despite the awful crimes he has committed, and is potentially redeemable. They also encourage us to think about issues of perspective in the novel. In some of the most painful scenes in *Crime and Punishment*, poverty and despair emerge as a kind of horrifying spectacle that divides characters into those directly affected and bystanders, witnesses, or spectators. We too as readers seem to join the crowds in pressing in to see Marmeladov wheeze out his last breath or to watch Katerina Ivanovna drive her weeping children through a grotesque street performance. We often seem to spy on characters when they are having private discussions in closed rooms—much as Svidrigailov pressed his ear to Sonya's door to eavesdrop on her conversations with Raskolnikov. Perhaps such narrative sequences are meant to make us uncomfortable; in the context of nineteenth-century efforts to explore the slums, they almost seem to hint at the educated classes' apathy and their privileged, largely detached position as observers.

Although *Crime and Punishment* reads as a rebuttal of simplistic determinist explanations of crime as caused by the environment, in a variety of places characters affirm the negative effects that unhealthy living conditions and circumscribed opportunities can have on urban inhabitants. Raskolnikov may not have killed the pawnbroker because he was destitute and underfed, but his circumstances at the beginning of the novel certainly played a role in his fate. As Raskolnikov notes to Sonya following his confession, "low ceilings and cramped rooms oppress the soul and the mind" 'низкие потолки и тесные комнаты душу и ум теснят' (Dostoevsky, *Crime* 459; *Prestuplenie* 320). Svidrigailov notes in his final interview with Raskolnikov, "There are few places where you can find so many gloomy, harsh, and strange influences on man's soul as you can in Petersburg" 'Редко где найдется столько мрачных, резких и странных влияний на душу человека, как в Петербурге' (*Crime* 514; *Prestuplenie* 357). Part 1 of *Crime and Punishment* is riddled with references to coincidences that propel Raskolnikov forward even as he considers abandoning his plan to commit murder (e.g., 67–69). He repeatedly evokes the devil or hell (depending on the translation) as he strolls through the town and at various points seems pulled along to his fate, unfree, or potentially at the mercy of outside forces (54, 67–68, 121). As coincidences propel him forward, his astonishment is "replaced by terror, as if a chill were running up and down his spine" 'сменилось ужасом, как будто мороз прошел по спине его' (*Crime* 67; *Prestuplenie* 52). Things act on him "almost completely mechanically: it was as if someone took him by the hand and pulled him along behind, irresistibly, blindly, with unnatural strength, without resistance" 'почти совсем механически: как будто его кто-то взял за руку и потянул за собой, неотразимо, слепо, с неестественной силой, без возражений' (*Crime* 77; *Prestuplenie* 58). For the experienced reader of nineteenth-century Petersburg fiction, such passages evoke the phantasmagoric and grotesque city of Nikolai Gogol, where urban space represents a site of temptation and spiritual ruin. When I am teaching *Crime and Punishment* as part of a St. Petersburg course, I generally assign at least a few of Gogol's Petersburg stories ("The Overcoat," "Nevsky Prospect," The Portrait") as well as two key Pushkin works set in the city ("The Queen of Spades" and *The Bronze Horseman*) b fore we start working with the novel. I can then ask my students to trace which elements of descriptions of Petersburg by Gogol and Pushkin Dostoevsky is echoing and why.

On either the first or second day of discussing *Crime and Punishment*, I usually show my students slides of a typical tour of Dostoevsky's Petersburg, including images of the most commonly identified models for Raskolnikov's house, the pawnbroker's house, Haymarket Square, Tairov Lane, and local bridges and canals. Good images for such a presentation can easily be found online, including on the website of the Dostoevsky Museum in St. Petersburg ("Peterburg Dostoevskogo"). As I talk students through these slides, I emphasize that for all the topographic detail in the novel, attributions are often approximate. As Nikolai Antsiferov, the pioneering scholar who created the Haymarket district route that underlies excursions to Dostoevsky's Petersburg, noted in his 1923 guidebook *Dostoevsky's Petersburg* (Петербург Достоевского; *Peterburg Dostoevskogo*), identifying the perfect model for Raskolnikov or the pawnbroker's house is not the most important thing: Dostoevsky may not have based Raskolnikov's house on a real structure (251). The topographic markers in *Crime and Punishment*, for all they may appear exactly measured in numbers of steps, often turn out, when we examine them more closely, not to match real locations. As A. M. Konechnyi and K. A. Kumpan explain, the Petersburg that we see in *Crime and Punishment* appears before us "in the form of the city's double, as if reflected in a fun house mirror" 'в виде города-двойника, отраженного как бы в кривом зеркале' (17). Its "streets and distances do not correspond to reality, and the houses of the protagonists and their locations are mobile and impossible to pin down" 'улицы и растояния не соответсвуют реальным, а дома героев и их местонахождение подвижны и неуловимы' (17–18; for more on this point, see Kumpan and Konechnyi). The main point of showing students slides of the setting of the novel is to provide them with visual clues that will help them better understand the novel. Given how much the Haymarket district has gentrified in recent decades, old engravings and photographs can be more helpful to students in many instances than contemporary images.

My slide presentation always includes parts of Petersburg that Dostoevsky largely ignores in his novel, such as the grand and glittery panorama of architectural ensembles (the Summer Palace, the Winter Palace, the Admiralty, the mansions of the English Embankment, Senate Square) that lines the Neva in the central district of the city and is praised to such great effect in the introduction to Pushkin's *The Bronze Horseman* (151–52). Raskolnikov notices this "majestic panorama" 'великолепную панораму' from the Nikolaevsky Bridge when he is returning from visiting Razumikhin in part 2 of the novel (*Crime* 126; *Prestuplenie* 90). He recalls the many times he stopped at the exact same spot to gaze at it while studying at the university. The impressions the great vista inspires in him are, however, negative: "An unaccountable chill always came over him as a result of this splendid sight; for him this opulent picture was filled with a deaf and mute spirit . . ." 'Необъяснимым холодом веяло на него всегда от этой великолепной панорамы; духом немым и глухим полна была для него эта пышная картина . . .' (*Crime* 126; *Prestuplenie* 90). Logically, Svidrigailov too would have a marvelous view of this most magnificent section of the city when he passes from the Haymarket district to Vasilievsky Island (where he sees his underaged fiancée) and then on to the Petersburg Side on the night leading up to his suicide, but Dostoevsky never has his character look up and does not mention the imperial magnificence that he passes. Instead, Svidrigailov looks down from the Tuchkov Bridge into the "black water of the Little Neva with particular curiosity and even a question in mind" 'с каким-то особенным любопытством и даже с вопросом посмотрел на черную воду Малой Невы' before heading off to find a hotel room for the night and descending into fevered dreams (*Crime* 553; *Prestuplenie* 388).

It can be helpful to ask students to think about why Dostoevsky chooses to provide such a circumscribed view of the capital in his novel. How is it that the characters in *Crime and Punishment* live just blocks away from the glittering center of the imperial capital and yet so seldom seem to glimpse it? Obviously, the routes that the characters travel, what they notice and what they seem to miss, are tremendously important. In *Crime and Punishment*, Dostoevsky uses the aspects of the Petersburg myth and text that he inherited from Gogol and Pushkin selectively, crafting a world that speaks to the problems of alienation and exclusion. His characters seem trapped geographically as well as by poverty, addiction, and, in the case of Raskolnikov, bad ideas. Notably, Raskolnikov is reborn and redeemed only once he leaves the confines of the city for penal servitude. And yet the geographic boundaries that seem to confine Dostoevsky's characters are to some extent illusory—as are so many aspects of literary Petersburg. What holds characters back is psychology, spiritual sickness, and circumstances—not distance per se. On the last day devoted to discussing the novel, it is always helpful to ask students to think about who escapes from the Petersburg underworld in Dostoevsky's novel and how.

NOTES

1. I cite the 2018 edition of the translation by Michael Katz throughout this essay.
2. For more information on conditions in the park, see Konechnyi 39–41.

Reading Money in *Crime and Punishment*

Vadim Shneyder

The challenge and the promise of paying close attention to money in *Crime and Punishment* is that, once we look for it, money turns out to be everywhere, and when we interpret it, almost everything in the novel turns out to be connected to (and by) money. Once students start to follow its movements, they are likely to realize that it connects the largest themes to the smallest details and leads readers in innumerable directions, both within and beyond the text. For example, Raskolnikov's lack of money helps define his place in the novel's character system, where some people are poor and others are rich. From there, we can examine how poverty and wealth become literary categories that interact with other major themes in the novel, such as the different kinds of indebtedness and obligation that characters assume, or the consequences of trying to reject the irreducible sociality of human beings (a rejection that is often abetted by money). Taking a different approach, readers can trace the links that money forms between the fictional world of *Crime and Punishment*, with its particular novelistic social imaginary, and various literary and social contexts. The novel clearly goes to considerable lengths to establish Raskolnikov's poverty and suggests connections between his poverty and the crime he decides to commit. As potential explanations for his murder accumulate, the possibility emerges that the cause of his crime lies in his poverty (here the instructor could assign an excerpt from the nineteenth-century critic Dmitry Pisarev's review of the novel, in which he argues that social factors are, indeed, crucial for understanding Raskolnikov's character in general and his crime in particular).

Following the lead of a critic like Pisarev, historicist readers can approach *Crime and Punishment* as a realist novel set in a distinctly modern, impoverished urban milieu. In that case, the constant intrusion of money into the quotidian experience of every character can indicate to students that Raskolnikov, Sonya, and the others live on our side of the great historical transformation that has rendered estates, duels, and matters of honor quite unfamiliar to twenty-first-century undergraduates. This is certainly important, but Fyodor Dostoevsky's self-description as a realist "in a higher sense" 'в высшем смысле' (Diary entry) also gives readers a cue to read a more protean discourse of money in *Crime and Punishment*.[1] In this expanded sense, a kind of money that is unstably metaphorical and rich in suggestions and implications emerges. Ethical questions in Dostoevsky are often closely tied to economic ones. The frequency with which his characters interact with money in an ostensibly irrational manner tells us something important about the moral contours of his fictional world, in which reciprocity, responsibility, and community are so important, and where calculation, rationalism, and hypertrophied individualism are often deadly. Both of these perspectives can help readers make sense of Raskolnikov's story. On the one hand, he is desperately poor, relies on remittances from his mother to survive, and fantasizes about the great things that he could accomplish if he could only acquire some money. Yet, when he steals the money and pledges from Alyona Ivanovna's apartment, he tries to hide it all, considers dumping it in the Neva River, and finally buries it under a rock, which is where it remains until his confession to the police.

We might regard this abandoned and buried money as a narrative false start. While Raskolnikov and the other characters make their way through the novel, it slowly decays under the rock. What is its use, then, whether in the novel or in the classroom? The question of why Raskolnikov does not do anything with the money can shed light on some of the values implicitly expressed by this novel. The protagonist commits a terrible crime based on a muddle of ideas, but he is not a calculating, rational utility maximizer. He is prone to spontaneous compassion and generosity, and in that, perhaps, lies the possibility of his redemption. Beyond this, the broader classroom uses of this unused money, and of all the other sums that appear in the novel, depend on the kind of course one is teaching. For example, in single-author courses on Dostoevsky's work, students can compare the strange things that characters do with money in *Crime and Punishment* (burying it under a rock [120–21]), *The Idiot* (throwing it into a fire [171–74]), and *The Brothers Karamazov* (sewing it up in a pouch and wearing it [489–99]). What happens—or doesn't happen—to this money? What new kinds of meaning or value does it accrue from being handled in this fashion? What does this kind of economic behavior tell us about the characters who perform it?

In what follows, I will focus on several key moments in the novel where money can serve as the focal point for wide-ranging discussion and exploration. Each scene provides a way into a major theme, such as the importance of mutual responsibility in Dostoevsky's moral universe, or a topic that is likely to be of interest to contemporary students, such as the crucial importance of women's labor for keeping the plot of *Crime and Punishment* going. In the classroom, the use of these scenes as starting points for discussion has the additional benefit of drawing students' attention to the intricate details of the text. This is important both as a corrective to the long tradition among Western readers of assuming that Dostoevsky was an undisciplined and sloppy writer and as a counterpoint to the tendency of some enthusiastic students to get carried away by the ideas in Dostoevsky's novels at the expense of the words in which those ideas are formulated. Such an approach forces students to read carefully. An online summary of the novel will tell the skimmer about schism, murder, Napoleon, the redemptive potential of poverty and humility, the criminal investigation, the dreams, and the epilogue. It is unlikely to mention Raskolnikov's emotional roller coaster at the beginning of part 2 as he wakes up to a summons from the police, walks to the station with the certainty that he stands accused of the murder, and then experiences enormous relief when it turns out that they just want to collect his unpaid rent.

We can think through the calculated effects of this scene's construction. Students well acquainted with the narrative devices of television will easily recognize how the scene builds up suspense, pulling readers into the first pages of the novel's second serialized installment (published in *The Russian Messenger* in February 1866). This little bit of narrative misdirection, where, for a moment, both Raskolnikov and the reader are probably convinced that he has been found out, opens the way for a discussion of Dostoevsky's writing as a commercial venture. The instructor can explain some of the particular circumstances in which *Crime and Punishment* was written: the money problems that Dostoevsky experienced in the mid-1860s, when he needed to support the family of his deceased brother Mikhail after the failure of their joint ventures in publishing the journals *Time* and *The Epoch*; his crippling gambling addiction; the infamous contract that he signed with the publisher Fyodor Stellovsky, which forced him to interrupt the writing of *Crime and Punishment* to dash off *The Gambler* in a matter of weeks or face the loss of royalties from all current and future publications for the next nine years; and how his extraordinary productivity in late 1866 was made possible thanks to the work of a young stenographer, Anna Grigoryevna Snitkina, who would soon become his second wife. This little scene illustrates one reason why money is so important in this novel: *Crime and Punishment* was itself a commodity, written by a man struggling to survive as one of the first professional writers in Russia's tiny publishing world, a man burdened by creditors and writing repeatedly to his publisher, Mikhail Katkov, for advances on the novel.[2] For *Crime and Punishment* to justify the large sums Katkov repeatedly lent to Dostoevsky—a middle-aged writer whose reputation did not equal that of Leo Tolstoy or Ivan Turgenev and who had only returned to literature in the late 1850s after a decade-long absence—it had to sell subscriptions to *The Russian Messenger.*

The material that the scene at the police station offers for class discussion is by no means limited to Dostoevsky's biography and the publishing context of the Russian classics. Raskolnikov responds with confusion to the police officer's announcement that he owes money: "But I don't owe anyone" 'Да я . . . никому не должен,' he says (*Prestuplenie* 77). What does this mean? What kinds of debt is Raskolnikov talking about here? What other kinds of indebtedness, besides the strictly monetary, are at work in this novel? The adjective that Raskolnikov uses—*dolzhen*, related to the noun *dolg*, meaning debt—means not just "owe" but also "should": read between the lines, Raskolnikov's words suggest that he has renounced any sense of obligation to others. He implies what the narrator repeatedly tells us: that this young man has fallen under the spell of certain ideas and has cut himself off from everyone around him. Questions about what people owe each other, what binds them together, and what happens when these bonds are torn apart by the deracinating ideology creeping in from the West are central to the novel. Later, in a dispute with Luzhin, Raskolnikov drives the point home: the logical conclusion of the pursuit of calculated self-interest is that people may murder each other (107). Luzhin tries to object, but it is the novel's two rich men—Luzhin and Svidrigailov—who are in many respects its most disturbing characters, and it is they who most readily treat people as things that can be bought or disposed of at will.

What makes money much more than just a theme among many in this novel is that it is both an alienating and destructive force and a generator of innumerable linkages between characters. One of the best places to illustrate this is a minor episode that takes place near one of the novel's most crucial scenes. During Raskolnikov's febrile wandering early in the novel, after passing out on Vasilievsky Island, where he has his famous dream of the mare, he meanders back into the city and through the Haymarket, where he is about to have a decisive chance encounter with Alyona Ivanovna's half-sister Lizaveta. The narrator, temporarily zooming out from his habitual close-up view of Raskolnikov, gives us an anticipation of the future: we learn that the hero would always wonder how this meeting, described as both "accidental" 'случайная' and "decisive" 'решительная' should have occurred when it did (*Prestuplenie* 50). In part 1, chapter 5, while walking among the stalls that are closing for the evening, Raskolnikov glimpses Lizaveta. Two sellers at the market are trying to arrange a meeting with her next evening. The purpose of this encounter for the novel's plot is clear: Raskolnikov finds out that Alyona Ivanovna will be home alone the following evening (that Lizaveta returns at the most inopportune moment is, of course, crucial: Raskolnikov's calculation, based on economic considerations, fails). Empowered by this evidence, he decides that he is free to carry out his crime.

The next chapter resumes the discussion of this meeting. The particulars are easy to miss because this chapter and the next are so dense with memorable details, including the murder itself. In the very first lines of the chapter, the narrator again jumps forward in time to give us temporary access to the perspective of the future Raskolnikov. Now we learn why Lizaveta was out of the house the following day. It turns out that she—perhaps surprisingly, if students expect a saintly character like Lizaveta to remain untainted by money—worked by arranging business transactions between buyers and sellers. At this point, a curious shift occurs in the narrative perspective, and the instructor might ask students what the point of it is: the narrator slips into the authoritative tone of someone who knows more than Raskolnikov. We learn that "[t]he matter was most ordinary and didn't involve anything unusual at all. An impoverished family that had recently arrived was selling some items, dresses and so on, all women's goods" 'Дело было самое обыкновенное и не заключало в себе ничего такого особенного. Приезжее и забедневшее семейство продавало вещи, платье и проч., все женское' (*Crime* [2018] 69; *Prestuplenie* 52). Lizaveta is being asked to arrange a private sale of these things. All of this, the narrator insists, is absolutely commonplace. The only reason to introduce these details, it seems, is to contrast the plausible explanation of Lizaveta's presence in the market with Raskolnikov's hermeneutic of suspicion, which endows every event somehow related to the murder with great prophetic significance.

In reality, that is, from the point of view of the judicious narrator, there is nothing the least bit unusual in the situation of a family moving to the capital, falling into poverty, and needing to sell off all its women's clothes. This is simply a bit of background detail, a slice of real life that Dostoevsky expected his readers to understand. If students encounter this passage in a course where they read novels by other writers, especially nineteenth-century novels from outside the Russian tradition, this scene is rich in contrastive potential. What typically happens when people from the countryside arrive in the big city in the novels of Honoré de Balzac, Charles Dickens, or Émile Zola? What change of social status awaits someone like Rastignac in *Père Goriot* or Pip in *Great Expectations*? Students are likely to find that Dostoevsky is unusual in focusing on the relentless downward mobility of these newcomers. Urban migration in *Crime and Punishment* seems to function as a conveyor belt moving people inexorably into poverty. Among the other newcomers, Raskolnikov has not met with much success since he moved to St. Petersburg in hopes of attaining a university education and a career. At the time of the novel's events, he cannot even give lessons because he cannot afford presentable clothing. We soon meet the Marmeladovs, who are also caught in a vicious cycle of diminishing opportunities. Raskolnikov predicts that his mother will have no means for survival in the city and will have to turn to barely remunerated sewing to survive, and Dunya's plan to marry Luzhin to save her mother and brother further indicates the lack of economic opportunities for working people in the big city.

What could be more natural, the narrator of *Crime and Punishment* suggests, than a family moving to St. Petersburg and finding itself destitute? In Dostoevsky's fictional world, the imperial capital, from its narrow, dirty streets to its huge and dingy buildings filled with tiny rooms and filthy back staircases, is a city of the poor. If students are reading *Crime and Punishment* alongside works by Alexander Pushkin, Nikolai Gogol, or Tolstoy, they can see that the great palaces, monuments, and public spaces are all marginal in Dostoevsky's representation of the capital. It can be hard to imagine that this is also the city of "The Queen of Spades," "Nevsky Prospect," or parts of *Anna Karenina*. Here students can take note both of Dostoevsky's different socioeconomic background, as compared to these other writers, and of the effect of this novel's different class setting on its style, themes, and narrative possibilities. How do Raskolnikov's ambitions of enrichment and their consequences compare to Hermann's? What is the meaning of his indebtedness compared to that of Stiva Oblonsky or Aleksei Vronsky?

The scene in the marketplace offers a point of departure for another discussion: the sign of the family's desperate circumstances is that they are selling off their women's clothes. It is not just poverty in general, but women's poverty in particular that seems to be a constant feature of urban life in *Crime and Punishment*. Raskolnikov is surrounded by women who struggle to support themselves in conditions where their opportunities for work are limited; selling themselves more or less literally seems to be by far the most remunerative occupation available to them. Raskolnikov himself makes the connection between Sonya's selling herself for her family and his own sister Dunya's similar sacrifice in giving herself to the despicable Luzhin to secure the future of her brother and mother.

Yet it is not only women's poverty that is on display in this novel. Women also control a considerable portion of its wealth. From the landlady to whom Raskolnikov owes several months of rent to the pawnbroker Alyona Ivanovna herself, women are central to the economic life of St. Petersburg in *Crime and Punishment*. Sonya supports her family with sex work, and Dunya was pressured to do the same as a governess in the household of the Svidrigailovs. Her former boss explains to Raskolnikov that he was rescued from debtor's prison by Marfa Petrovna, a wealthy landowner, whom he married and then (probably) murdered. An aside about the property rights enjoyed by noblewomen in imperial Russia can clarify that an independently wealthy woman like Marfa Petrovna was not such an unusual case.[3] Furthermore, the numerous working women in this novel open the way for wide-ranging discussions about Dostoevsky's representation of women and the narrative work that they do. Students may notice that Raskolnikov is able to wander the city streets thinking about the great men of the past because his mother sends him money, his landlady allows him to accumulate debt, and her servant keeps bringing him food. Sonya is able to follow Raskolnikov to Siberia thanks to the money left her by Svidrigailov, who got his money from his late wife. If not for this last financial detail, Sonya could not have been there in Siberia for the transformative moment at the end of the epilogue. These tiny details, impossible to find in any summary, are what make Raskolnikov's story possible within the generic rules of the nineteenth-century novel. Reading them, students will learn to be better readers of novels and better readers in general.

NOTES

1. All translations are my own unless otherwise indicated.
2. The work of William Mills Todd, particularly his chapter "Dostoevskii as a Professional Writer," would be a useful secondary reading here.
3. The work of Michelle Marrese is a useful source on Russian noblewomen's property rights.

Poverty and Privilege: Teaching *Crime and Punishment* for Social Justice

Rachel Stauffer

As a novel that vividly describes systemic injustice, socioeconomic disparity, and gender inequality in nineteenth-century St. Petersburg, Fyodor Dostoevsky's *Crime and Punishment* offers instructors and students a unique opportunity to explore broad questions of social justice, both in Dostoevsky's time and in the present. Social justice education (SJE) emphasizes equity literacy, civic and democratic engagement, critical thinking skills, and the recognition and dismantling of systemic injustice and inequity: "Social justice educators interrogate the status quo and seek to disrupt oppression by calling for and acting toward transformation of oppressive structures and practices" (Mthethwa-Sommers 220). SJE can be applied in any content area by any instructor who wishes to illuminate and dismantle systemic injustice and inequity experienced by members of groups historically underrepresented in socially dominant culture because of race, ethnicity, religion, gender identity, sexual orientation, class, socioeconomic status, ability, or intersecting categories. This chapter will discuss how the guiding principles of SJE may be applied in the teaching of *Crime and Punishment* among increasingly diverse student populations at colleges and universities in the United States.

Social Justice Education

Multicultural educators and researchers generally agree on the following objectives for SJE: the recognition of inequality and injustice in order to foster action for equality and justice; the teaching of critical thinking and problem-solving skills to cultivate civic and democratic engagement in order to resolve systemic problems of inequity and injustice; and the acknowledgment that society consists of groups and classes that are unequally valued by socially dominant culture, which means such groups and classes are not equitable beneficiaries of societally determined advantages. An important foundational principle of SJE, therefore, is the distinction between *equality* and *equity*. As multicultural educator Sonia Nieto differentiates the two, "*equal* education implies we are giving every student the *same* thing and an *equitable* education provides students with what they *need to achieve equality*" (Nieto and Bode 9). Therefore *equality* and *equity* are not synonymous, and SJE practitioners must be equipped to tell the difference. As Paul Gorski writes, "Whereas many popular approaches ask us to focus on culture—the *culture* of poverty, *cultural* competence—equity literacy asks us to keep *equity* at the center of our conversations, to focus on how to create and sustain equitable learning environments free of even the subtlest biases and inequities" ("Equity Literacy" 6). The development of equity literacy requires instructors and students to be attuned to injustice and bias in course content; subsequently, it often requires diligent, self-aware reflection on our own biases, suggested practices for which will be discussed further below.

Another important function of SJE is the preparation of students for civic and democratic engagement. Applicable skills identified in this area by educators include "[c]ollaborating, building coalitions; negotiating and seeking consensus; making decisions; learning cooperatively; working with diverse groups (in race, culture, ideology)" (Gottlieb and Robinson 22). Critical thinking skills are essential to democratic engagement, and *Crime and Punishment* connects the law and the respective roles of government and law enforcement with criminality and social issues while maintaining its artistic purpose: "The most important task of literary works of art is the true rendering of social and philosophical issues of the era the author lives in. An important aspect of social reality is law as the people's special relationship system, involving the recognition of rights and duties of the people" (Skorohovoda et al. 290). As Paulo Freire, one of the founders of critical pedagogy, a foundational ideology for the field of SJE, wrote in 1970,

> Education either functions as an instrument which is used to facilitate integration of the younger generation into the logic of the present system and bring about conformity or it becomes 'the practice of freedom', the means by which men and women deal critically and creatively with reality and discover how to participate in the transformation of their world. (34)

The capacities of young people to think critically and to challenge the status quo of high-stakes testing and federally mandated curricula are essential for the recognition and dismantling of injustice. Such skills are often developed in SJE approaches, for example, by asking students to identify and consider voices that are not represented in a text or other medium, or to consider the potential biases of authors and information sources. In the analysis of history or literature, for example, SJE practitioners threaten injustice by challenging orientalist, nativist, and purely socially dominant frames of interpretation and inquiry.

Russian Literature and Cultural Dilemmas

American scholarship on the teaching of Russian literature is largely concerned with theoretical frameworks, historical or comparative contextualization and analysis, and close investigation of specific themes, motifs, tropes, ideas, thoughts, or philosophies. There is less discussion as to how or why *Crime and Punishment*, for example, is considered a canonical work of nineteenth-century Russian literature. SJE requires questions about the canon in order to challenge the status quo. The very establishment and recognition of a canon are acts of privilege. Any prioritization of certain works of literature selected by socially dominant groups, without the benefit of non-socially-dominant and intersectional perspectives, will be more likely to emphasize and perpetuate socially dominant categories. Although the very nature of a canon is allegedly immutable, such inflexibility is an affront to humanistic inquiry, which compels reconsideration and redefinition in light of new discoveries and theories, social movements, and technological advances. The notion of how any canon is defined and sustained is worthy of a larger discussion in Slavic studies, and perhaps also in our classrooms. This is not to say that *Crime and Punishment*, or Dostoevsky's many other works, do not belong in the canon of Russian literature. However, the implementation of SJE compels the reexamination of canons and their contributions to the maintenance of certain types of authority and conformity that sustain the privilege of socially dominant groups.

In the context of SJE, *Crime and Punishment* differentiates itself from many other works in the accepted canon of classic Russian literature by illuminating injustice, particularly in its unfiltered depictions of people experiencing poverty and of the systemic oppression of girls and women. As Boris Christa has observed, "Where Dostoevskii becomes strongly emotionally involved is when he takes up the theme of money and sexual power. In this area, he was a pioneering publicist totally aware of the realities of sexual power and the deplorable economic position of women" (Leatherbarrow 100). Dostoevsky's biography contains experiences of non-socially-dominant culture, given his near execution and time spent imprisoned, as well as his various health-related and financial struggles, particularly during the time he was writing *Crime and Punishment*: "By the end of his life his financial affairs were more or less in order, but the period between . . . 1865 . . . and . . . 1872 were years of acute financial hardship, not helped by his pathological addiction to roulette" (Leatherbarrow 18). SJE requires us to go a bit further in order to recognize that while Dostoevsky struggled financially, perhaps particularly in comparison with contemporaries like Tolstoy (who had the noble title of Count), he simultaneously had enough privilege that he was able to sustain his gambling addiction and continue writing *Crime and Punishment* despite temporary financial strain, in comparison with the characters in the novel, such as Raskolnikov and Sonya, who struggle to survive financially in St. Petersburg. Raskolnikov, despite having legitimate sources of funds, nevertheless resorts to murder and theft, even though these acts do not really help him financially, while Sonya has no choice but to engage in sex work for the survival of her family.

SJE also requires us to acknowledge that the audience of *Crime and Punishment* in the 1860s and 1870s largely consisted of privileged, socially dominant groups, according to what we know about Russian literacy rates in the second half of the nineteenth century.[1] Both the author and the audience of *Crime and Punishment* represented the socially dominant culture and the urban elite. As we acknowledge that fact of the novel's history, we can examine the themes of poverty and privilege in *Crime and Punishment* more closely.

Poverty and Privilege in Crime and Punishment

Raskolnikov rejects socially dominant culture, both in terms of the personal liberty of others—for example, that of the pawnbroker and her sister—and the rule of law, which considers murder to be a crime. Stepping over the culturally understood line between crime and non-crime is the genesis of the etymology of the Russian word used in the title of the novel for *crime*, *prestuplenie* (*pre* means "over, with exaggeration," and *stup* means "step" or "foot"; this noun therefore literally means "overstepping" or "stepping too far"). Certainly this was not accidental, as Dostoevsky himself oversteps many different lines in the novel, such as the disparity between how systemic poverty affects men (by creating circumstances that, perhaps, contribute to Raskolnikov's state of mind, leading him to commit a crime) and how it affects women, whose very survival, as well as social mobility, more often than not depend on subjugation. Although the murder Raskolnikov commits is likely the crime to which the author refers, for the women in *Crime and Punishment*, whose lives are dictated by marriage, poverty, or sex work, the idea of stepping across the line is an altogether different experience. Instructors can dedicate several class discussions to the topic of sex work in the novel, which would be an acceptable approach in the context of SJE. An inevitable theme, however, is poverty.

Crime and Punishment addresses societal byproducts of poverty, and the way that poverty disenfranchises and further marginalizes non-socially-dominant groups. By understanding poverty in the modern world, instructors and students may be able to more deeply connect with Dostoevsky's depictions of the poor in *Crime and Punishment*. Instructors could encourage students to challenge common perceptions, assumptions, and stereotypes about poverty, namely, as Gorski asserts, that people experiencing poverty do not value education, are lazy, are substance abusers or addicts; are linguistically deficient or poor communicators, and are ineffective and inattentive (Gorski, *Reaching* 74–82). Gorski notes that these incorrect stereotypes about people experiencing poverty are persistently and widely believed by Americans at all educational levels—indeed, such stereotypes often pervade higher education. In a recent article in the *Chronicle of Higher Education*, for example, Adam Kirk Edgerton laments the treatment of Southern, rural students by academics who are not from the South, which he specifies as a type of discrimination that has increased since the 2016 presidential election:

> In the age of Trump, anti-Southern attitudes seem to have crystallized and worsened throughout higher education. Any Trump-voting area, in fact, seems to be fair game for ridicule. These attitudes undercut the efforts of those seeking to advance the rights of marginalized groups in regions of the country where evidence-based scholarship might be needed the most.

Gorski notes, "[P]overty is everywhere. It's even in schools people presume are filled with 'upper-middle-class' students. And increasingly so" (*Reaching* 53). In classroom discussions of poverty in *Crime and Punishment*, for example, there may be triggering moments for some students around Raskolnikov's own precarious situation as a student, which includes food insecurity, inhospitable living conditions, and his family's inability to support him financially, and he believes that his struggle in this regard is unique. The terrible choice that Sonya must make between prostitution and watching her younger siblings go hungry may not be a situation many students find triggering, but those who have experienced or are experiencing poverty may have faced similarly impossible decisions. Instructors must anticipate the emotions, often associated with trauma, that some students may feel as a result of discussions of these difficult topics.

Dostoevsky's characterization of Raskolnikov encodes all five of Gorski's stereotypes about people experiencing poverty, which provides an excellent topic of discussion in the SJE context. Raskolnikov was once a student but no longer wants to teach or to finish his schooling; having abandoned both pursuits, he may be perceived as a person experiencing poverty who does not value education. In Dostoevsky's characterization of him, Raskolnikov also demonstrates some laziness. He spends much of his time in bed in his apartment, likely because of his mental and physical challenges, largely brought about because of poverty. Drinking and alcoholism occur throughout the novel; in particular, Marmeladov's alcoholism is funded by his adolescent daughter's sex work. Many of those who drink in the novel are also living in poverty. However, Raskolnikov is not linguistically inferior as a beneficiary of education. He is literate, which makes him part of the privileged few in the context of nineteenth-century Russia, but his neuroses, extreme circumstances of poverty, and poor health coincide to make him an unusual person to communicate with. In the first one hundred pages of the novel, many of Raskolnikov's utterances are incomprehensible or ineffectual. And, perhaps as a result of mental and physical illness brought on by financial poverty, Raskolnikov is inattentive and ineffective. His inattention may be (as is the case with children experiencing poverty in schools) the product of hunger, malnutrition, anxiety, psychological distress brought about by poverty, and other trauma-inducing circumstances. The author seems to suggest that Raskolnikov could bring himself out of poverty if he wished to, but this reinforces many stereotypical perceptions of people experiencing poverty.

The novel reveals many injustices that Raskolnikov has endured by his early twenties, some as the result of his own actions and others that were out of his control. We learn in the novel that his brother and his father died when he was a child, leaving him, as the only male member of the family, to care for his mother and sister. As such, he ran out of money and support while seeing to his education, which he clearly viewed, as do many college students in the United States, as a means to achieve greater financial security. The text tells us that Raskolnikov has been experiencing poverty for a while, evidenced by his clothes and hat, which are routinely ridiculed. Raskolnikov is ill, mentally, physically, psychologically, although the cause of his various sufferings is not made clear to us. College students are likely to identify and empathize with Raskolnikov's precarious financial situation, considering that ninety percent of undergraduates experience some level of financial anxiety (Goldrick-Rab 119). A robust discussion of the novel might be oriented around the categories of poverty that people experience[2] and the category into which Raskolnikov best fits. Similarly, an examination of Gorski's stereotypes of poverty in the novel might be complemented by an examination of themes of crime and punishment in popular television series such as *Orange Is the New Black* or *Narcos* in order to show students a modern parallel to the historical, social, and entertainment context of Dostoevsky's serially published novel.

Social Justice Outcomes and Objectives for Crime and Punishment

It may be useful to have a sample framework for SJE that can be customized to align with instructors' personal teaching style and methods. There is no uniform set of SJE outcomes or objectives. The outcomes and objectives suggested below align with the broader goals of SJE as they have been defined in this chapter. Table 1 offers a sample of how student learning outcomes and course objectives for a unit in a literature course on Dostoevsky's *Crime and Punishment* could be designed and implemented. Student Learning Outcomes (SLOs) are the things that students will learn to do in the course, Course Learning Objectives (CLOs) are the assignments that instructors will assess to determine students' level of achievement of the SLOs, and Community Action (CA) items are the opportunities for students to take the SLOs and the CLOs into the campus community, the community outside of the college or university, or other external groups that may benefit.

There are also several existing SJE-oriented experiential programs and courses at colleges and universities in the United States that take Russian literature into juvenile detention centers or prisons. The University of Virginia's Books Behind Bars program focuses on Russian literature exclusively, taking students, professors, and course content beyond the classroom into social and criminal justice contexts into which *Crime and Punishment* clearly fits. Experiential and community engagement programs fully advance the goals of SJE in that they require equity literacy, increase the visibility of non-socially-dominant groups and experiences, provide opportunities to identify and examine privilege and cultural dilemmas, and provide educational equity to people who are currently incarcerated. Dostoevsky would likely have embraced many of the objectives of SJE, as Peter Roberts suggests:

> A Dostoevskian approach to education stands opposed to the linear, outcomes-based constructions of learners and learning that tend to domi-

Table 1. Example of SJE Framework

Social Justice Competencies	*Equity Literacy*	*Civic and Democratic Engagement*	*Critical Thinking*	*Non-Socially-Dominant Perspectives*
Student Learning Outcomes	Recognize bias and injustice in Dostoevsky's authoring of *Crime and Punishment* as well as in the novel.	In the reading of *Crime and Punishment*, identify contemporary parallels to Raskolnikov's circumstances (poverty, limited access to education, poor health), the means whereby local, state, and federal governments in the United States address such problems today, and the ways in which constituents can engage actively toward dismantling these injustices.	Through close reading, observe implicit and explicit systems and conditions of oppression in the novel.	Identify the ways in which marginalized people and communities are treated in *Crime and Punishment*.
Course Learning Objectives	Respond to biases and injustices in *Crime and Punishment* in an essay or a presentation for the class.	Reflect on the similarities and differences in student life in nineteenth-century St. Petersburg and in the contemporary classroom, considering financial aid, accessibility, and socioeconomic status.	Keep an ongoing record throughout our reading of *Crime and Punishment* of a theme or themes in the novel (this may involve but does not require tracking a theme that illuminates issues of injustice or inequity).	Create a product or activity to present to and engage classmates that illuminates the suffering of marginalized groups (people experiencing poverty or illness; women; sex workers) in *Crime and Punishment*.
Community Action	Engage others on campus or in the community with *Crime and Punishment* in order to work toward and compel others to work toward the dismantling of systemic injustice.	Participate as a class in a campus-wide or community political event on income inequality, poverty reduction, education, health care, or human rights.	Write a research paper on the theme tracked, and discuss it, supporting commentary with textual evidence and peer-reviewed scholarship.	Deliver instruction, a presentation, or an activity to a group of people outside the class to cultivate compassion and action against unjust treatment of marginalized people.

> nate policy discourse. It also rubs against any psychological model of education that emphasizes development through ordered, sequential stages, each with their own measurable behaviors and attributes. Dostoevsky shows us what is wrong with these dominant ways of thinking by depicting human beings "living on the edge"—on the margins of society, on the brink of insanity, and in the throes of desperate daily struggles. . . . Dostoevsky's characters are outsiders—strangers, we might say, but not altogether unlike us, and this is, in part, what allows them to speak to us so powerfully. . . . We may, of course, be far less extreme in our thoughts, feelings, and actions than many of Dostoevsky's troubled souls, but we often suffer as they do, experiencing deep existential anxiety and finding no relief in education. Indeed, education can contribute to our suffering, prompting painful reflection on the muddied events of our lives, on our shortcomings as well as strengths, and on the challenges that still lie ahead of us. Becoming educated in this manner can be a disturbing, sometimes deeply traumatic, experience—but we are, as Dostoevsky shows, not alone in this process, and an encounter with others who suffer, in fiction as in "real life," can make a difficult pedagogical journey more bearable. (383–84)

Ultimately, SJE has the potential to steer the teaching of *Crime and Punishment* toward innovation in the teaching and analysis of Russian literature. More broadly, SJE also contributes to the greater purposes of humanistic inquiry that include the recognition of common humanity, the depiction of and compassion for the many diverse struggles of human experience, and working for the common good.

NOTES

1. According to Boris Mironov, by 1897, thirty years after the publication of *Crime and Punishment*, "the average literacy of both sexes of the population in European Russia was 30 percent; of the urban population it was 58 percent and of the rural, 26 percent; among men it was 43 percent and among women, 22 percent" (Mironov 235).
2. One multicultural educator, for example, identifies six types of poverty: situational, generational, absolute, relative, urban, and rural (Jensen 6).

Teaching Religious Subtexts in *Crime and Punishment*

Olga Meerson

Unlike other religious intertexts, Orthodox subtexts are primarily liturgical, even when they stem from a biblical source. A given intertext may have both levels of allusion: the biblical source and a liturgical use. The latter would have been known to Russian speakers in Fyodor Dostoevsky's time, whether Orthodox, nominally or actively, or heterodox and surrounded by an Orthodox population. All readers, for example, would have registered any allusions to the paschal service. The examples below will address both levels of allusion and how and why they should be taught. Since liturgical allusions appealed to the subconscious, Dostoevsky's Russian contemporaries or characters would have registered them more readily than the purely biblical ones.

Alerting students to religious subtexts in *Crime and Punishment* has twofold importance: it provides a strong example of intertextuality per se, something essential for decoding any work of art, and if students register the specific liturgical allusions, they will get into the minds of Dostoevsky's contemporaries, thereby gaining an insider's insight into Russian culture. This process de-others the other for American students.

Just as liturgical awareness informs the original intended readers' perception of *Crime and Punishment*, so the novel itself is also structured in a quasi-liturgical way: its narrator and characters invite readers to participate in a religious event rather than merely observe it as outsiders. Also, we shall soon see that the most crucial theme in the novel is sacrifice and what may go wrong with it. According to Dostoevsky, sacrifice is right only when one sacrifices oneself—as Christ sacrificed himself for everyone—rather than someone else. Consequently, the main structuring element in the novel is the opposition between Raskolnikov's ideology of sacrificing another person for the general good and the motif of self-sacrifice—be it Sonya's or Dunya's or Pulkheriya's. A biblical intertext to be discussed later will oppose the right sacrifice to the wrong one.

The novel itself has a quasi-liturgical event at its center—Sonya reading, out loud, the passage from John 11:1–45 about the resurrection of Lazarus. This episode, key to the novel and its understanding, must be discussed with students in any case, and in doing so I stress its liturgical form and genre. The episode even refers to rubrics—the specifications of the reader's intonation fluctuations. The narrator compares Sonya's "ringing" voice to a "high-strung wire"—a description that may apply equally to an extremely emotional reading and to liturgical chanting (in the Orthodox liturgy, all scriptural readings are chanted): "'Now, a certain man was sick, named Lazarus, of Bethany . . .'—she finally uttered with effort, but suddenly, from the third word on, her voice started ringing and broke off like too high-strung a wire" '«Был же болен некто Лазарь, из Вифании . . . » произнесла она, наконец, с усилием, но вдруг, с третьего слова, голос зазвенел и порвался, как слишком натянутая струна' (Dostoevsky, *Prestuplenie* 250).[1]

An earlier section in the same episode, part 4, chapter 4, illustrates the priority of liturgical over scriptural experience in the novel. Before she finally summons the courage to read the Gospel passage out loud, Sonya first asks Raskolnikov if he has ever read the Gospels—to which he nervously replies, "long ago, when I was a student" 'Давно . . . Когда учился'—and then she asks if he perhaps has heard the reading in the church ("а в церкви не слыхали?"; *Prestuplenie* 249). Unlike most Orthodox, Sonya herself actually reads the Scriptures rather than relying on hearing them in the church: as a prostitute, she feels embarrassed to attend church and goes only rarely. She is aware of both contexts for the narrative of the resurrection of Lazarus, the scriptural and the liturgical.

Before, however, making any structural claims about liturgy in *Crime and Punishment*, let us turn to biblical allusions, closely reading a relatively short example of religious allusion. In the classroom, this example will aim to facilitate discussion among students as to why these allusions, religious and markedly Orthodox, may matter to them as readers of Dostoevsky as well as of any novel or piece of fiction or poetry.[2] (A side benefit of discussing these subtexts is acquainting students with material that may be unfamiliar to them from the Old and New Testaments.)

In the passage in question, in part 1, chapter 2, Marmeladov says of his benefactor Ivan Afanasievich, "Do you, Sir, happen to know his Excellency Ivan Afanasievich? No? Then you do not know one who is truly a man of God. [He is mild like] wax, real wax, before the face of the Lord—'as wax melts' . . . His excellency even shed a tear after listening to my story" 'Его превосходительство Ивана Афанасьевича изволите знать? . . . Нет? Ну так божия человека не знаете! Это—воск . . . воск перед лицом господним; яко тает воск! . . . Даже прослезились, изволив все выслушать' (18).

Marmeladov is alluding here to a text used in the paschal service and in exorcisms, based on Psalm 68.1–2: "Let God arise! Let His enemies be scattered, let all those who hate Him draw back! As smoke vanishes so let them vanish, as wax melts before the fire, so let sinners [for exorcisms, *demons*] perish before the face of God." The liturgical and scriptural contexts of these words each carry their own allusive power. The irony of Marmeladov's description becomes evident when we consider both the biblical and the liturgical layers of this subtext. The liturgical reference is itself twofold, entailing two separate liturgical orders of the Orthodox church, one public (the paschal service) and one private but no less significant (the rite of exorcism).

On the scriptural level, Marmeladov's phrase alludes to Psalms 68.3 (67.3 in the Septuagint [*Bibliia*])—"[К]а́къ таетъ воскъ отъ огня, та́къ нечестивые да погибнутъ отъ лица Божія" '[A]s wax melts before the face of fire—so let the evildoers [רשעים] perish before the face of God.' Of course, even this purely biblical allusion conveys irony: being mellow as "wax before the face of God" hardly suggests the force that causes God's enemies to melt before his face "as wax melts before the face of fire" (cf. verses 1–2: "Да возстанетъ Богъ, и расточатся враги Его" 'Let God arise, let His enemies scatter'). Even in the psalm, these defeated evildoers are by no means "true men of God" but rather God's enemies.

Yet this allusion by Marmeladov also appealed to those readers, Dostoevsky's contemporaries and compatriots, who did not read the Bible daily. To put it in Sonya's terms, they might have heard it in the church. Both the paschal and the exorcist contexts were known widely. The verses are sung, recited, and used as responses, many times over, during the paschal matins and liturgy. The best testimony to the popularity of these verses for a non-Russian is Nikolai Rimsky-Korsakov's *Paschal Overture* (a.k.a. *Russian Easter Festival Overture*), where the first trombone solo is set to the chant for these verses. In that version, through the Septuagint, "מיעשר" is rendered as "грешницы" ("sinners").[3]

The exorcism version, no less popular, is a prayer addressed to the Holy Cross as the instrument of casting out demons. The prayer is common for healing the sick, as well as for various blessings, so people in Dostoevsky's time used to hear and recite it more often than they would go to church. In the exorcism version, the word used to translate the original "מיעשר" is neither "sinners" nor "evildoers" (semantically the closest to the Hebrew) but "бѣси" ("demons").

The exorcism text continues as shown below in italics. The expressions Marmeladov uses, albeit in a different combination, are in bold:

> Let God arise, and let His enemies be scattered; and let those who hate Him flee from **His face**. As smoke vanishes, let them vanish; and **as wax melts** from **the face/presence** of fire, so let the sinners/*demons* perish from **the face/presence of** *those who love* **God** *and who sign themselves with the Sign of the Cross. . . .* [4]
>
> Да воскреснет Бог и расточатся врази Его и да бежат от **лица Его** ненавидящии Его. Я́ко исчеза́ет дым, да исче́знут; **я́ко та́ет воск** от лица́ огня́, та́ко да поги́бнут *бе́си*/грешницы от **лица́ Божия**/*лю́бящих Бо́га и зна́менующихся кре́стным зна́мением Его. . . .*

Though overtly praising him, Marmeladov covertly compares his "benefactor" Ivan Afanasievich to a demon to be defeated by the Cross.[5] Dostoevsky thus manages to flesh out the complexity of Marmeladov's own character. Although sophisticated, this type of quotation does not characterize an intellectual, let alone a snob. Rather, Marmeladov opens a whole gallery of prophetic drunks, derelicts, or even pathological liars, such as Lebedev, Ivolgin, Lebyadkin, Smerdyakov—a whole cast of very unlikely authorities on truth.[6] In Dostoevsky, just as in Shakespeare or according to Bakhtin's idea of the Carnival, *argumentum ad hominem* never works, since all of us are fallen. These themes are crucial to discuss in class.

Most important, Marmeladov's example can teach students to link style to its function—the "how" to the "to what end" or "why bother"—in a Bakhtinian way. The way Marmeladov quotes sets a pattern for characterizing him as a subject, not as the object of a description.

How does one teach all this? By asking Socratic questions of the right kind. Fortunately, modern technology allows us to ask those questions with the expectation that the students can do some research online. Here is a sample homework assignment to give to students for subsequent discussion in class:

> In an online biblical concordance, find the relevant reference to melting wax. NB: in the original Russian, the conjunction "as" is given in Church Slavonic (*iako* instead of *kak*), which immediately marks the whole expression "as wax melts" as something a Russian contemporary of Dostoevsky would have heard in the Church.
>
> Find out, through any means available, when and how the phrase "as wax melts" is used in an Orthodox liturgical context. This question will inform our next discussion in class: Depending on your findings, what do you think Marmeladov's real attitude to Ivan Afanasievich is? Does the biblical/liturgical allusion characterize only Ivan Afanasievich, or also Marmeladov, Raskolnikov, or Dostoevsky?
>
> Do you think Marmeladov impresses Raskolnikov the same way he impresses us? Do you think Dostoevsky lets Raskolnikov see everything he himself sees in the figure of Marmeladov?

The same teaching process may also involve slightly less arcane intertexts, such as the above-mentioned John 11.1–45, on the resurrection of Lazarus, in book 4, chapter 4. The questions below stress to students the importance of who is reading the passage and to whom, and of how the narrator describes this reading. The prompt for these questions is as follows: Only once in the novel (book 4, chapter 4) does the narrator use the shockingly direct terms "a murderer and a harlot" to refer to Raskolnikov and Sonya (251–52). The term "harlot" (блудница) is rather biblical, which also tints the word "murderer" with the same connotations.

> Explain the importance of book 4, chapter 4, as this phrase's context.
>
> Do you think the voice here is the narrator's own? Why or why not? What would differ if the voice were not the narrator's own, and whose might that be?
>
> What is the importance of the previous question, considering that this is the only time the narrator seems to label these two characters so overtly?
>
> What can you tell about Dostoevsky's own attitude toward the authority of the Scriptures?
>
> Do you think the narrator in any way identifies the characters with any of the figures in the excerpt they are reading, or elsewhere in the Bible? Why or why not? Why would he?
>
> Are we as readers empathizing or identifying with "the murderer and the harlot" in the novel?

Is there a liturgical element to the reading activity of "the murderer and the harlot" here? What does it tell us about the way these two characters see themselves and each other, or the way we see them?

Answering these questions may help students experience the force of religious allusions in *Crime and Punishment* on their own, without any further mediation by their professor.

On the other hand, the same exercise may give them a firsthand Bakhtinian experience—of being implicated in various characters' subjective perspectives and sore spots. For further study of the clashing stances and voices of Dostoevsky's narrator, John's narrator, Sonya, and Raskolnikov, and their possible links to axiology in Dostoevsky's poetics, I may eventually refer students to Bakhtin and some Bakhtinian scholars, or to other secondary literature, but not before they do their own close readings. First, students read Dostoevsky, and only then, if needed, do they read about Dostoevsky. This order especially matters for religious subtexts and allusions, whose relevance students should experience firsthand. Only afterward may other scholars' solutions become relevant.

The next example concerns my personal research and addresses a well-known controversy about the novel. Dostoevsky's readers often find the epilogue to *Crime and Punishment* as mechanical or artificial as that to the Book of Job: the resolution of the conflict is too easy for the way the conflict itself has been presented. After all, even after turning himself in, Raskolnikov never repents. So why now, on the last page of the epilogue, does he suddenly emerge as a *poenitens ex machina*, without any psychological or ideological motivation to his change of heart or mind?

My solution—of which I am yet to persuade my students with the right kind of questions—is relevant to the liturgical centrality of the motif of sacrifice in *Crime and Punishment*. The seemingly unmotivated appearance of the *poenitens ex machina* has a subtext—from Genesis 22, the sacrifice of Isaac. Rather than deciding to sacrifice another, a project that has driven Raskolnikov's intentions since the beginning of the novel, he now experiences firsthand what it is to be in the position of Isaac, about to be sacrificed: climbing up the hill and then sitting on a pile of firewood and contemplating "the times of Abraham and his herds" 'века Авраама и стад его,' he finds himself in the physical position of Isaac placed on a pile of firewood (*Prestuplenie* 421). Like Isaac, Raskolnikov gets up from the pile a completely changed person. This parallel pinpoints the fault of Raskolnikov's original argument: up to that moment, he believed that, for a lofty purpose, human life could be sacrificed, but that life was another's, not his own (see Meerson, "Raskolnikov"). The unexpected parallel between Raskolnikov and Isaac signals three things: first, for Dostoevsky, true repentance is rarely speculative, or even conscious, but is experienced existentially; second, this experience leads the protagonist to discover that any redemption for the world's wrongs entails self-sacrifice rather than the sacrifice of others (Raskolnikov finds himself in the position of Isaac, not of his father); and, finally, the reader is implicated in the protagonist's experience as immediate and nonintellectual. Hence the need to present his penitence as *ex machina*—out of the blue. Here then are my questions for discussing the epilogue problem in class:

> Compare the passage at the end of the epilogue where Raskolnikov comes to sit and ruminate on the riverbank slope to Genesis 22, and find as many possible parallels or connections as you can between the two descriptions.
>
> Like Isaac, Dostoevsky survived his own near-execution. Explain what possible bearing this fact may have on Raskolnikov's change of heart.

As discussion guidelines, such questions allow us to introduce our interpretations without imposing them. In research we first present our thesis and then substantiate it. As teachers, we may only ask questions.

NOTES

1. Unless otherwise attributed, all translations are mine.

2. What follows partly draws from an example I discussed twenty years ago, in a very early article, in Russian, and as only one of many biblical—not yet liturgical—subtexts ("Bibleiskie interteksty").

3. It is worth mentioning which specific scriptural and liturgical allusions Dostoevsky makes in Russian versus the Russified Church Slavonic used in the church and familiar to Orthodox parishioners, even if only by hearing. The Gospel reading about Lazarus's resurrection and the allusion to the sacrifice of Isaac from Genesis in the epilogue to *Crime and Punishment* are in Russian, from the then newly available Synodal Translation. By 1863, when Dostoevsky was beginning to work on *Crime and Punishment*, both Genesis and all four Gospels, as well as most of the New Testament, were available in Russian, and Dostoevsky was quoting the Synodal Russian Bible text quite extensively throughout his corpus. On the availability of those biblical texts, and Dostoevsky's use of them in Russian—not Church Slavonic—compare Meerson, "Bibleiskie podteksty" (see especially 40n3).

As to liturgical quotations, by Marmeladov, as often elsewhere, we will see that they are in Church Slavonic. These quotes and allusions are quite clear to the Russian ear in meaning, but they also bear clear stylistic markers of the liturgy. For example, the use of яко, instead of как, which I discuss here, immediately marks liturgical use as the source of the quotation.

4. Cf., for example, saintgregoryoutreach.org/2010/01/let-god-arise-holy-cross.html.

5. Dostoevsky may have learned this rhetorical trick from Archpriest Avvakum, whose allusions are almost exclusively liturgical, even when they are biblical (see Meerson, *Personalizm* 55). Here, it suffices to note that Dostoevsky has fully adapted Avvakum's device to his own needs. Avvakum's *Vita* was printed in 1861 and thus became available to diverse readers outside the Old Belief community (see Babitskaya). This continuity between Avvakum and Dostoevsky matters because it presents a case of a purely liturgical polemical quotation: as a formula, the subtext in Avvakum's alleged missive to Pashkov can be recognized solely from the liturgy, not from the Bible itself.

6. On Ivolgin, see Meerson, "Ivolgin." On Lebedev, see Meerson, "Skeletom." On the unexpected importance of Smerdyakov's view of the plot in *Brothers Karamazov*, see Meerson, *Dostoevsky's Taboos*.

Crime and Punishment on Trial: Reading Dostoevsky with Kafka

Susan McReynolds

> The past should be altered by the present as much as the present is directed by the past.
>
> —T. S. Eliot, "Tradition and the Individual Talent"

The encounter with *Crime and Punishment* can startle student readers with uncanny feelings of simultaneous intimacy, recognition, and repugnance. What young person hasn't at some point felt crowded, perhaps even hounded and driven to despair, by well-meaning friends, counselors, and family members? Or harbored some anger against those same caretakers and interventionists? This text in particular creates feelings of being recognized, drawn in, and repelled by the traumas it portrays.

These traumas are specific and individualized yet also grounded in mythopoetic universals. Sonya's experience as a stepdaughter in an unhappy household, pushed out onto the streets as a teenage prostitute; Dunya's story as a fatherless young woman subjected to a series of indecent proposals before finally accepting the third, appropriate suitor; Raskolnikov's situation as an impoverished but physically and psychologically hungry young man alone in a city full of false and true paths, and his vicious, violent dreams—the novel insists on the irreducible, nonfungible nature of these characters while also endowing them with the universal stuff of folk and fairy tales. *Crime and Punishment* thus manifests one of the key features of great art: the power to impress upon us what distinguishes each individual from all others while also releasing us from illusory forms of isolation.

When a work of literature "does this to them," so to speak, students not surprisingly want to know *how*: how did Fyodor Dostoevsky think this up? Equally unsurprising is their desire to know how, or if, they can tell if their reading experience is "right." If the first question concerns the nature of literary creativity, this second question is about the role of the reader and occurs to students as, "Are there any wrong readings?" or "What makes some readings better or more persuasive than others?" Addressing these concerns is especially important when working with STEM students, who may be more familiar with using measurement and the scientific method to ground their judgments.

We can concretize the nature of literary inspiration and the role of the reader by providing students with an example of a strong reading of *Crime and Punishment*. Exposure to such a reading ideally illuminates dimensions of the novel students may not have otherwise accessed and allows them to compare the results of their interpretive efforts with the insights of this other reader; this is not unlike the familiar exercise of having students exchange papers or post reading responses on a course site. When this other reader is a writer like Franz Kafka, and his reading response takes the form of a novel—in this case, *The Trial*—then students can also witness the creative process.

The approach I describe here is obviously similar to other ways of teaching *Crime and Punishment* together with the myriad adaptations and transpositions it has inspired. *The Trial* could be included as one adaptation or transposition of *Crime and Punishment* among others in a course or unit studying Dostoevsky's legacy. Kafka's potential as a fascinating interlocutor in the Dostoevsky classroom extends beyond *The Trial*: "The Judgment" and "The Metamorphosis" also offer stimulating examples of how Kafka grappled with the complex philosophical and aesthetic questions he perceived in Dostoevsky's writing. Kafka referred to Dostoevsky as one of "the four men I consider to be my true blood relations" (in a 1913 letter to his fiancée, Felice Bauer; qtd. in Dodd 4), and maintained a lifelong interest in the Russian author.

The bond Kafka felt with Dostoevsky played a crucial role in the intimate emotional relationship he constructed for himself with an image of Russia. In a diary entry from 1912, reflecting on the marginality and loneliness that characterize his existence, Kafka invokes Russia's geographical isolation on the fringe of Europe and describes his personal condition as "an experience . . . that one can only call Russian" (Dodd 15). Russia's exile from the center of European culture, like his own self-imposed exile from cultural institutions like marriage and fatherhood, was accompanied by a reservoir of creative power. "The endless fascination of Russia," a diary entry from 1915 argues, lies in its uncontainable, "unbounded" spaces and rivers with the potential to overwhelm their surroundings (16).

Kafka's sense that Russia, and Dostoevsky's art in particular, manifested something urgently important was shared by many in Europe in the first decades of the twentieth century, especially in its German-speaking regions; "a general fascination with Russia" was "endemic to German intellectual life at the turn of the century" (19). His contemporary Rainer Maria Rilke, also a member of Prague's German-speaking cultural milieu, felt so drawn to Russian language and culture that he made spiritual-aesthetic pilgrimages to Kiev and Moscow (in the company of his muse and mentor Lou Andreas Salome), and even attempted to write poetry in Russian.

Dostoevsky was central to German-speaking Europe's fascination with Russia. Landmarks in the reception of Dostoevsky included an 1899 biography by Nina Hoffmann and Dmitri Merezhkovsky's *Tolstoy and Dostoevsky* (1903). It was the violent conflicts of the era, however, that truly launched Dostoevsky's fame among German readers. The revolution of 1905 heightened interest in Russia and Dostoevsky and was quickly followed by the first volume of what was to become one of the most influential German publications of the twentieth century: the *Gesamtausgabe* (*Collected Works*) of Dostoevsky in translation, edited by Merezhkovsky and Arthur Moeller van den Bruck. *Demons* came first, in 1906; *Crime and Punishment* was published as *Rodion Raskolnikoff* in 1908; *The Idiot* and *The Brothers Karamazov* appeared in 1909. The outbreak of World War I in 1914 led to even greater demand, and the second edition of the *Collected Works* was published in 1915.

The years immediately preceding and during composition of *The Trial* were a time of Kafka's especially intense interest in Dostoevsky, when he was using his Russian predecessor "as a foil as well as a kindred spirit" (Dodd 12). *The Trial* is widely acknowledged to be Kafka's deepest and most sustained engagement with Dostoevsky, and I will focus on how we can use this novel in the classroom as one of the most remarkable readings of *Crime and Punishment*. The relationship between Dostoevsky's *Notes from Underground* and Nikolai Chernyshevsky's novel *What Is to Be Done?* provides a helpful model for comparison when approaching *Crime and Punishment* through the lens of a strong reading. Many of us provide our students with selected passages from Chernyshevsky's novel—scenes, images, and situations that provoked Dostoevsky to present them in recognizable but transformed guise in his own story. It is this dialogical relationship—the call and response that can be identified first in *What Is to Be Done?* and then in *Notes from Underground*—that I believe also characterizes the relationship between *Crime and Punishment* and *The Trial*.

Ideally, we read *The Trial* after thorough discussion of *Crime and Punishment*, weaving any new perspectives on Dostoevsky throughout our analysis of Kafka. Rereading *Crime and Punishment* through Kafka's eyes can reveal what Kafka perceived in the novel that we—and even many professional critics—might have missed and lead to some reevaluation of Dostoevsky's central themes of sexuality, authority, transgression, guilt, and justice. This kind of reevaluation is a macro-level goal that we approach through close comparative textual analysis.

There's no indication that Kafka experienced a polemical reaction against *Crime and Punishment* similar to the one *What Is to Be Done?* elicited from Dostoevsky, but his reading of *Crime and Punishment*, as manifested in *The Trial*, does selectively amplify and diminish different elements of Dostoevsky's novel. It's important to examine both the amplifications and absences in order to appreciate the depth of Kafka's immersion in the world of Raskolnikov as well as the critical eye he trains on it.

The textural surface of Kafka's novel looks remarkably like Dostoevsky's in many ways. We can identify, follow, and analyze the presence and function of common elements from the hyperspecific, such as the fact that the persecuting authority initially confuses the protagonist with housepainters, to the broadly atmospheric, like the stuffy, bad air of claustrophobic spaces. To read *Crime and Punishment* with *The Trial* is to witness repeated invasions of personal space; absurd crowding; inappropriate self-exposure, both bodily and spiritual; and the blurring of boundaries between the public, decent, and sanctioned, on the one hand, and the private, sexually and psychologically intimate, and transgressive, on the other.

Each novel is structured by an open question that drives the plot, but the questions are inverse. *Crime and Punishment* has readers and characters, including the protagonist himself, wondering why he committed a heinous crime; the protagonist of *The Trial*, and its readers, ask why he is being persecuted when he hasn't done anything wrong. In Dostoevsky's novel, we want to know why Raskolnikov butchered two women—what was his motive? In Kafka's, we want to know why the Court is accusing Joseph K.—what, if anything, has he done, and what is *their* motive in persecuting him?

Most of *Crime and Punishment* takes place while a murderer roams the city, un-apprehended and indeed not even suspected of the crime we witnessed in brutal detail. *The Trial* opens with an innocent man's being arrested, accused of committing crimes that are never named. Porfiry Petrovich, the detective who knows that Raskolnikov is guilty, even in the absence of any evidence—going on "psychology" alone—allows Raskolnikov to remain free, out of the conviction that a guilty conscience and desire to confess will reel the culprit in. An analogous logic informs the actions of the Court that persecutes Joseph K., who is arrested but allowed to continue his daily life unimpeded. Like Porfiry, who believes in Raskolnikov's guilt without any evidence and doesn't see the need to imprison him, the Court is supremely confident in its ability to determine and attract guilt.

What's most striking about Kafka's reading of *Crime and Punishment*, however, is what he leaves out. Generations of professional readers, scholars such as Joseph Frank, have claimed that the "the main plot line" of *Crime and Punishment* is "the commission of a murder as the result of ideological intoxication" (*Dostoevsky: The Miraculous Years* 97). The professional consensus (of course not unchallenged) among scholars—here we can take Frank as representative—has been that *Crime and Punishment* is an ideological and psychological novel, one that examines the social and emotional consequences of utilitarianism; the personal and historical dilemmas posed by the existence of "great men" such as Napoleon; a Nietzschean Superman-syndrome *avant la lettre*; and the dilemmas faced by ordinary people living in a diseased age who become infected with a desire to test themselves, to find out if they are capable of transgressing the rules of society—and, of course, whether or not a young man who kills women ostensibly due to such an infection can be redeemed.

There is none of this in *The Trial*. No musings about history, great men, being a benefactor, or daring to do extraordinary things. Kafka leaves it all out. What he finds in the pages of *Crime and Punishment*, rather, is transgressive male sexuality hiding in plain sight among the poor, the young, and the vulnerable female population of a city. He sees men evading the traditional responsibilities and honor that attended to male maturity in St. Petersburg and Prague, choosing humiliation, dishonor, even infamy instead, with deadly consequences for others.

What, if anything, Joseph K. might be guilty of is never clarified, not even when the Court kills him. Readers can, however, derive a picture of Joseph K. over the course of the novel that suggests some objectionable aspects to his character and some intriguing similarities with Raskolnikov. Joseph K. exhibits in extreme form some behaviors and attitudes that are present in Raskolnikov but have been largely passed over by scholars—actions motivated by nonnormative male sexuality. An eligible young man with a promising career, Joseph. K. seems to be evading traditional gender relations. He assaults Fraulein Burstner, an unmarried young woman of questionable virtue, who is a fellow lodger in his boarding house; he makes late-night visits to another young woman, Elsa, who receives male callers from her bed; and he finds another lover's physical deformity, her webbed fingers, so attractive that he kisses them. One object of his desire is a hunchback; young girls who seem to be prematurely sexually aware make appearances.

Raskolnikov is attracted to childlikeness, sickness, deformity, and transgression. He was in love with and engaged to the landlady's daughter, who, Razumikhin says, "was not very attractive, that is, they say she was even rather plain . . . and so sickly, and . . . and strange" 'была собой даже не хороша, то есть, говорят, даже дурна . . . и такая хворая, и . . . и странная' (Dostoevsky, *Crime* 151; *Prestuplenie* 166).[1] Raskolnikov, too, dwells on the deceased young woman's illness and unattractiveness. "She was a sickly girl," he recalls, "Very ill"; "She was very plain . . . I really don't know why I felt attracted to her; perhaps it was because she was always sickly . . . If she'd been lame or a hunchback, I probably would've loved her even more . . ." 'Она больная такая девочка была . . . совсем хворая . . . Право, не знаю, за что я к ней тогда привязался, кажется за то, что всегда больная . . . Будь она еще хромая аль горбатая, я бы, кажется, еще больше ее полюбил . . .' (*Crime* 160; *Prestuplenie* 177).

Sonya is repeatedly called childlike, thin, pale, with a "thin, very thin, pale little face, rather irregular, somewhat angular, with a pointed little nose and chin" 'Это было худенькое, совсем худенькое и бледное личико, довольно неправильное, какое-то востренькое, с востреньким маленьким носом и подбородком' (*Crime* 166; *Prestuplenie* 183). Her activity as a prostitute clashes with her childlike attitude and physically immature demeanor. The first time

Raskolnikov sees her, she is "humiliated, crushed, decked out, and embarrassed" 'приниженную, убитую, расфранченную, и стыдящуюся' (*Crime* 130; *Prestuplenie* 145), and she is described as looking "very young indeed, almost like a girl" 'очень еще молоденькая, почти похожая на девочку' (*Crime* 164; *Prestuplenie* 181), a quality the narrator singles out for special emphasis.

> There was, in addition, one special trait reflected in her face and in her entire figure: in spite of her eighteen years, she still seemed like a young girl, much younger than her years, almost a total child, and that fact sometimes appeared engagingly in several of her movements. (*Crime* 166)

> В лице ее, да и во всей ее фигуре, была сверх того одна особенная характерная черта: несмотря на свои восемнадцать лет, она казалась почти еще девочкой, гораздо моложе своих лет, совсем почти ребенком, и это иногда даже смешно проявлялось в некоторых ее движениях. (*Prestuplenie* 183)

There is nothing womanly or sexually mature about her, aside from her hypersexualized status as a prostitute. Raskolnikov was attracted to his fiancée because she was unattractive, odd, and ill; he admits to being drawn to the childlike Sonya because of her spiritual sickness, her status as a great sinner.

Many influential readings of *Crime and Punishment* gloss over these phenomena, either passing over them in silence or subordinating them to the "reality effect" of a Russian realist novel of the 1860s. Svidrigailov, who more fully realizes the consequences of being beyond good and evil, has probably murdered his wife; he is drawn to the age-inappropriate and vulnerable Dunya, who is employed in his household; and he has allegedly raped a fourteen-year-old mentally disabled girl. Readers have largely accepted Svidrigailov as a double for Raskolnikov in their roles as murderers; the implications of Svidrigailov's sex crimes for this doubling, however, have yet to be fully acknowledged.

These elements of the novel are also commonly read as evidence in the physical, material world of the ethical confusion plaguing the hero, confusion over utilitarianism and whether he is extraordinary and has exceptional privileges. Frank, for example, subsumes all this into the Superman/Napoleon story, one that traces the consequences of some sort of "immutable egoism of personal self-affirmation"—Raskolnikov is testing his strength, it is "some sort of self-exalting as well as morally heroic deed" (*Dostoevsky: The Miraculous Years* 124).

Reading Kafka and Dostoevsky together forces us to linger with these dimensions of the novel. Kafka emancipates them from the swirl of contradictory explanations for what Frank calls "the fearsome slaughter" of women, dispelling "the mirage of serving any moral cause," and calling into question the significance of any Napoleonic/Nietzschean extraordinary man theory (122). Reading *Crime and Punishment* together with *The Trial* stimulates discussions that could potentially lead to new perspectives on the heart of the novel, the commission of violence against women, against "the individual marked out as the sacrificial victim" (105). It is a dialogue that powerfully illustrates the global nature of art and inspiration, allowing us to witness the encounter between a twentieth-century central European Jew and a nineteenth-century Russian nationalist anti-Semite on the field of literature.

We may find ourselves questioning the hierarchies of significance we perhaps unconsciously impose on *Crime and Punishment*: history, politics, male characters at the top; sexual behavior, women, domestic spaces lower down. By prompting such questions, reading *Crime and Punishment* with *The Trial* provides an opportunity to practice a skill useful in any future profession, from STEM fields to art: the ability and willingness to ask ourselves, What did Kafka (or my colleague, for example) see that I didn't see?

NOTE

1. This essay quotes from the translation by Michael Katz (2019).

Crossing Thresholds: Tracking Poe's Footprints

Jamie Brummer

A hard fact must be reckoned with when teaching Fyodor Dostoevsky's *Crime and Punishment* in an American high school: there's a good chance that not a single student in a typical English class will have any previous experience with Russian literature. The reasons may be varied, but the result is the same: few students will have any familiarity with one of the world's richest literary traditions. Experience suggests that few will have even heard of an author named Dostoevsky.

Most high school students in America, however, have encountered the works of Edgar Allan Poe, especially atmospheric and claustrophobic tales of psychological torment such as "The Raven," "The Tell-Tale Heart," or "The Cask of Amontillado." They are drawn to Poe's lurid and transgressive world, captivated by his haunting and surreal descriptions, and fascinated by the desperation of his obsessed protagonists. It comes as an enormous surprise to my students that Dostoevsky knew of Poe's work and that he translated some of his stories into Russian only a few years before serializing *Crime and Punishment*. A quick review of the way Poe manipulates the external and physical and relates it to the internal and psychological primes students to follow Raskolnikov into the oppressive heat, noise, and sensory assault of St. Petersburg. As they wander with Raskolnikov and the city seethes about them, students draw connections between the spaces he inhabits (his cramped garret, bridges and street corners, restaurants and taverns, an endless array of thresholds and doorways) and the psychological trauma he suffers. So we make a shaky bargain. We agree to let Poe act as our guide. We will place our trust in one author to help us understand another as we seek to grasp how Dostoevsky uses exterior space as a means of gesturing toward Raskolnikov's inner state of being.

This essay maps key passages from *Crime and Punishment*—the initial description of the city and of Raskolnikov's lodging in it; the first conversation between Raskolnikov and Svidrigailov, which concerns ghosts, eternity—and spiders; and, finally, Raskolnikov's exile to the vast open spaces of Siberia and the liberation he experiences as a result—alongside selections from Poe's oeuvre. The pedagogical focus is twofold: to help students comprehend the novel's surface details as well as some of the psychological, structural, and symbolic elements that have made it timeless; and to challenge students to pay special attention to space, to liminality, to marginalization—both literal and figurative—as central elements in the novel and as key points of connection with Poe. Raskolnikov's Great Man theory pushes him to extremes, but all teenagers know what it feels like to be outsiders, aliens even in the most crowded urban (or digital) spaces. Raskolnikov's search for a place to belong is not so foreign after all.

Something in Poe's work spoke to Dostoevsky just as something in Dostoevsky's work speaks to us. The most effective approach I have found to teaching *Crime and Punishment* is to encourage my students to listen to the intertextual conversation between these two masters and enter into it themselves.

Poe Inside and Out

The students I teach are bright, funny, and more capable than adults tend to recognize.[1] When it comes time to introduce "that big Russian novel" shortly after we return from our winter break, I like to throw them a curveball.

First we take a poll. I know my students have read Poe's "The Tell-Tale Heart," because we cover it in the first semester in a unit on short fiction. What else have they read? Usually "The Cask of Amontillado" and "The Raven" make the cut and sometimes "The Fall of the House of Usher" or, less often, "The Black Cat." We spend a class period re-creating the sordid and quotidian biographical details that have contributed to Poe's lasting mythology. Situating both Poe and Dostoevsky in the magazine business accomplishes at least two things: my students can appreciate how one artist devoted to his craft would recognize the mastery of another, and they can understand the desire to capitalize on another author's fame and infamy to promote one's own work. When we discover that Dostoevsky first introduced several of Poe's works to a Russian readership in *Time* not long before he began serialization of *Crime and Punishment*, you can almost see the light bulbs switch on.

We recall the tortured narrator of "The Tell-Tale Heart," a profoundly disturbed man who immediately reveals, "I heard all things in heaven and in the earth. I heard many things in Hell." When he reveals that "[i]t is impossible to say how the idea first entered my brain; but, once conceived, it haunted me day and night," we are already witness to a consciousness losing the ability to distinguish between the internal and the external, and conventional boundaries between personal identity (and responsibility) and external reality are dissolving before our eyes (187). By the time we reach the story's conclusion, the narrator has lost all psychological mooring: "I talked more freely," he rants, "to get rid of the feeling; but it continued and gained definiteness—until, at length, I found that the noise was not within my ears" (191). Identity, agency, and sanity itself are merging and roiling with external stimuli beyond the narrator's control. The more desperately this man struggles to find solid ground on which to justify his actions, the more adrift he becomes. In just a few pages, then, the narrator of "The Tell-Tale Heart" serves as a case study for the psychological schism we will watch Raskolnikov endure for an entire novel.

St. Petersburg: Lost in Dreams

Dostoevsky's *Crime and Punishment* vividly re-creates the haunted and increasingly destabilized inner world of its protagonist, Raskolnikov. In the opening paragraphs the reader learns that Raskolnikov "has become so completely absorbed in himself, and isolated from his fellows that he dreaded meeting, not only his landlady, but anyone at all" 'до того углубился в себя и уединился от всех, что боялся даже всякой встречи, не только встречи с хозяйкой' (*Crime* 5; *Prestuplenie* 5)[2] and for several hundred more pages accompanies him deeper and deeper into his monomania and loneliness.

Yet, paradoxically, it is almost impossible to consider Raskolnikov apart from his surroundings, especially the city of St. Petersburg. Dostoevsky spoke of this relationship between external and internal realities in the preface he wrote in *Vremia*, which included Poe's stories. Poe "chooses as a rule the most extravagant reality, places his hero in a most extraordinary outward or psychological situation, and, then, describes the inner state of the person with marvelous acumen and amazing realism" (Dostoevsky, "Three Tales"). Like Poe, whose work he clearly admired, Dostoevsky endeavors to create a symbiotic relationship between his protagonist's inner struggles and his external circumstances. This symbiosis is immediately on display when Dostoevsky describes Petersburg for the first time.

> The heat in the street was terrible: and the airlessness, the bustle and the plaster, scaffolding, bricks, and dust all about him, and that special Petersburg stench, so familiar to all who are unable to get out of town in summer—all worked painfully upon the young man's already overwrought nerves. The insufferable stench from the pot-houses, which are particularly numerous in that part of the town, and the drunken men whom he met continually, although it was a working day, completed the revolting misery of the picture. (*Crime* 6)

> На улице жара стояла страшная, к тому же духота, толкотня, всюду известка, леса, кирпич, пыль и та особенная летняя вонь, столь известная каждому петербуржцу, не имеющему возможности нанять дачу, – все это разом неприятно потрясло и без того уже расстроенные нервы юноши. Нестерпимая же вонь из распивочных, которых в этой части города особенное множество, и пьяные, поминутно попадавшиеся, несмотря на буднее время, довершили отвратительный и грустный колорит картины. (*Prestuplenie* 6)

The periodic structure of the first sentence does more than simply place Raskolnikov in the city; it places the city in him. The sentence surrounds Raskolnikov, who we sense will forever be "unable to get out of town." The "special Petersburg stench" has not only permeated his clothing but has begun to infect his mind as well. We reread these opening paragraphs carefully to analyze the extreme care the author takes to place Raskolnikov in this precise setting. The teeming city is both sprawling and claustrophobic. The "heart of St. Petersburg" is an outward manifestation of the "accumulated bitterness and contempt in the young man's heart" 'злобного презрения уже накопилось в душе молодого человека' (*Crime* 6; *Prestuplenie* 6), and in its opening paragraphs we have unearthed a motif that runs through the novel.

"I Sat in My Room Like a Spider"

In Dostoevsky's universe, what is true on a macro scale is true on a micro scale as well. Throughout the novel Raskolnikov returns to his tawdry garret hoping in vain to find some refuge from the torments that descend from all corners of the city. His room, of course, offers no such refuge and instead distills and personalizes the vast and looming anxieties that Raskolnikov encounters in the city's streets.

> It was a tiny cupboard of a room about six paces in length. It had a poverty-stricken appearance with its dusty yellow paper peeling off the walls, and it was so low-pitched that a man of more than average height was ill at ease in it and felt every moment that he would knock his head against the ceiling. The furniture was in keeping with the room: there were three old chairs, rather rickety; a painted table in the corner on which lay a few manuscripts and books; the dust that lay thick upon them showed that they had been long untouched. (*Crime* 29)

> Это была крошечная клетушка, шагов в шесть длиной, имевшая самый жалкий вид с своими желтенькими, пыльными и всюду отставшими от стены обоями, и до того низкая, что чуть-чуть высокому человеку становилось в ней жутко, и все казалось, что вот-вот стукнешься головой о потолок. Мебель соответствовала помещению: было три старых стула, не совсем исправных, крашеный стол в углу, на котором лежало несколько тетрадей и книг; уже по тому одному, как они были запылены, видно было, что до них давно уже не касалась ничья рука. (*Prestuplenie* 25)

Rather than providing a refuge or sanctum, Raskolnikov's room serves as a constant reminder of his inner turmoil. Its material poverty represents his psychological poverty; its disorder and dirt symbolize his intellectual and emotional disorder. The "dusty yellow paper peeling off the walls" emblematizes Raskolnikov's fraying and decayed mental state. The cumulative effect of words such as "dusty," "stricken," "peeling," and "rickety" that describe the room's interior serve only to magnify the teeming interior frailties of its inhabitant. At the critical moment when Raskolnikov finally chooses to confess his crimes, he tells Sonya:

> I sat in my room like a spider. You've been in my den, you've seen it. . . . And do you know, Sonya, that low ceilings and tiny rooms cramp the soul and the mind? Ah, how I hated that garret! And yet I wouldn't go out of it!

> I wouldn't on purpose! I didn't go out for days together, and I wouldn't work, I wouldn't even eat, I just lay there doing nothing.
>
> (*Crime* 396; ellipsis in source)

> Я тогда, как паук, к себе в угол забился. Ты ведь была в моей конуре, видела. . . . А знаешь ли, Соня, что низкие потолки и тесные комнаты душу и ум теснят! О, как ненавидел я эту конуру! А все-таки выходить из нее не хотел. Нарочно не хотел! По суткам не выходил и работать не хотел,и даже есть не хотел, все лежал.
>
> (*Prestuplenie* 320; ellipsis in source)

Dostoevsky's description of the cramped and rotting garret perfectly encapsulates his protagonist's mental state. Once more, the repetitions, the exclamations, even the stacked monosyllables echo Poe.

Crossroads and Thresholds, Shreds and Fragments

Throughout *Crime and Punishment* Raskolnikov encounters a vast array of liminal spaces. Doorways, thresholds, paper-thin walls, bridges, rivers, and crossroads appear and reappear, and each represents an opportunity and challenge for our splintered protagonist. In the novel's first sentence, Raskolnikov is walking "slowly, as though in hesitation, towards K—— Bridge" 'медленно, как бы в нерешимости, отправился к К-ну мосту' (*Crime* 5; *Prestuplenie* 5). An idea has become an obsession; he has memorized the number of steps from his garret to the pawnbroker's apartment, and the bridge and canal it spans represent a point of no return. When he crosses another bridge in chapter 5 of part 1, his physical and psychological condition has deteriorated even further. He collapses in exhaustion and instantly falls asleep. Here, again, Dostoevsky's prose takes on a decidedly Poe-like quality:

> In a morbid condition of the brain, dreams often have a singular actuality, vividness, and extraordinary semblance of reality. At times monstrous images are created, but the setting and the whole picture are so truth-like and filled with details so delicate, so unexpectedly, but so artistically consistent, that the dreamer . . . could never have invented them in the waking state. Such sick dreams always remain long in the memory and make a powerful impression on the overwrought and deranged nervous system.
>
> (*Crime* 54–55)

> В болезненном состоянии сны отличаются часто необыкновенною выпуклостию, яркостью и чрезвычайным сходством с действительностью. Слагается иногда картина чудовищная, но обстановка и весь процесс всего представления бывают при этом до того вероятны и с такими тонкими, неожиданными, но художественно

> соответствующими всей полноте картины подробностями, что их и не выдумать наяву этому же самому сновидцу . . . Такие сны, болезненные сны, всегда долго помнятся и производят сильное впечатление на расстроенный и уже возбужденный организм человека. (*Prestuplenie* 45–46)

"Morbid," "monstrous," "sick," and "deranged," Raskolnikov, like so many protagonists in Poe's fictional universe, is losing the ability to distinguish between his internal nightmares and external reality. The dream pulses with themes of shattered innocence, suffering, and moral responsibility. Having transgressed another boundary of sorts by crossing the bridge onto Vasilyevsky Island, Raskolnikov descends deep into a nightmare world where innocents are butchered.[3] He resurfaces "sweating, gasping for breath, his hair soaked with perspiration, and [stands] up in terror. 'Thank God, that was only a dream!'" 'весь в поту, с мокрыми от поту волосами, задыхаясь, и припоынялся в ужасе. «Слава богу, это только сон!»' he offers, and "his whole body felt broken; darkness and confusion were in his soul" 'Все тело его было как бы разбито; смутно и темно на душе' (*Crime* 60; *Prestuplenie* 49). Crossing the bridge has brought Raskolnikov to a tipping point.

> He rose to his feet, looked round in wonder as though surprised at finding himself in this place, and went towards T—— Bridge. He was pale, his eyes glowed, he was exhausted in every limb, but he seemed suddenly to breathe more easily. . . . "Lord," he prayed, "show me my path—I renounce that accursed . . . dream of mine." (*Crime* 60; ellipses in source)

> [В] удивлении осмотрелся кругом, как бы дивясь и тому, что зашел сюда, и пошел на Т—в мост. Он был бледен, глаза его горели, изнеможение было во всех его членах, но ему вдруг стало дышать как бы легче. . . . «Господи!» – молил он, – «покажи мне путь мой, а я отрекаюсь от этой проклятой . . . мечты моей!» (*Prestuplenie* 50; ellipses in source)

He crosses the bridge and is free. For reasons he cannot fathom, however, a more circuitous route takes him through the Haymarket, another liminal space asserts itself (the corner of K—— Alley), and in a chance encounter with a huckster, his wife, and the pawnbroker's sister, Raskolnikov's moment of freedom evaporates. By the time he finds himself back home, "he went in like a man condemned to death. . . . [H]e felt suddenly in his whole being that he had no more freedom of thought, no will, and that everything was suddenly and irrevocably decided" 'Он вошел к себе, как приговоренный к смерти. . . . [Н]о всем существом своим вдруг почувствовал, что нет у него более ни свободы рассудка, ни воли и что все вдруг решено окончательно' (*Crime* 63; *Prestuplenie* 52). Dostoevsky, like Poe, amplifies the internal struggle of his protagonist by situating him within a set of carefully crafted external circumstances. Raskolnikov feels his agency and identity leaching away as the city reasserts itself around him. The city is a surreal and synaesthetic dreamscape threatening to erase conventional boundaries separating internal and external experience. Both the city and Raskolnikov seem diseased.

By this point in our reading the students can appreciate how Raskolnikov's "disease" seems particularly acute in his encounters with Svidrigailov. Though Raskolnikov feels haunted by Svidrigailov from the time he reads his mother's letter early in the novel, it is not until the end of part 3 that the two come face to face. Building to this moment for hundreds of pages, Dostoevsky manipulates the physical scene to maximize its psychological impact. A raving Raskolnikov lies in a state of semiconsciousness in his crumbling garret; his guilt-ridden mind drags him back to the scene of the crime. Everything is at once familiar and fantastic, partaking of that dreamlike quality that preys upon reality by distorting it. In another passage eerily reminiscent of Poe, Raskolnikov kills the old woman again, striking her repeatedly with an axe, only to hear her shaking with laughter. "He drew a deep breath—but his dream seemed to persist strangely: his door was flung wide open and a man he had never seen stood in the doorway watching him intently" 'Он тяжело перевел дыхание, – но странно, сон как будто все еще продолжался: дверь его была отворена настежь, и на пороге стоял совсем незнакомый ему человек и пристально его разглядывал' (*Crime* 264; *Prestuplenie* 213–14). The fly that troubled his dream now "buzze[s] and flutter[s] against the window pane" 'жужжала и билась какая-то большая муха, упаряясь с налета об стекло' (*Crime* 264–65; *Prestuplenie* 214), and Arkady Svidrigailov calmly introduces himself.

Their first conversation opens part 4. Soon pleasantries turn to talk of ghosts and of the sick men haunted by them. Svidrigailov then perfectly channels Poe[4] as he details his argument to perhaps the only other man in the novel capable of hearing it:

> [G]hosts are, as it were, shreds and fragments of other worlds, the beginning of them. A man in health has, of course, no reason to see them, because he is above all a man of this earth and is bound for the sake of completeness and order to live only in this life. But as soon as one is ill, as soon as the normal earthly order of the organism is broken, one begins to realise the possibility of another world; and the more seriously ill one is, the closer becomes one's contact with that other world. (*Crime* 277)

> Привидения – это, так сказать, клочки и отрывки других миров, их начало. Здоровому человеку, разумеется, их незачем видеть, потому что здоровый человек есть наиболее земной человек, а стало быть, должен жить одною здешнею жизнью, для полноты и для порядка. Ну, а чуть заболел, чуть нарушился нормальный земной порядок в организме, тотчас и начинает сказываться возможность другого мира,

> и чем больше болен, тем и соприкосновений с другим миром больше, так что, когда умрет совсем человек, то прямо и перейдет в другой мир. (*Prestuplenie* 221)

Much earlier in the year, when we are studying Poe, I surprise my students with this passage and ask them to write the rest of the story using these sentences as their springboard. When we arrive at this part of Dostoevsky's novel, then, we can dust off those old pieces and experience at first hand just how deep the connections are between the Russian author and the American one. The intentional destruction of "the normal earthly order of the organism" in order to depict the resulting psychological torment is essential in both authors' work. To destabilize one's firm sense of reality, to blur the boundaries between this world and whatever lies beyond, between reason and emotion, logic and fantasy, sickness and health . . . and to spend eternity in "one little room, like a bathhouse in the country, black and grimy and spiders in every corner" 'будет там одна комнатка, эдак вроде деревенской бани, закоптелая, а по всем углам пауки' (*Crime* 277; *Prestuplenie* 221)—that is a sentence and a fate that demonstrates as clearly as any the intimate imaginative connection between Poe and Dostoevsky.

"What You Need Now Is Fresh Air, Fresh Air, Fresh Air"

Raskolnikov is doomed to just such a fate if, like Svidrigailov, he refuses to abandon his Great Man theory and insists on alienating himself from the rest of humanity. And if this were a tale told by Poe, one could imagine the story ending in a black and grimy room of the sort Svridgrigailov fears, with only spiders and one's own guilt for company for eternity. Dostoevsky, however, offers his hero another path. Porfiry tells Raskolnikov, "You must fulfill the demands of justice. I know that you don't believe it, but life, in fact, will bring you through. You will live it down in time. What you need now is fresh air, fresh air, fresh air!" 'Вот исполните-ка, что требует справедливость. Знаю, что не веруете, а ей-богу, жизнь вынесет. Самому после слюбится. Вам теперь только воздуху надо, воздуху, воздуху!' (*Crime* 437; *Prestuplenie* 351). Sentenced to Siberia for his crimes, Raskolnikov has the chance to resurrect himself. The claustrophobia and sensory chaos of St. Petersburg have been replaced by "a broad landscape [which] opened before him, the sound of singing floated faintly audible from the other bank. In the vast steppe, bathed in sunshine, he could see, like black specks, the nomads' tents. There there was freedom, there other men were living . . . there time itself seemed to stand still" 'берега открывалась широкая окрестность. С дальнего другого берега чуть слышно доносилась песня. Там, в облитой солнцем необозримой степи, чуть приметными точками чернелись кочевые юрты. Там была свобода и жили другие люди . . . там как бы самое время остановилось.' Another version of eternity, joined with the human family, awaits Raskolnikov as the novel closes. Dostoevsky intentionally contrasts this setting with Petersburg, and paradoxically, Raskolnikov's confinement allows him his first true opportunity of freedom.[5] In the Easter season, the time of spring and rebirth, the faces of Sonya and Raskolnikov become "bright with the dawn of a new future, of a full resurrection into a new life" 'сияла заря обновленного будущего, полного воскресения в новую жизнь' (*Crime* 519; *Prestuplenie* 421). As the narrator says in the closing paragraphs, "life had stepped into the place of theory and something quite different would work itself out in his mind" 'Вместо диалектики наступила жизнь, и в сознании должно было выработаться что-то совершенно другое' (*Crime* 521; *Prestuplenie* 422).

NOTES

1. At Christian Brothers High School, an all-boys school of approximately eight hundred students in Memphis, Tennessee, serving grades 9 through 12.
2. Quotations from *Crime and Punishment* in English are from the translation by Constance Garnett published in 2007.
3. The dream of "the poor horse" 'бедную лошадку' (*Crime* 59; *Prestuplenie* 49), which comprises nearly five full pages, is one of the novel's most poignant and memorable windows into Raskolnikov's youth as refracted through his anguished adult consciousness.
4. Consider how this passage from Poe's "The Imp of the Perverse" functions almost as a palimpsest for Dostoevsky's portrayal of the corrupted great men, Raskolnikov and Svidrigailov: "No sooner had I spoken these words [I am safe], than I felt an icy chill creep to my heart. I had had some experience in these fits of perversity (whose nature I have been at some trouble to explain), and I remembered well that, in no instance, I had successfully resisted their attacks. And now my own casual self-suggestion, that I might possibly be fool enough to confess the murder of which I had been guilty, confronted me, as if the very ghost of him whom I had murdered—and beckoned me on to death" (206–07).
5. One of my students, Jack Jerit, put it this way: "The claustrophobic nature of his setting eventually strangles him the same way Porfiry attempts to strangle him psychologically, the same way Luzhin attempts to deceitfully, and the same way Svidrigailov does intellectually by challenging his Great Man theory. Only when thrust into the open setting of Siberia can Raskolnikov, while ironically in prison, stop feeling so constrained and end his psychological suffering."

The Allure of the Outlaw: Teaching *Crime and Punishment* to High School Students

Karen R. Smith

Why are we drawn to literary characters we would condemn in real life? What makes us identify with protagonists who break the laws we value? How is it that we can care for, and even root for, a criminal? These questions framed a world literature course that I taught using Fyodor Dostoevsky's *Crime and Punishment* as an anchor for exploring "the allure of the outlaw." While I originally designed the course as an undergraduate elective, I reconceived it for seniors at the high school where I currently teach. The problem at the heart of its theme—our willingness to sympathize, as readers, with seemingly unforgivable characters—can hold special relevance for college-bound students newly exploring the complexities of their personal and social identities.

I teach English at the Alabama School of Mathematics and Science, a public, STEM-focused, honors high school enrolling high-achieving sophomores, juniors, and seniors from across the state. Like those in similar schools, or in Advanced Placement, International Baccalaureate, or dual enrollment programs, these students are eager for challenges, and the perceived difficulty of an author like Dostoevsky may add to the appeal of reading *Crime and Punishment*. At the same time, these students constitute a diverse group of twenty-first-century citizens. Getting *Crime and Punishment* to speak to them requires developing the novel's status as "world literature" in David Damrosch's sense—as a text that "gains in translation," or that becomes more meaningful in its relations to other texts, eras, and locales (281). For this reason, a theme-based course provides an effective approach. Through pairings with different texts that pose the problem of the alluring outlaw, it can enrich the meaning of *Crime and Punishment* as exemplar of a continually transforming genre, the modern crime narrative, whose relevance and appeal endures.

Crime and Punishment *in Relation to Other Texts*

I structured The Allure of the Outlaw as a survey course when I taught it to university undergraduates. We read six novels, starting in the nineteenth century with *Crime and Punishment* and spanning the twentieth century with works from Europe and North America that continue the novel's legacy.[1] We began by reviewing authors who influenced Dostoevsky and ended with student presentations that discussed crime narratives in popular culture. This survey structure was appropriate for a college course, where its broad scope helped to build students' knowledge of literary history and cross-cultural intertextuality. For the high school unit, I cover fewer works to emphasize skills needed for college-level scholarship: close reading, argument, research, and comparative analysis. In the sections that follow, I introduce ways of using different texts—a short story, three novels, and two television series—to practice these skills while illuminating aesthetic, philosophical, and historical aspects of Dostoevsky's novel.

Reading for Narrative Technique: "The Tell-Tale Heart"

Understanding how authors use narrative technique to engage their readers in protagonists' conflicts is essential to analyzing the archetype of the alluring outlaw. For this reason, Edgar Allan Poe's "The Tell-Tale Heart," familiar to most high school seniors, makes an ideal text to pair with *Crime and Punishment* early in the course. Dostoevsky introduced Poe's tale to Russian readers five years before writing his crime novel. As students read closely for evidence that this American story influenced Dostoevsky's work, they should focus on the way that Dostoevsky's distinctive use of a limited omniscient narrator internalizes in Raskolnikov the dialogue that Poe's first-person narrator conducts with the reader.

Because of its brevity, "The Tell-Tale Heart" can be read in class or as an overnight assignment as students are finishing part 1 of Dostoevsky's novel. To facilitate a close, comparative analysis, I would direct students to consider the opening lines of Poe's story together with the last three paragraphs of part 1's chapter 6, in which Raskolnikov visits the pawnbroker to implement his murderous plan. After these passages are read aloud by student volunteers, students may free-write or brainstorm what they notice.

Students may recognize that Poe's opening sentences create an intimacy between the first-person narrator and his reader (". . . why *will* you say that I am mad?") that is undermined by the narrator's hyperbolic claims ("I heard all things in the heaven and in the earth . . .") ("Tell-Tale Heart" 303). They should also detect parallels to Poe's story in the passage from *Crime and Punishment*: the reference to a heart that "pounded harder, harder, harder" 'сердце . . . стучало сильней, сильней, сильней'; a preternatural sense of hearing ("Either his senses were especially sharp . . . or it was indeed quite audible, . . . he . . . discerned something like the cautious sound of a hand on the door-latch" 'чувства ли его были так изощрены . . . или действительно было очень слышно, . . . он различил как бы осторожный шорох рукой у замочной ручки'); the criminal's knowledge of his targeted victim's ways ("He was somewhat familiar with her habits" 'Он отчасти знал её привычки'); the obsessive planning of the crime (Dostoevsky, *Crime* 74; *Prestuplenie* 61). With guidance, they should also note how the omniscient narrator changes the effect of these parallels in Raskolnikov's story. Poe's narrator confidently addresses the reader, but Dostoevsky's narrator reveals Raskolnikov's self-questioning ("Am I not too excited?" 'не в особенном ли я волнении?') and highlights his uncertainty ("[H]e could not understand where he got so much cunning . . . his reason seemed clouded at moments" '[О]н понять не мог, откуда он взял столько хитрости . . . ум его как бы померкал мгновениями') (*Crime* 74; *Prestuplenie* 61).[2] Closely analyzing these distinctions shows that, whereas Poe's first-person narrator loses our trust, Dostoevsky's outside narrator plunges us into the consciousness of his disturbed protagonist. A short creative writing assignment can reinforce the significance of this effect: students can be asked to select a brief passage from the first two parts of the novel and rewrite it using the first-person point of view, adopting Raskolnikov's persona to defend his thoughts or actions.

Responding with Argument: The Stranger

While textual comparisons can show students the impact of specific details in reading and writing about the alluring outlaw, they can also widen their perspectives on philosophical debates raised by the course's theme. Following Dostoevsky's *Crime and Punishment* with a reading of Albert Camus's *The Stranger* provides opportunities for students to grapple with ideas about the social nature of justice. A short novel that some students may know from French classes, *The Stranger* offers a plot that centers on the succession of crime, confession, and punishment, but the character of its alienated protagonist, Meursault, and the circumstances of his crime differ from Raskolnikov's in ways that raise questions about what constitutes guilt and redemption.

With an eye toward argument, comparisons between *Crime and Punishment* and *The Stranger* can productively focus on the nature of the crime (premeditated in Raskolnikov's case; spontaneous in Meursault's), the mode of confession (Raskolnikov seeks out Sonya; Meursault is brought to a public trial), and the justice of the punishment (Raskolnikov is exiled to Siberia and reforms through Sonya's influence; Meursault is executed after a period of solitary confinement). Examining these three points highlights the philosophical differences underlying Dostoevsky's narrative, in which moral choice and spiritual redemption are possible, and Camus's, in which social convention arbitrarily shapes ideas of morality. Students can debate whether Dostoevsky's planned and justified murder of Alyona Ivanovna deserves more condemnation than Meursault's unmotivated shooting of the Arab man; they can take a position on whether Raskolnikov's feelings of remorse about Lizaveta and his charitable deeds toward the Marmeladov family make him more worthy of forgiveness than the unrepentant Meursault: they can argue that Meursault is unfairly punished for his atheism and lack of conventional feelings about his mother's death rather than for the killing of a human being, and consider whether Sonya is right to instruct Raskolnikov to ask for public forgiveness before formally confessing; they can contend that a private, self-motivated confession such as Raskolnikov's to Sonya serves a better purpose than a compulsory public one; they can argue for or against the use of exile, solitary confinement, and execution as methods of restoring justice; or they can attempt to persuade their classmates that each of these protagonists is or is not punished in a way that matches the nature of his crime. These activities encourage students to apply the ethical issues raised by both novels to contemporary debates concerning criminal justice. They can also show how Dostoevsky's novel provides seeds that germinate in Camus's existentialist philosophy, which exposes the arbitrary nature of social and moral codes. Formal papers may develop from positions taken in the debates, and students should be encouraged to support their claims about justice with examples from the novels.

Research for Historical Context: Beloved *and* Alias Grace

Connecting students to the world of its nineteenth-century Russian characters is one of the challenges of teaching *Crime and Punishment*. Two relatively recent literary variations on the novel's theme of the alluring outlaw, Toni Morrison's *Beloved* and Margaret Atwood's *Alias Grace*, provide strategies for addressing this challenge. Based on actual events from the 1800s, both novels feature sympathetic heroines accused of horrible crimes. Their stories evoke intersections of gender, race, class, and mental illness that speak not only to current social conflicts but also to those of Dostoevsky's time and place, creating opportunities for different student research projects that can highlight the relevancy of Raskolnikov's world for these narratives.

Beloved is based on the account of Margaret Garner, a woman who fled slavery in 1858 with her family and, in a desperate attempt to prevent them from being returned to bondage upon discovery, killed one of her children (Reyes). In Morrison's novel, which takes place ten years after the abolition of slavery, the protagonist, Sethe, is haunted by the ghost of her victim as she and others in her community of former slaves adapt to life as free human beings. Sethe's struggle with her reincarnated daughter, symbolic of the survivor contending with slavery's past, provides the novel's crime and punishment narrative, but flashbacks to the unpunished sins of slaveholders, and references to Sethe's time in jail, reinforce the theme of justice. Assigned aspects of Garner's story to research, students will discover that Morrison departs from historical fact when she has Sethe tried and sentenced. They will learn that, despite her abolitionist lawyer's efforts, Garner was never given the chance to defend her case but instead was returned as property to the Garner estate, and that the infanticide sparked debate about the morality of slavery and the agency of slaves (May). Morrison's artistic choice develops Sethe's fallible humanity and her need—comparable to Raskolnikov's—for redemption from the human community she has betrayed.

Despite this point of comparison, students may have trouble relating *Crime and Punishment* to a novel about American slavery. However, if they research Russian serfdom, including changes to the justice system following its abolition, they will appreciate how the novels treat similar social problems. Written around the same time that *Beloved* is set, *Crime and Punishment* comparably portrays an environment of civic upheaval. While Morrison explores the transition in consciousness that occurs as former slaves adjust to recognition of their full humanity, Dostoevsky exposes how conventions built upon human ownership and exploitation persist in post-abolition St. Petersburg society. Students should examine how this persistent mindset is expressed through the character of Svidrigailov, who is at once Raskolnikov's nemesis and his alter ego, and is comparable to the sadistic character of the schoolteacher in *Beloved*. They may also see parallels between Sethe's sexual exploitation as a female slave and the degradations that Dunya and Sonya endure to support their families financially.

Indeed, multiple examples of sexual exploitation in *Crime and Punishment*—Dunya, Sonya, the girls whom Svidrigailov molests, the intoxicated young woman whom Raskolnikov protects—all prompt questions about how criminals and criminal activity are gendered in *Crime and Punishment*. For exploring these questions further, Margaret Atwood's *Alias Grace* provides another historically based narrative with parallels to Dostoevsky's novel. As in *Crime and Punishment*, female characters in *Alias Grace* are doubly victimized by gender and class, serving as maids in households where, like Svidrigailov's victims, they are sexually targeted by their male employers. But Atwood's female protagonist is not just a victim; she is accused of turning the tables on one such employer, killing a wealthy landowner and the housekeeper carrying his child. Atwood modeled her "murderess" on real-life Grace Marks, a teenage Irish-Canadian immigrant who was accused in 1843 of being an accomplice to a double murder. Despite Marks's conviction and prison sentence, her role in the crime mystified the public of her time—her femininity belied the viciousness of the acts of which she was accused—and students researching the case can trace Atwood's departures from fact into crime fiction that subverts conventional ideas of female powerlessness.

Nineteenth-century beliefs about the relationship between mental illness, culpability, and criminality provide additional research topics that illuminate parallels between the characters of Atwood's Grace, whose criminal impulses appear to derive from a multiple personality disorder that initially lands her in an insane asylum, and Dostoevsky's Raskolnikov, who is suspected of "madness" and whose name and behaviors suggest a split personality. Students may also want to research Dostoevsky's biography to determine how his own experiences with prosecution and imprisonment influenced his novel and to what extent his family background complicated his portrayals of social inequality.

Comparative Analysis: Dexter *and* Dead to Me

The genre of the crime story continues to develop not only in literary fiction but also in popular television, where it has been a successful serial form for decades. While many shows reinforce the conventional triumph of good over evil, showing police officers, detectives, lawyers, and judges prevailing over lawlessness, recent twists on the genre that complicate this binary provide productive material for analyzing the allure of the outlaw. Two examples, the series *Dexter* and *Dead to Me*, can inspire students to practice comparative analysis across media genres.

The eponymous hero of *Dexter* is both a forensic detective and a serial killer who brings vigilante justice to other serial killers by murdering them in a way that mimics their crimes. Like Raskolnikov, Dexter kills for good; he believes his victims are evil and that murdering them is a way to exact justice. The first season of the show stressed the likeability of Dexter, focusing on his charm and on the incongruency between the sadistic murders he commits and the way he fulfills the roles of father, husband, son, and colleague. The ethical nature of his activity is not fully addressed until after the first season, but students need watch only the show's trailer or introductory episodes (available for streaming online) to understand its premise and relevancy to ethical questions raised in *Crime and Punishment*. For example, students can discuss the idea of vigilante justice and whether the term can be applied to Raskolnikov's murder of the pawnbroker, whom he sees as a symbol of exploitation as well as an abuser of her younger sister. Students can also discuss how Dexter's allure is built up through the show as his gentler roles are emphasized and we are encouraged to root for him as an avenger. Does it matter that Dexter, like Raskolnikov, could be considered "remarkably good-looking" 'Кстати он был замечательно хорош' and well loved by those who know him best (Dostoevsky, *Crime* 4; *Prestuplenie* 6)? The revelation of Dexter's secret can also be compared to the way that Raskolnikov reveals his crime to Sonya. Finally, the scenes of graphic violence, so much more vivid in visual form, can lead students to discuss whether and how violence should be portrayed in the media. They might be surprised to learn that this is not a new issue: copycat axe murders followed the original publication of *Crime and Punishment*.

In Netflix's *Dead to Me*, the central crime is an unsolved case of hit-and-run manslaughter, and the story centers on the friendship between Jen, the grieving widow of the victim, and Judy, the driver who killed him. Jen is consumed from the beginning with the need to track down the driver and bring "him" to justice, not knowing that the woman who pursues her at a grief therapy session is the object of her search. As the friendship develops, viewers vacillate between sympathy and antipathy for Judy (What are her reasons for befriending Jen? Is she a stalker, or is she motivated by remorse? Do we want her to be discovered or to turn herself in?). In the final episode, when Jen ultimately acknowledges her guilt, references to different spiritual practices of redemption may remind students of Raskolnikov's confession to Sonya—and of whether they were satisfied by its outcome. Comparison can prompt discussion about the relationship between confession and redemption, including the role that the criminal justice system plays in formalizing these processes. To prompt a comparative analysis, students may view one or two scenes in class, then, in brainstorming sessions, note parallels to *Crime and Punishment* in theme, plot, and characterization. Students may then choose an additional episode to watch and analyze on their own time, and they can share their results in a later class session.

When *Crime and Punishment* is approached through the theme of the alluring outlaw, students have reasons to pay attention to narrative technique, take positions on justice, delve into history, figure out the relationship between fact and fiction, and compare Dostoevsky's novel to other texts. In addition to developing skills, these activities guide students toward important questions about social authority and identity. Pursuing the allure of the outlaw—the problem of why we identify with literary characters whose deeds appall us—can help students become more conscious of themselves as readers and come to understand reading itself as an ethical activity.

NOTES

1. The novels in the survey included Albert Camus's *The Stranger*, Vladimir Nabokov's *Lolita*, Toni Morrison's *Beloved*, Margaret Atwood's *Alias Grace*, and Bernhard Schlink's *The Reader*.
2. This essay cites the translation by Richard Pevear and Larissa Volokhonsky (1993).

Contrasting Approaches: What I Learned in Prison

Priscilla Meyer

Teaching undergraduates to read literary fiction involves moving beyond story line and character by revealing authorial crafting. Motifs and subtexts are two literary devices that students can explore themselves to discover verifiably systematic principles of construction. One easily accessible and globally determining subtext for Fyodor Dostoevsky's *Crime and Punishment* is Honoré Balzac's *Père Goriot* (*Old Goriot*). In a course on French and Russian novels (called Murder and Adultery), my students and I analyzed this subtext to highlight Dostoevsky's creative process—what he transformed, how, and why—and to show how the Russian nineteenth-century novel evolved in dialogue with the French prose tradition. In this essay, I will contrast this scholarly reading of *Crime and Punishment* with the insights that an experience-based identification can supply, which I gained from teaching the novel not only in a university setting but also in a maximum security prison. The essay analyzes *Père Goriot*, *Notes from the House of the Dead*, and the Gospel of John as subtexts of *Crime and Punishment*.

Crime and Punishment *and* Père Goriot

In *Crime and Punishment*, Dostoevsky sets French novels about prostitutes and young men who abandon virtue for vice in opposition to the Russian cultural universe.[1]

Dostoevsky had devoured the best French novels as a youth. He spent the summer of 1838 reading everything that Balzac had published and wrote to his brother Mikhail, "Balzac is great! His characters are products of a universal mind. Not the spirit of the times, but the struggles of whole millennia prepared this development in the human soul" 'Бальзак велик! Его харатеры – произведения ума вселенной! Не дух времени, но целые тысячелетия приготовили бореньем своим такую развязку в душе человеке' (Letter to Mikhail Mikhailovich Dostoevsky 51; my trans.). Dostoevsky's first publication was a translation of *Eugénie Grandet*; *Père Goriot* was the first book Dostoevsky recommended to his new bride, Anna Grigor'evna Snitkina, four months after he completed *Crime and Punishment*.

Leonid Grossman was the first to outline the relationship between these two novels. He notes the parallels between the French and Russian casts of characters: Rastignac and Raskolnikov are both young law students from the provinces who leave their beloved mothers and sisters behind; in the capital they are torn between compassion, whose objects are Goriot and Marmeladov on the one hand, and immorality, represented by Vautrin and Svidrigailov on the other.

In his Russian "translation" of *Père Goriot*, Dostoevsky renders what is literal in Balzac metaphorical, metaphysical: Vautrin plans to go to America to start a tobacco plantation using slave labor, while Svidrigailov, speaking of "going to America," is contemplating suicide. Dostoevsky thus represents "two variants of false salvation" 'двух вариантов ложного спасения,' as V. N. Toporov puts it, the literal journey and the figurative one to the other world (251n52; my trans.).

Having established the character parallels, methods of transposition, and cultural dialogue of Dostoevsky's detailed response to *Père Goriot*, students themselves can look for and interpret textual parallels. They write a paper on how Dostoevsky recasts Balzac's material, analyzing a scene, a motif, a theme, or a pairing of characters as part of Dostoevsky's argument with Balzac. Some points of contact are discussed by Grossman; for example, the "sister motif" as part of the heroes' motivation for their respective crimes. Both heroes in the capitals receive letters from home in the village; Rastignac calls his sisters "angels" as Raskolnikov's mother calls Dunya an angel (Grossman 41). Rastignac's mother tells him, "Love your aunt; I won't tell you all she's done for you" (Balzac 96); Raskolnikov's mother writes, "Love your sister Dunya, Rodya. Love her as she loves you, and know that she loves you infinitely more than she loves herself" 'Люби Дуню, свою сестру, Родя; люби так, как она тебя любит, и знай, что она беспредельно, больше себя самой любит' (Dostoevsky, *Crime* 47; *Prestuplenie* 34).[2] Rastignac's sisters are happy to sacrifice their savings to their beloved brother. Raskolnikov's mother writes that Dunya is prepared to sacrifice her entire life for Raskolnikov by marrying Luzhin, a man she cannot love. Rastignac happily takes his sisters' money to buy clothes so that he can enter high society; Raskolnikov, in despair over his mother's letter, refuses Dunya's sacrifice, one she hoped would help her brother to a career in law.[3] Rastignac eagerly turns his sisters' and mother's gifts to use in visiting Madame de Beauséant; Raskolnikov, in an act of spontaneous compassion, gives his mother's money to the Marmeladov family. What is material and morally faulty in Balzac becomes redemptive in Dostoevsky.

Dostoevsky's recasting of Balzac's material aspect of human motives is particularly striking in his description of Marmeladov's death; rewriting Père Goriot's passing, he links the scenes by several details. Rastignac and Raskolnikov send for the doctors and provide for the funerals of the fathers. Both deathbed scenes are illuminated by "a single candle" 'Один только огарок освещал всю сцену' (Balzac 269; Dostoevsky, *Crime* 177; *Prestuplenie* 143). Rastignac supports Goriot as his shirt is changed (Balzac 268); Raskolnikov "carefully support[s] Marmeladov's head" 'осторожно поддерживал голову' (Dostoevsky, *Crime* 187; *Prestuplenie* 138) as he is carried from the street and "wipes Marmeladov's face with a moistened towel" 'стал обмывать залитое кровью лицо Мармеладова' (*Crime* 187; *Prestuplenie* 140). After Goriot's death, dinner at the maison Vauquer proceeds as usual: "fifteen diners were soon chattering in their usual way. . . . But the sounds of forks and spoons, the laughter and the talk, the varied expressions on the gluttonous impassive faces of the boarders, their lack of concern, froze the young men with horror" (Balzac 271). Raskolnikov is similarly appalled by the uncaring, rowdy guests at Marmeladov's wake:

"Amalia Ivanovna stormed around the room, shrieking, wailing, and throwing everything she could get hold of on the floor in a fuming rage. The lodgers shouted in an incoherent medley of voices—some commenting each in his own way on the events that had just taken place; others arguing and swearing; others struck up songs . . ." 'Амалия Ивановна металась по комнате, визжала, причитала, швыряла все, что ни попадалось ей, на пол и буянила. Жильцы горланили кто в лес, кто по дрова – иные договаривали, что умели, о случивемся событии; другие ссорились и ругались; иные затянули песни . . .' (Dostoevsky, *Crime* 394; *Prestuplenie* 311).

Most important is the inverse relationship between the fathers and the daughters. Joel Hunt has shown Goriot and Marmeladov to be similarly obsessed outcasts who are responsible for their own misery, guilt-ridden and driven to confession and self-punishment. To this may be added some dramatic parallels: Goriot, dying, calls out for his daughters—"Nasie! Fifine!" (Balzac 268)—but they don't come; in contrast, Marmeladov's daughter immediately runs to his bedside, where he cries out "Sonya! My daughter! Forgive me" 'Соня! Дочь! Прости!' (Dostoevsky, *Crime* 189; *Prestuplenie* 145). Goriot's daughters don't want to compromise their social positions by associating with their father. Marmeladov's daughter, who has already compromised her own position to maintain him and his second family, comes despite her shame at appearing at Amaliya Fyodorovna's apartment: "Sonya . . . looked like a lost soul, not understanding, apparently, anything, forgetting her fourth-hand silk indecent bright dress with the long and absurd train and huge crinoline that filled the entire doorway [. . .] 'Соня . . . глядела как потерянная, не сознавая, казалось, ничего, забыв о своем перекупленном из четвертых рук шелковом, неприличном здесь, цветном платье с длиннейшим и смешным хвостом, и необъятном кринолине, загородившем всю дверь [. . .]' (*Crime* 187; *Prestuplenie* 143). Dostoevsky's detailed description of Sonya's finery implicitly parodies Balzac's elaborate depictions of Goriot's daughters' clothing, the expense of which contributes to their father's ruin (Hunt 316). The implication that Goriot's daughters are simply expensively kept prostitutes, conveyed by the boarders' gossip about their backstairs visits to Goriot, is inverted by Dostoevsky's rendition of Sonya. She is an honest prostitute, sacrificing herself out of love for her family, strengthened by her religious faith; her "finery" is so external to her spiritual nature and love for her family that she is able to forget about it entirely when she runs to her father's deathbed.

The systematic parallels between the two novels highlight the conspicuous point of departure from Dostoevsky's elaborate parallel: in *Père Goriot* Sonya has her counterpart in Victorine, a devout, pale, "excessively slim" young woman who resembles a medieval statuette and whose eyes "express Christian gentleness and resignation" (Balzac 17). But Dostoevsky uses the favorite device of the *école frénétique*, combining opposites: Sonya is "a very small, thin girl of about eighteen . . . blonde" 'малого роста, лет восемнадцати, худенькая . . . блондинка' (*Crime* 187; *Prestuplenie* 143), "still very young, almost like a child, with a meek and modest manner" 'очень еще молоденькая, почти похожая на девочку, с скромною и приличною манерой' (*Crime* 234; *Prestuplenie* 181), imbued with Christian faith—and is a prostitute. Dostoevsky's contrast goes beyond the startling effect to argue with all the French prostitute tales: unlike Balzac's other prostitutes, or Victorine, Sonya has found faith, strength, and love through suffering, loving others as herself, and reading the Bible. In *Crime and Punishment* Dostoevsky recasts Balzac's version of social and monetary "salvation": Raskolnikov's moral and spiritual salvation is brought about not by killing the pawnbroker but through his compassion and eventual acceptance of suffering.

Students are excited to become capable of this degree of close reading and understanding of subtextual literary argument. The hive mind always finds new parallels, making the exploration fun for both students and instructors.

Crime and Punishment *and* Notes from the House of the Dead

After fifty years of teaching *Crime and Punishment* in several different contexts to undergraduates in a small private university, I designed a course on prisons in Russian literature for a men's maximum security prison where I had taught before. The range of student responses in any literature program teaches instructors about the texts; here, the juxtaposition of the prison setting with the private liberal arts classroom can provide an instructive polarity between the experiential and the intellectual modes of reading fiction. While the two methods overlap, of course, the vivid experience of reading prison literature with students in prison suggested that my earlier efforts to avoid simple identification with a text's characters had privileged literary analytical methods over self-aware identification as a way to access the richness of a text. When students have personal experience with a highly particular circumstance such as imprisonment, it provides an intensity of insight quite different from the puzzle-solving pleasures of subtext analysis. This kind of identification has the potential to reverse simple personal projection that distorts the fictional character by subsuming artistic creation into the limits of self; rather than reduce the fictional to the familiar, it enlarges personal experience through the fictional in a particularly powerful way, an ideal response to fiction.

Approaching *Crime and Punishment* through the prison theme by first reading the shorter and immediately accessible *Notes from the House of the Dead* gave incarcerated students a sense of kinship with Dostoevsky—as they wrote, only someone who has been in prison can understand it—and led to insights about Dostoevsky's creation of Raskolnikov.

The students in Prisons in Russian Literature, despite the distance in time and place between them and the novelist, related *Notes from the House of the Dead* to their own experiences, particularly the psychological and emotional impact of being imprisoned. Many remarked on the surprising constants between incarceration in Russia in the 1850s and in the United States in 2018: once his shackles are removed, Dostoevsky describes his incredulity that he had worn them for four years (*Notes from the House of the Dead* 247); one student compared this to being moved to a lower-security area where only the corridor, not the individual cell where he had spent ten years, was locked and he was free to move around. Both writer and reader marvel that they could have lived under these conditions for as long as they did, a fully commensurate mode of identification with a literary text. Another student noted the assumptions, sometimes based on race, that people in prison make about each other and related that to the incarcerated peasants' rejection of the gentleman political prisoners. The kinship with Dostoevsky that *House of the Dead* establishes for students helps them relate *Crime and Punishment*'s themes of poverty, relationship to the environment, guilt, and murder to their own experience and recognize their own rationalizations of their crimes by tracking Raskolnikov's: students wrote of the psychological effects of crime and of how they devalued others' lives as well as their own. These readers were moved by the truth of Raskolnikov's thoughts in Siberia, "that [those in prison] valued life more in prison than they had when they were at liberty" 'в остроге ее еще более любят и ценят и более дорожат ею, чем на свободе' (*Crime* 516; *Prestuplenie* 418), which reading *House of the Dead* had prepared them to see.

House of the Dead adds an autobiographical dimension to Raskolnikov's epiphany in *Crime and Punishment*'s epilogue. Joseph Frank shows that the "regeneration of [his] convictions" that Dostoevsky wrote of in his *Diary of a Writer* in 1873 relates not specifically to his religious faith, as is often assumed, as much as to the evolution of his relationship to his fellow prisoners (*Dostoevsky: The Miraculous Years* 87), an insight also contained in one student's response paper, which suggested that one can read the ending of *Crime and Punishment* as a rebirth not into Christianity but into humanity. During his first year in prison Dostoevsky was horrified by the brutality and lack of conscience he saw in many incarcerated with him; it challenged the humanitarian and idealized vision of the peasantry that had motivated members of the Petrashevsky Circle, which in turn had led to his imprisonment (Frank, *Dostoevsky: The Miraculous Years* 96–106). Frank identifies the Easter when Dostoevsky was twenty-nine as the beginning of his "regeneration," using the story "The Peasant Marey" (1876) from the *Diary* to explicate Dostoevsky's epiphany (120). Dostoevsky had suffered intensely from the revulsion he felt on coming into close contact with the common people during his first year in prison (106). *House of the Dead* recounts his growing ability to recognize the "kernel" in the "husk" of each man's character, with the Christmas performance as centerpiece (126); it enables Dostoevsky to reach a new, positive, understanding of the People and their intuitive Christian compassion as displayed in his later account of the serf Marey's maternal comforting of the nine-year-old Dostoevsky.

This insight suggests that Raskolnikov's epiphany mirrors Dostoevsky's. Dostoevsky was hurt to be rejected as a "gentleman." In Raskolnikov's prison camp, the other men recognize his rejection of them, something implicitly overcome when he is ready to accept Sonya's views—"How can her beliefs not be my beliefs now too?" 'Разве могут ее убеждения не быть теперь и моими убеждения?' (*Crime* 522; *Prestuplenie* 422). "It even seemed to him that all the convicts who had been his enemies looked at him differently now. He even began chatting with them himself, and they replied affectionately" 'ему даже показалось, что как будто все каторжные, бывшие враги его, уже глядели на него иначе. Он даже сам заговаривал с ними, и ему отвечали лаского' (*Crime* 521; *Prestuplenie* 422). Working backward, then, it appears that in *Crime and Punishment*, Dostoevsky recognizes his own admiration for the fearless strength of the "superman" Orlov in *House of the Dead* who observes no law but his own (Frank, *Dostoevsky: The Miraculous Years* 150), takes it to extremes in creating Raskolnikov, and tests its limits by transposing the "superman" into the confined reality of the Petersburg poor, a metaphorical prison. Dostoevsky adds conscience and the capacity for compassion as essential missing aspects of the superman, aspects of humanity that connect the individual to the collective that had shunned Dostoevsky.

The Gospel of John

The opposition between the benefits of a literary analytic reading (through *Père Goriot*) and those of an experiential one (through *House of the Dead*) can be resolved through reading the Gospel of John. In my experience, incarcerated students are more familiar with the Gospels than most undergraduates; once alerted to its presence early in the reading process (we read John before starting *Crime and Punishment*), they quickly identify many points of contact with John and through that come to understand the methods of subtextual reference.

Crime and Punishment may be seen as a modern Gospel, in particular, the Gospel according to John, from which Sonya reads at such surprising length to Raskolnikov.[4] Dostoevsky translates the gospel into modern dress in order to have the Word made, if not flesh, then at least newly vital; by transposing the good news into the world of the Petersburg poor, he shows Raskolnikov's miraculous transformation to be possible for any reader. Even the sudden change of tone and focus from that teeming world to the biblical Siberian landscape of the epilogue has its origin in the conclusion of the Gospel of John.

John had particular significance for Dostoevsky. In mid-January 1850, on his march to Siberia, the wife of one of the Decembrists gave him a copy of the New Testament, which he kept under his pillow during the four years he spent in prison. Dostoevsky made fifty-eight marginal markings in John, four times more than in any of the other Gospels (Kjetsaa 5–8; Kirillova 42).

Dostoevsky recasts the passion story in novelistic terms. Luzhin plays the role of Judas, Porfiry is Pilate, although both are also briefly identified with Peter. Sonya and Raskolnikov play dual parts, one secular and the other sacred. In the first of these, they follow the prototypes of French novels, and in the second, of the Gospels: Sonya is a prostitute and is hence associated with Mary Magdalene, while Raskolnikov, as an ambitious young man from the provinces, is a mock Jesus who tries to play the role of God and fails. The Gospel's not-so-hidden presence adds a sacred plane to the novel, in which Svidrigailov represents the lack of any faith while Sonya represents the ideal of Christ toward which Raskolnikov moves from the opposite pole of a false Christ.

The synthesis of the sacred and profane can be reached either through Dostoevsky's argument with the French novel, whose focus on the material aspect of human existence he corrects, or through his personal alienation from his fellow prisoners as described in *House of the Dead*. Both approaches are countered and resolved through the subtext of John, which provides a way to transcend the limits of reason through the irrational acceptance of religious faith. In deeply personal responses as compared to the more abstract literary detective work of subtext study, my students in prison appreciated the way the novel legitimated their own experience: one of them wrote that he had been wrestling with guilt similar to Raskolnikov's for many years and felt that Raskolnikov would understand.

The looks on the faces in the prison yard in *Shawshank Redemption* when Andy plays a duet from *The Marriage of Figaro* over the PA system provide an image of the effect *Crime and Punishment* had on the incarcerated students, a sense of awe that we'd like all our students to experience in all our classes.

NOTES

1. For a fuller discussion of this topic, and of the Gospel of John in *Crime and Punishment*, see chapter 3 of my *How the Russians Read the French* (89–151).
2. This essay cites the translation by Sidney Monas.
3. I am grateful to my students for their observations on these parallels.
4. That several of the passages Sonya reads were inserted in the final stages of composition to replace censored material (see Dostoevsky, *Polnoe sobranie sochinenii*, 7: 326, 386) substantiates the importance of John for the novel.

Crime and Punishment in the Context of Philosophy

Brian Armstrong

A philosophical approach to Dostoevsky's *Crime and Punishment* is quite natural, given Dostoevsky's reputation as a philosophical novelist. It is also a challenge, as there are many conceptions of philosophy, which in turn lead to many possible approaches. Another challenge is that, as philosophers, we can all too easily reduce literature to mere illustrations of preexisting claims, which does a disservice to what makes literature what it is. Still, there are philosophical approaches to literature that can shed light on what interests the student of a novel such as *Crime and Punishment.* This is especially the case when addressing the many significant concepts that are at issue in the novel and the many instances of explanatory reasoning at play in the novel and for which the novel calls.

In what follows, I will illustrate some philosophical approaches using the concepts of *reason* and *conscience.* Other concepts would also work, such as those within epistemology regarding how we know self, others, and the world, or those within metaphysics dealing with the nature of consciousness, free will, and personhood. The concept of a *person*, for instance, might lead one to distinguish between a *human* as a living being and a *person* as a kind of consciousness and to then deny personhood to some humans (as Raskolnikov seems to do). And, of course, there are the central concepts of ethics. I find that those concepts that we tend to take for granted or that receive less attention in either philosophy or literature often work especially well, and that *conscience* is one of these.

Definitions: Reason and Philosophy

When approaching Dostoevsky's novel, we should keep in mind that there are multiple implicit conceptions of reason and, by extension, philosophy. We should also keep in mind that, although Dostoevsky is often considered an irrationalist of some kind, those who claim or are accused of irrationalism are (generally) taking issue not with reason as such but with a particular conception of it. Thus, we would do well to think of *Crime and Punishment* as offering a critique of certain conceptions of reason, which in turn requires that we understand what conceptions of reason (and philosophy) are at work in the novel.

A useful starting point is found in the work of the literary critic Vissarion Grigor'evich Belinsky, who influenced the young Dostoevsky. Belinsky provides a definition of a philosopher that seems straightforward at first: "The philosopher speaks with syllogisms, the poet with images and pictures, but they both speak one and the same thing" 'Философ говорит силлогизмами, поэт – образами и картинами, а говорят оба они одно и то же.' He then elaborates: "The one *proves*, the other *points*, and both *convince*, only one with logical arguments and the other with pictures" 'Один *доказывает*, другой *показывает*, и оба *убеждают*, только один логическими доводами, другой – картинами' (35).[1] In both cases, they (the philosopher and the poet) convince insofar as they work on the consciousness of the reader; both use words in order to actualize something within us that in turn affects how we act.

However, the way in which the philosopher does this, according to Belinksy, might sound odd: the philosopher does this with statistics. It is in "furnishing himself with statistical numbers" 'вооружась статистическими числами' that he *proves* (*доказывает*), thereby "acting on the minds of his readers" 'действуя на ум своих читателей' (35). The statistician had, by that time, come to occupy a role at which philosophers have traditionally aimed: the thinker who presents a view of reality that is abstract yet objective, grounded in particulars yet universal, and seen as essential to the good of the whole. These calculating thinkers were engaged in the creation of a new kind of objective *thing*—the statistical fact—which could then be used to justify an instrumental approach to members of the state and one's neighbor.

A possible philosophical approach to the novel would thus have us attend to the various appearances of reasoning in the novel. The reasoning of Raskolnikov and Luzhin in particular is described in terms of calculation (расчет): mathematics, numbers, percentages, probabilities. Following Belinsky, we could say that they are engaging in "philosophy." But to attack such a mode of problematic reasoning is hardly to attack philosophy and the value of reason as such. Instead, it should lead us to conceive of philosophy and reason more carefully. We should ask, "What are the different ways we can reason—and which are better?" rather than "Is reason good or bad?"

Exercise

Ask students to articulate different conceptions of a concept, such as philosophy or reason. See if they can find instances in the novel that illustrate each particular conception. And, for a more advanced activity, ask students to use the conceptions to explain relevant parts of the novel with an eye toward which one works best.

Definitions: Conscience

One surprisingly protean concept that might be chosen for the above activity is conscience. The philosophical approach helps us attend to the fine-tuned presentation of conscience in the minds, words, and deeds of Dostoevsky's characters. We can even view these conceptions as phenomena that Dostoevsky is testing, such that a failure of conscience in a character might actually be the failure of a particular conception of conscience.

Here are some questions that can help students to articulate conceptions of conscience:

- Is it cognitive (enabling knowledge of moral truths), affective (producing unpleasant feelings in response to certain actions), or conative (producing not justifications or feelings but dispositions to act)? In other words, do I *know* that this is wrong, do I *feel* that this is wrong, or do I simply find myself *disposed* to not perform this action?
- Is it a voice? If so, what is its origin, the source of its authority, and the qualities that distinguish it from other voices in my head? Does it originate in a divine being, a society, my physiology, or my "authentic" self?
- Is it a unified thing within me or such that I can be of "two minds," as if I had *two* consciences?
- Can my conscience transform me? If so, is it more likely to do so when I dwell on it alone or when I engage it in dialogue with others?

Exercise

As above, ask students to articulate conceptions of conscience and then use them to identify illustrative moments and explain confusing moments in the novel.

Articulating the Claim

Questions are essential to any philosophical approach. And just as they can help us distinguish among different possible articulations of a concept, they can also help us articulate a claim. Porfiry Petrovich provides an excellent example of this as he presses Raskolnikov to articulate his theory of the extraordinary person (EP). Here are possible articulations of Raskolnikov's claim that emerge in the course of their conversation (in book 3, chapter 5):

- "Some people have the right to kill innocent others."
- "EPs have the right to kill innocent others."
- "EPs have the right to kill innocent others in the pursuit of a 'new word.'"
- "EPs have the right to kill 'innocent' others in the pursuit of a new word."
- "EPs grant themselves the right to kill 'innocent' others in the pursuit of a new word."

Exercise

Articulate the claims of a character, testing them against what the character actually does and elsewhere says. In particular, ask students to note how questions (whether explicitly stated or somehow implied) lead characters to articulate their beliefs more clearly, and on what conceptual distinctions these articulations depend. Ask students to do the same with their own claims about the novel.

Deducing

Deductions can be especially useful when trying to articulate not just what *exactly* someone is saying but also *all* that someone is saying, in the sense that many claims involve the implicit endorsement of other claims. For instance, if we take the premises of Raskolnikov's theory to be true, we can deduce how he ought to feel before, during, and after his crime.

1. The EP does not experience "bad conscience" while performing an action that society considers a crime.
2. A sign of having no "bad conscience" is that one's mental activity proceeds normally during the "criminal" action.
3. Thus, an EP's mental activity proceeds normally during the "criminal" action.

We can therefore infer that if Raskolnikov is an EP (who is not bound by an ordinary conscience), and if such a person experiences no "bad conscience" while performing an action judged morally wrong by an ordinary conscience, then Raskolnikov will not experience impaired mental activity while planning, executing, and moving on after the action. But he does, and so he is not.

This can also be stated as a classic *modus tollens*: If Raskolnikov is an EP (*p*), then he will think clearly when committing a "crime" (*q*); he was not thinking clearly when he committed a "crime" (~*q*); ergo, he is not an EP (~*p*).

Exercise

Have students create syllogisms that capture a character's implicit belief (either because it must be assumed given that character's speech, or because it follows from that speech). Does the character seem to accept or avoid these implications? Does the character revise a belief in the face of these inferential consequences?

Finding Patterns

Given Raskolnikov's early rant against statistical reasoning ("A percentage!" 'Процент!' he cries out at one point [Dostoevsky, *Prestuplenie* 43)], it may seem ironic to use inductive inferences to gain insight into the novel. However, there are powerful reasons to do so. As an example, let's use the explicit mentions of conscience (совесть), of which there are twenty-three.[2] We find the word used in a range of activities, such as Raskolnikov reflecting on his mother's "having agreed to sacrifice" 'согласилась пожертвовать' his sister (*Crime* [2018] 44; *Prestuplenie* 36), a student claiming he could murder without a pang of conscience, Raskolnikov presenting his extraordinary person theory, Svidrigailov claiming that his conscience is clear with respect to his wife's death, and Porfiry claiming that Raskolnikov's crime was, with respect to his conscience, only an obscuration ("помрачение"; 350). What patterns do we observe in Dostoevsky's use of the word?

> **Exercise**
>
> Ask students to observe patterns and then seek to explain them. For instance, one likely explanation of the use of "совесть" is that Raskolnikov and Dostoevsky have different conceptions of conscience. Raskolnikov deploys his to justify and explain things that he finds troubling, but he generally fails to reflect meaningfully on the actual operations of his conscience. Where are instances of his actual conscience at work?

Thinking through Translations

Translations can often have philosophical bearing: the translation of key terms can vary across editions and even within an edition, and we can often find meaningful patterns in these alterations and omissions that help us to better articulate the concept under consideration.

Let's look at four translations of a key moment in which conscience plays a role: Dunya's reply to Svidrigailov's explanation of Raskolnikov's behavior. Dunya says to Svidrigailov, "А угрызение совести? Вы отрицаете в нем, стало быть, всякое нравственное чувство? Да разве он таков?" (Dostoevsky, *Prestuplenie* 378) The translations below were written by Michael Katz, Oliver Ready, Richard Pevear and Larissa Volokhonsky, and myself, respectively:

> "And *pangs of conscience*? Are you therefore denying him *any moral feeling*? Could he really be like that?" (*Crime* [2018] 541)
>
> "And the *voice of conscience*? Are you denying him *all moral sense*? Is he really like that?" (*Crime* [2015] 462)
>
> "And *remorse of conscience*? You mean you deny him *all moral sentiment*? Is that what he's like?" (*Crime* [1993] 491)
>
> "And *a twinge of conscience*? You are, therefore, denying him *any moral feeling*? Is he really like that?" (my trans.)

Philosophically, Ready's "voice" is highly problematic: conscience is clearly something *felt* in these and related passages, not something *heard*; the figure of speech risks obscuring what's at play. Pevear and Volokhonsky's "remorse" is also problematic, as remorse and conscience are different things. My own "twinge" is problematic, as it is too literal and might suggest that Dostoevsky is talking about something different from what we mean by these "pangs." The proper English equivalent of "угрызение совести" is "pang of conscience." Katz alone has that (using the more idiomatic plural found in English). And how, exactly, are we to understand "чувство," rendered here as "feeling," "sense," or "sentiment"?

Exercise

What difference does each translation make to our larger philosophical concerns? How might our conceptions of conscience lead us to misperceive or misread the novel, and how might a more focused reading of these passages shed light on what conscience is (and is not)? Ask students to look at the translation of other key passages.

Finding the Question

The *question* matters greatly in philosophy. And, at times, we can fail to make sense of something if we assume the wrong question. For instance, one can frame Raskolnikov's theory of conscience as a response to the fact that some people get away with crimes while others do not. That fact is a strange phenomenon of which he is trying to make sense. As the narrator notes, "From the beginning—or, rather, for a long time before—he'd been preoccupied by one question: why are almost all crimes so conspicuous, so easily discovered, and the traces of almost all criminals revealed so obviously?" 'Сначала – впрочем, давно уже прежде – его занимал один вопрос: почему так легко отыскиваются и выдаются почти все преступления и так явно обозначаются следы почти всех преступников?' (*Crime* [2018] 77; *Prestuplenie* 58). Raskolnikov hypothesizes that the answer is found in the consciousness of the person: if we consider the psychological state of the criminal throughout the course of the crime, we will find that it is accompanied by an illness that obscures reason and will. What's left unstated at this point is the answer to the question implied in his still-vague theory: if I don't *experience* something as a crime, then I don't experience the obscuration ("помрачение"). In other words, Raskolnikov hypothesizes that the relativity of conscience can explain how some get away with murder.

Exercise

In order to assess Raskolnikov's overall theory, we must know what evidence he seeks to explain. What, then, are the phenomena that his theory must explain? How well does his theory explain those phenomena? Are there better explanations of all the available evidence regarding crimes and conscience? Can students find evidence or reasons that Raskolnikov might have overlooked?

Contrastive Analysis

One way to generate explanatory hypotheses in an intentional fashion is through the use of foils, which in this context are things that are similar to the fact we wish to explain but, in a crucial respect, different (Lipton 34). Medicine provides classic examples: if two people are very similar, and both are exposed to an illness, we would expect both to get sick; however, if just one of the two becomes ill, we would want to explain that fact, and we can do that by looking more closely for relevant differences—ones that could explain the contrast. In doing that, we have two things to explain: why did one fall ill (the expected fact) and why did the other (the otherwise similar foil) not fall ill? If we stick to the fact, we might be inclined to say, "He fell ill because he was exposed to a virus." However, while that's true, it doesn't (in the relevant way) explain what happened, because someone similar was exposed and did not fall sick. Thus, we need to explain the difference, which will in turn put us closer to the heart of the matter.

A classic example in *Crime and Punishment* is the ending: one might not expect Raskolnikov to change after finding his conscience clear, and yet the narrator tells us that he does change. This is unexpected and needs to be explained. Here, the foil is implicit: it is our expectation of how such a change should go.

With respect to making sense of Dostoevsky's conception of conscience, one can ask why Raskolnikov's conception of conscience seems "inoperative" (meaning that it does not lead to his conversion). We can contrast this with a conception of conscience that *does* work. A reader might feel that, if one's conscience is clear upon inspection, then a later conversion makes no sense; this feeling implies that, for there to be a conversion, one's conscience cannot be clear. But is that so? And if it isn't so, then what does that imply about our everyday conceptions of conscience?

Exercise

Provide students with a view of conscience, as a foil, that might contrast with the everyday one noted above. Paul, in his letter to the Philippians, provides a good example, as he appears to have had a clear conscience prior to his conversion: he prosecuted those whom he has now joined but claims that he was "as to righteousness under the law, blameless" (*Bible* [New Revised Standard Version], Phil. 3.6). Nor does he now seem to experience remorse; rather, he says, "[T]his one thing I do: forgetting what lies behind and straining forward to what lies ahead . . ." (Phil 3.13). Here, introspection—even after the fact—seems to suggest the presence of a clear conscience; it also suggests that a new sense of things does not require introspective self-flagellation while looking at the past. How might this conception of conscience help us to explain the novel's ending?

Abduction: Explain Something Strange

Dostoevsky was clearly very interested in explanatory reasoning, especially when people offer theories of one another and themselves. This points to another philosophical approach: assessing the quality of various explanations in the novel, such as those offered of Raskolnikov's motives (including the role played by conscience). There is, of course, Svidrigailov's explanation. And Raskolnikov runs through a series of possibilities in his confession to Sonya (to steal, to follow the example of Napoleon, to save his mother and sister, to spite, to dare, or to know if he's a man). None of these, however, holds up from a philosophical perspective.

Any good theory must first pass the coherency tests (it must not contradict the evidence or itself). Those that pass can then be assessed by a set of criteria: testability (Can I test it?); scope (Can it explain more than the target phenomena?); fruitfulness (Can it generate predictions?); simplicity (Does it avoid ad hoc postulates?); and humility (Does it challenge too much of what we already believe is known?).

Exercise

Using these criteria, ask students to test explanations (their own and those found in the novel) against the evidence offered by the narrator. Doing this well should generate insight into the concepts one wishes to investigate, insofar as a proper explanation of Raskolnikov (or another character) should help us to make sense of each other and ourselves, too.

NOTES

1. Translations not otherwise attributed are my own.

2. Appearances of the word "conscience" 'совесть' in the original Russian are listed here by book and chapter: two in 1.4, three in 1.6, one in 2.3, two in 2.6, five in 3.5, two in 4.1, one in 5.1, one in 6.1, two in 6.2, two in 6.5, and two in chapter 2 of the epilogue. The Russian "совесть" may not consistently be translated as "conscience" in every English translation. Students can work together to make a full list of all the relevant passages in the translation(s) they are using.

Teaching Ethics through *Crime and Punishment*

Ani Kokobobo

A few years ago, my university adopted a series of distributive requirements, which prompted me to apply for an NEH course development grant that brought Russian literature into dialogue with different ethical theories. Although, on the surface, morality in Fyodor Dostoevsky's novel seems thoroughly shaped by religion, *Crime and Punishment* lent itself well to considerable explorations of ethics and ethical questions. With a crime at its center and extensive evaluation of the processes of intention, self-incrimination, and remorse and retribution that come with it, the novel seems made to order for the undergraduate ethics distributive requirement. Focusing at times on Raskolnikov, and at times on other characters, like Sonya or Razumikhin, and with the help of an ethics reader (James Rachels's *The Elements of Moral Philosophy*),[1] my class managed to tease out different normative ethical philosophies in the novel, including egoism, utilitarianism, deontology, and feminist ethics of care. In keeping with his polyphonic talent, Dostoevsky captures several abstract ethical perspectives in *Crime and Punishment* but pushes for a version of ethics rooted in community and human connections outside strict ideological divisions. My students and I defined this ethics of community as a version of the feminine ethics of care, which was formulated by feminist philosophers as a response to more abstract masculine ethical theories. Situating *Crime and Punishment* in such an ethical context resulted in interesting observations by students on the nature of community, and the moral responsibilities that members of a community have toward one another.

Given that *Crime and Punishment* has a strong Christian component, the first step my students and I took toward exploring ethics in the novel was to address the relationship between the ethical theories represented in it and the overall Christological arc. For this reason, we started the course by reading a chapter in *The Elements of Moral Philosophy* that addressed the relationship between morality and religion. Rachels argues that although traditionally human beings perceive moral views as grounded in religious ideas, we tend to misconstrue this connection. So rather than religion informing and driving morality, it is often the case that individuals "make up their minds about the moral issues first and then [interpret] the Scriptures, or church tradition, in such a way as to support the moral conclusion they have already reached" (Rachels 58–59). I brought this idea to the students, who also applied it to their own lives and considered the ways in which their moral codes interacted with their religious ideas. With this overarching idea in mind, we disentangled the novel's ethical and Christian dimensions, which resulted in my teaching the novel quite differently than in the past. Rather than focusing on the religious content directly, I worked with students to excavate the polyphony of moral views in *Crime and Punishment* while determining where the author's alliances fell and how those were reinforced by biblical messages. In fact, this portion of the course was conducive to an interesting discussion of politics and religion, both in Dostoevsky's time and in our own. We compared Dostoevsky's conservatism and religiosity to contemporary conservatism and religiosity. The students felt that Dostoevsky's Christian conservatism was less aimed at prohibitions and more geared toward building communities of care. One of the questions that came up was whether Dostoevsky's brand of Christian conservatism was more closely aligned to the contemporary position of the Christian left in America—meaning that he embraced Christianity while still holding socially liberal views.

When we turned away from religion and into a direct discussion of ethics, portions of Immanuel Kant's *Foundations of the Metaphysics of Morals* were essential reading for the course. This text informed our overall approach to ethics and morality in *Crime and Punishment* while also launching us into a broader discussion of ethics. Through Kant we began to wonder about the nature of ethics and moral absolutes: are there things that we simply cannot do as human beings, and are there moral rules that hold true without exception? Kant, who insists that such clarity is possible, outlines the notion of a moral idea, or a "categorical imperative," that has to hold true at all times for all rational individuals. In his *Foundations of the Metaphysics of Morals*, he describes the categorical imperative, or the moral absolute, in the following way: "Act only according to that maxim whereby you can, at the same time, will that it should become a universal law" (30). According to this principle, if an act, like murder, is not something that we could envision growing into a universal law, then this is where we must draw our ethical limits. As students pointed out, when Raskolnikov thinks about murder, both before and after his crime, he considers the moral imperative of preserving human life as something incidental that can and should be overcome by the truly strong individual. Beyond individual morality, we discussed some complications that arise where states are concerned: Kant supported capital punishment for murderers, and as part of Raskolnikov's argument for his murder he notes the double standard of allowing the state or military heroes to murder with impunity whereas individuals cannot.

One of the main ideas discussed in class in the context of ethics was Raskolnikov's perception of the pawnbroker as less than human—and here is where Kant's related ideas about the dignity of human beings were relevant to the course. Toward the end of *Crime and Punishment*, Raskolnikov rants about the pawnbroker in dehumanizing language. "I only killed a louse, Sonya, a useless, nasty, pernicious louse" 'Я ведь только вошь убил, Соня, бесполезную, гадкую, зловредную,' he says. This remark prompts Sonya to contradict him by exclaiming in outrage that a human being cannot possibly be a louse. As she puts it, "A human being—a louse!" 'Это человек-то вошь!' (Dostoevsky, *Crime* 416;

Prestuplenie 320).[2] By this later point in the novel Raskolnikov himself is evolving and is shaken in the ideas that make his murder justifiable. He responds to Sonya by acknowledging the pawnbroker's humanity. In class, we connected this conversation between the two characters to Kant's ideas about the uniqueness of human beings on account of their rationality. "Act so that you treat humanity, whether in your own person, or in that of another, always as an end, and never as a means only," writes Kant (30). Indeed, we concluded, Dostoevsky uses the murder in the novel to present the inalienable humanity of the pawnbroker and every other person. The intentionally animalistic and ugly aesthetic that Dostoevsky applies to the pawnbroker seems aimed at dehumanizing her—as though the author is tempting us to see her as less than human, thereby justifying her murder. In *Crime and Punishment* and in other novels, it seems as though Dostoevsky leads us into jarring and unethical thinking—such as, for instance, denying someone's humanity, only so that we may catch ourselves in it and repent or self-correct. We also observed in class that, just as Dostoevsky dehumanizes humans, he gives animals a great deal of personality at times. We considered animal cruelty in *Crime and Punishment* and interrogated the limitations of Kant's ideas of morality in this context. In fact, the dream sequence with the horse seems to prefigure the murder of the pawnbroker, or is at least connected to it in some way. But in the Kantian system of morality animals are not accounted for in the same way as humans.

Besides Kant's ideas, much of the narrative capturing Raskolnikov's thoughts about committing the murder, before and after the fact, was extremely ripe territory for the exploration of a range of ethical theories. For instance, at the start of the novel, Raskolnikov gets very agitated when he overhears a student and an officer at a tavern having a discussion about murdering the old pawnbroker, whom they also describe in dehumanizing language, as a "stupid, meaningless, worthless, wicked, sick old crone" 'глупая, бессмысленная, ничтожная, злая, больная старушонка.' One of the students in the tavern articulates a rationale for murder that closely echoes and partially exaggerates key precepts of ethical utilitarianism. He contrasts young and vibrant students, who are seeking to make their way in the world but lack the means to do so, with the old pawnbroker, who is "no good to anyone and, on the contrary, harmful to everyone" 'никому не нужная и, напротив, всем вредная.' He describes the great benefit that would come from the old woman's money if it were given out to others:

> A hundred, a thousand good deeds and undertakings that could be arranged and set going by the money that old woman has doomed to the monastery! Hundreds, maybe thousands of lives put right; dozens of families saved from destitution, from decay, from ruin, from depravity, from the venereal hospitals—all on her money. Kill her and take her money, so that afterwards with its help you can devote yourself to the service of all mankind and the common cause: what do you think, wouldn't thousands of good deeds make up for one tiny little crime? For one life, thousands of

> lives saved from decay and corruption. One death for hundreds of lives—it's simple arithmetic! (*Crime* 65)

> Сто, тысячу добрых дел и начинаний, которые можно устроить и поправить на старухины деньги, обреченные в монастырь! Сотни, тысячи, может быть, существований, направленных на дорогу; десятки семейств, спасенных от нищеты, от разложения, от гибели, от разврата, от венерических больниц, – и все это на ее деньги. Убей ее и возьми ее деньги, с тем чтобы с их помощию посвятить потом себя на служение всему человечеству и общем уделу: как ты думаешь, не загладится ли одно крошечное преступленьице тысячами добрых дел? За одну жизнь – тысячи жизней, спасенных от гниения и разложения. Одна смерть и сто жизней взамен – да ведь тут арифметика! (*Prestuplenie* 54)

We read these portions of the novel in conjunction with the utilitarianism chapter in the Rachels reader, which provided an overview of the ethical theory as well as fragments from Jeremy Bentham and John Stuart Mill, two core thinkers of utilitarianism. Bentham's "Principle of Utility" ostensibly requires that in the choice between different actions or policies we must opt for the one with the best overall consequences for everyone concerned. As he writes in *The Principles of Morals and Legislation*, "By the Principle of Utility is meant that principle which approves or disapproves of every action whatsoever, according to the tendency which it appears to have to augment or diminish the happiness of the party whose interest is in question; or what is the same thing in other words, to promote or to oppose happiness" (2). The idea behind these words is that actions are measured by the amount of happiness they produce, or the "Principle of Utility"—the extent to which an action can increase or decrease the happiness of those involved. Mill argues for similar views through his "Greatest Happiness Principle," which ultimately evaluates actions through the consequences that come from them with the object being an existence as free from pain and as rich in enjoyment as possible.

When students applied these ideas to *Crime and Punishment*, they first considered the argument made at the tavern that the pawnbroker has greater value dead than alive, in the sense that her death and the redistribution of her wealth could substantially benefit many poor individuals and families. We explored this argument further in a mock trial exercise. I split up students into three teams—the prosecution, the defense, and a judging panel—each of which adopted different ethical theories to support their arguments. The students representing the utilitarian view (which was also represented on the subject of euthanasia in the ethics reader) proposed that the murder could be seen as the release of an elderly and infirm person from a life of misery and unhappiness. Similar, and similarly problematic, arguments were also made about Raskolnikov's second victim, Lizaveta, in the polemical discussions that ensued in the mock trial.

Ultimately, we saw utilitarianism, with its quantitative approach to ethics, as the most productive moral outlook for justifying acts like murder.

Beyond utilitarianism, we also traced manifestations of the ethical theory of egoism in the novel. One of the largest questions that came up in the mock trial was whether Raskolnikov's crime was in any way self-serving. While utilitarianism was used predominantly by the defense and judging teams to rationalize the murder, egoism was used most broadly as a collective line of argumentation by all the teams in the mock trial. We considered two different strands of egoism in the course—psychological and ethical egoism. While psychological egoism, as a doctrine, puts forth the idea that human beings are by nature motivated to pursue their own interests, ethical egoism normalizes this course of action by presenting self-interested action as morally correct.

At various points in the novel, Raskolnikov discusses his selfish motives for committing the murder. As he says to Sonya at the very end,

> I wanted to kill without casuistry, Sonya, to kill for myself, for myself alone! I didn't want to lie about it even to myself! It was not to help my mother that I killed—nonsense! I did not kill so that, having obtained means and power, I could become a benefactor of mankind. Nonsense! I simply killed—killed for myself, for myself alone—and whether I would later become anyone's benefactor, or would spend my life like a spider, catching everyone in my web and sucking the life-sap out of everyone, should at that moment have made no difference to me! . . . And it was not money above all that I wanted when I killed, Sonya; not money so much as something else . . . I know all this now . . . Understand me: perhaps, continuing on that same path, I would never again repeat the murder. There was something else I wanted to know; something else was nudging my arm. I wanted to find out then, and find out quickly, whether I was a louse like all the rest, or a man? Would I be able to step over, or not! Would I dare to reach down and take, or not? Am I a trembling creature, or do I have the right . . .
>
> (Dostoevsky, *Crime* 419)

> Я захотел, Соня, убить без казуистики, убить для себя, для себя одного! Я лгать не хотел в этом даже себе! Не для того, чтобы матери помочь, я убил – вздор! Не для того я убил, чтобы, получив средства и власть, сделаться благодетелем человечества. Вздор! Я просто убил; для себя убил, для себя одного; а там стал ли бы я чьим-нибудь благодетелем или всю жизнь, как паук, ловил бы всех в паутину и из всех живые соки высасывал, мне, в ту минуту, все равно должно было быть! . . . И не деньги, главное, нужны мне были, Соня, когда я убил; не столько деньги нужны были, как другое . . . Я это все теперь знаю . . . Пойми меня: может быть, тою же дорогой идя, я уже никогда более не повторил бы убийства. Мне другое надо было узнать, другое толкало меня под руки: мне надо было узнать тогда, и поскорей узнать, вошь

> ли я, как все, или человек? Смогу ли я переступить или не смогу! Осмелюсь ли нагнуться и взять, или нет? Тварь ли я дрожащая или право имею . . . (*Prestuplenie* 322)

In the statement above, Raskolnikov negates the utilitarian argument of the novel, insisting that he did not kill for the general welfare of mankind or of his fellow students. Instead, he defines his motivations as selfish. As he asserts, he wanted to discover his own nature in the course of his confrontation with crime—would he have the ability to step over another human and murder with impunity, or would he be tormented by guilt?

In the mock trial, the prosecution, defense, and judging teams all asked whether Raskolnikov's murder was truly an act of egoism. Different teams argued that if, within the bounds of egoism, it is our ethical duty to pursue our self-interest and act to our own advantage, then Raskolnikov's murder was hardly self-interested. As we read in the ethics reader, there are differences between self-interested behavior, selfishness, and the irrational pursuit of pleasure. So, for instance, someone may smoke because that is what they wish to do in the immediate present, but this act is not necessarily a self-interested one (Rachels 70–72). Raskolnikov, for all his planning, commits the murder impulsively and irrationally, out of an irrational need for self-validation. He convinces himself that the ability to kill with impunity could make him into an Übermensch of sorts and allows this abstract idea to dictate his actions. In the end, although this idea may be gratifying in the moment, it is damaging in the long term because it does not serve Raskolnikov well. It causes him intense mental torture and eventually lands him in a penal colony in Siberia. Whereas the murder may be selfish, we argued that it was not, in fact, self-interested. This argument did not, however, take into account the idea that Dostoevsky saw Raskolnikov's suffering as edifying; what the character needed was precisely penance and suffering.

Even though *Crime and Punishment* is a book about a character who commits murder motivated by ideological reasons, and we spent considerable time addressing abstract ethical principles in class, in the final analysis, we felt that the most important ethical perspectives in *Crime and Punishment* were those rooted in the interpersonal experience. Discussion of feminine ethics of care was especially productive in class, as students noted that individuals like Razumikhin or Sonya bring healing and clarity to Raskolnikov's formerly isolated life. We read excerpts from a number of works by feminist philosophers like Nel Noddings and Carol Gilligan, who took a somewhat different perspective on ethics than Kant or Bentham. In fact, some feminist philosophers have felt that ethics and particularly abstract ethical principles are masculine in nature. The ethics of care, as they articulate it, is an ethics in which emotion and intuition are privileged over strict principles. There is also a relational element to this ethics, which suggests that we care more about members of our family or people we know than we do about absolute strangers. Raskolnikov's mother and sister, or Sonya, or Razumikhin—all bring a caring and grounding presence to his life. Students felt that his caring acts for the Marmeladov family helped Raskolnikov as well. For Dostoevsky, this human connectivity and the ability to relieve one's inner turmoil in dialogue with another is essential and perhaps far more important to ethics and a moral worldview than the abstract principles of Kant. Ultimately, Raskolnikov does not hear that murder is wrong in the abstract; he hears that murder is wrong because Sonya tells him it is, and because he knows Lizaveta was a meek and kind person. And while the reading of the Bible in isolation does help Raskolnikov recognize the error of his ways, it is as much the presence and fortitude of those around him that help in his redemption.

Reading *Crime and Punishment*, or any of Dostoevsky's works, it is hard not to feel that the author is testing us ethically as readers and putting us in a position—such as that of empathizing with a murderer's struggles and needs—where we question ourselves and our own morality. By raising questions of ethics in the classroom, we were able to anatomize all the ways in which the author significantly engages ethics in the novel—around the crime, the protagonist, and the readers themselves.

NOTES

1. Although I had initially intended to use more primary and sophisticated readings, my colleagues in philosophy advised me to rely on a reader for grappling with large complicated questions. I found this beneficial because it allowed for theoretical simplification that made my otherwise more ambitious pedagogical goals more tenable.

2. This essay cites the translation of *Crime and Punishment* by Richard Pevear and Larissa Volokhonsky (1993).

Hystericizing the Novel: *Crime and Punishment* and Psychoanalysis

Emma Lieber

When I teach *Crime and Punishment*, I speak from within two distinct roles: as a teacher of Russian literature, and as a psychoanalyst. Psychoanalysis and literature is a field of its own, and any piece of literature can be discussed with psychoanalysis in mind: not so much as an object of psychoanalytic scrutiny, but as a kind of codiscourse or parallel process. As Shoshana Felman writes, literature is "not simply a body of language to interpret, nor is psychoanalysis simply a body of knowledge with which to interpret, since psychoanalysis itself is equally a body of language, and literature also a body of knowledge, even though the mode of that knowledge may be different from that of psychoanalysis" (6). As equally adventures of language and of a certain kind of knowledge, psychoanalysis and literary texts can always be put in conversation with each other in order not to submit the one to the other but "to engage in a real *dialogue* between literature and psychoanalysis, as between two different bodies of language and between two different modes of knowledge." My task at the beginning of teaching *Crime and Punishment* is to indicate the ways in which Fyodor Dostoevsky's text in particular calls to psychoanalysis, or calls to it in particular ways, and vice versa.

My classroom approach to *Crime and Punishment* from a psychoanalytic perspective obtains on several registers. On one level, I will suggest here, as I do in class, that we might view Dostoevsky's text as housing many of the thematic elements in which psychoanalysis is interested, and that it delineates some of the psychic formations that Sigmund Freud and others have heard in the verbal texts of their patients. On another, I will indicate that the text specifically encodes something of the process and practice of psychoanalysis into its textual procedures: its understanding of the effects of speech and even its plot elements. Lastly, I will speak to the narrative and cultural factors that I believe are bound up in the ways in which Dostoevsky's novel might be considered "hysterical," under a psychoanalytic rubric—hysteria being the place at which psychoanalysis began and a diagnostic category in which the workings of the unconscious are especially evident. Doing so will allow me to suggest not only that the effect of *Crime and Punishment* on readers may have something to do with its participation in hysterical discourse but, more specifically, that Dostoevsky's novel aims to do to its imagined community of readers precisely what Jacques Lacan says is the first step of an analysis: that is, to hystericize the subject in question.

One might begin with Freud's interest in Dostoevsky: with the ways in which Dostoevsky, as a creative writer (one of the class of people who intuited the unconscious before Freud did, perhaps to Freud's chagrin), was giving voice in his works to many of the unconscious processes, formations, and dynamics that Freud would later theorize, often with literary texts in mind. Freud's "Dostoevsky and Parricide" names *The Brothers Karamazov* as a work of genius because, like *Hamlet* and *Oedipus Rex*, that novel gives shape to the Oedipus complex as a constitutive subjective formation (234). Among other things, *The Brothers Karamazov* bears the intuition that family romances and police procedurals have something to do with each other. To Dostoevsky as much as to Freud, there is something of guilt, punishment, and the law at stake in the subjective economy as it is formed in the sexual cauldron of the family.[1]

Crime and Punishment works similarly, and in fact in certain ways Raskolnikov can be seen as a perfect Freudian criminal: that is, a "criminal from a sense of guilt" (Freud, "Some Character Types" 333). To Freud, guilt precedes rather than succeeds many crimes, as often those who commit crimes actually seek relief from the guilt resulting from (infantile) incestuous and murderous Oedipal wishes. Better to attach the guilt to something in the world outside than to live with its psychic weight. Readers and critics of *Crime and Punishment* have long wondered about Raskolnikov's motivation for the murder, given that none of the reasons offered in the novel seem sufficient (to test out utilitarian principles, to prove himself an *Übermensch*, etc.). In class, I work with students to see that Raskolnikov's guilty feelings are evident from the first pages of the novel, before the murder occurs, as he avoids his landlady and social interaction generally with some vague and indefinite sense that he is in the wrong. Even here, the motivations given by the narration—which moves in and out of free indirect discourse, coming close to what is indicated to be Raskolnikov's inner monologue—for Raskolnikov's sense of anxiety and shame feel inadequate: he avoids his landlady because he is in debt to her, but he also avoids everyone. So what exactly is going on?

Here, as at many points in the book, the expository confusions that are both the narrator's and Raskolnikov's own sound like the muddle that many of my patients are in, or that I am in as a patient, when I attach some affective response to a cause that doesn't seem quite right. In a certain psychoanalytic reading, Raskolnikov's guilt might be related to early taboo infantile wishes rather than to anything contemporaneous, and this may be in part why all of his motivations seem so confused. In this Oedipal reading, further, one might look at the role of the missing father in the novel, whose death may have activated Raskolnikov's guilt for his own infantile psychic murder of him (this is essentially how Freud read Dostoevsky's response to his own father's death).[2]

At the same time, and as useful as such a reading of the opening of the novel and the question of criminality within it has been in class, I work not to reify the text or the psychoanalytic concepts that I introduce, or to use psychoanalysis as a way of "explaining" the text or its main character. Rather, in positing the ideas above I try also to underline their methodological and epistemological problems as well as the questions that they raise: that is, how can we approach a text psychoanalytically without reducing it to an object that manifests psychoanalytic concepts, and without psychoanalyzing its characters, who are not real people, or its author, who is not our patient? How to position oneself delicately, away from a kind of banal psychologizing and more on the side of the structures of subjectivity?

It is here that I introduce Lacan as a potential salve for these troubles, to the extent that his readings of Freud consistently underline structure over individual psychology. To Lacan, "to speak about the Oedipus complex" is not so much to speak about mother and father and hate and sexual longing (though it is also that) as it "is to introduce as essential the *function* of the father" (*Formations* 150; emphasis mine). Thus in Lacanian thought the Oedipus complex is the temporal and logical instance at which the symbolic register comes to be: that is, the moment at which language, law, and the injunctions of culture are installed in the subjective economy. Oedipus registers the institution of the superego, which takes on the internal function of judge and executioner, and the father in Lacanian thought means the fact of this installation. Thus the question of the function of the father, as Lacan reads Freud, *is* the question of the law, and we might read Dostoevsky with an ear to this intuition and ask what the missing father might mean on this register. By marking us as subjects of language and of culture, the Oedipus complex further makes possible sociality as such, which is one of the main questions of *Crime and Punishment*: that is, how it might be possible to live in the social world or be integrated into a community. Thus my task when delineating these ideas to students is not to posit anything about Raskolnikov's Oedipus complex or how he felt about his father or why he doesn't have many friends but to suggest that Dostoevsky's text bears associations that are similar to these Freudian and Lacanian ideas.

Many scholars have written about Raskolnikov's dream of the mare, and with students, I prefer to leave this section of class discussion radically open. I introduce the dream as an entry point into thinking through the question of the unconscious in, and in relation to, the text, as well as exploring the relationship between psychoanalysis and literature. What does it mean to include dreams within a literary work? How can we approach the matter of interpretation at such a juncture? What happens to meaning? If the students are interested, I discuss with them Freud's theory of dream interpretation as well as the radical intervention that psychoanalysis made in our understanding of dreams and of the act of interpretation more generally. In psychoanalytic work with dreams, the manifest content of a dream—what happens within it, what the dreamer sees—screens latent dream thoughts (taboo wishes, sometimes) that are the subject of censorship and can only be witnessed in distorted form. Dream elements are not so much symbols or signs to be assigned meaning as they are nodal points to be interrogated—and it is in the patient's associating to these elements that something like "meaning"—or unconscious truth—comes to be. At the same time that the mechanics of dream interpretation bear resonance with literary criticism, a consideration of them may open up investigation of what we are doing when we interpret or read text, especially text that is as close to the unconscious as Dostoevsky's. Sometimes, if students seem open to it, I ask them to keep a dream journal and bring in their own dreams, as a way of exploring (delicately, in a public context) such meta-interpretive issues.

At some point, I introduce Lacan's comments on Freud's famous dream of Irma's injection from *The Interpretation of Dreams*, which, as Lacan points out, is a dream that ends in a crowd. At a certain moment in Freud's dream, his ego, as such, disappears, and what emerges are its constituent identifications (other doctors and patients with whom Freud identifies and who take over in the dream), out of which the ego—our sense of who we are, our methods of identifying ourselves, which are generally more or less illusory—is constructed. To Lacan, Freud's Irma dream, in its cacophony of voices saying enigmatic things, bares the function and the formation of the ego and points to the work of the unconscious as such:

> If there is an image which could represent for us the Freudian notion of the unconscious, it is indeed that of the acephalic subject, of a subject who no longer has an *ego*. And yet he is the subject who speaks, for that's who gives all the characters in the dream their nonsensical lines—which precisely derive their meaning from their nonsensical character.

I believe that these comments open up something that Dostoevsky does in his writing, which resonates with the functions and registers of dreaming even when dreams are not explicitly invoked. Lacan's description of Freud's Irma dream might equally apply not only to the dreams in Dostoevsky's texts (in which the dreamer is identified with veritably everyone in the—often themselves crowded—dream scenes) but also to the crowd scenes of waking life (most notably, in *Crime and Punishment*, Katerina Ivanovna's memorial dinner), in which, as Lacan says of Freud's dream, "the discourse of the multiple *ego* makes itself heard in a great cacophony": everyone shouting, the subject lost in the din, surrounded by characters speaking nonsensical lines, nowhere to be seen and yet everywhere at once (*Seminar II* 167). Dostoevsky's work thus not only follows the logic of the unconscious but also—by iterating subjective and social formations, the novel a dream-text of crowds within which are dream-texts of crowds—gives shape to the places at which subjectivity aggregates and disaggregates in the matrix of the social. (That Dostoevsky's writing balances very delicately between social and subjective formations—that it reveals the extent to which the subjective is formed within and through the social, and that this has something to do with the functioning and extimacy of language—is quite close to Mikhail Bakhtin's insights about the author, which are likely more familiar to most teachers of the novel.)

If up to this point I have been mostly invoking psychoanalytic theories of unconscious mechanisms and formations, it is here that I introduce the question specifically of psychoanalytic practice as I believe Dostoevsky's text takes it up. It seems to me that *Crime and Punishment* charts the course—or perhaps the beginning—of an analysis *avant la lettre*. At its core, *Crime and Punishment* is interested in speech. More than anything, what the novel demands of Raskolnikov is that he say what he has done: not talk around it, not indicate it gesturally, not wait for other people to guess, which is what he spends most of the book doing. He has to take responsibility for his act, and this means that he has to speak it in its specificity, including by saying the names of his victims. Most readers don't remember the name of the murdered pawnbroker because Raskolnikov rarely speaks it throughout the book, calling her instead an old crone, a louse, et cetera.

This act of speech would mean not so much rectifying the fault that produced the murder as accounting for it. Raskolnikov needs to account for himself in language and, in a way, he needs to account *for* language and its effects. "Raskol" may mean "split" in Russian, but, according to Lacan, that is essentially what every name means. Lacan's famous dictum that "the unconscious is structured like a language" (*Seminar XI* 203) means many things, but one of them is that it is precisely our existence in language that alienates us from Being. In being named you are made subject to language and the social; in that subjection you are subjectivized, the unconscious is drawn, and you are constitutively split from yourself. This split is also what, for Lacan, makes us subjects of what he calls desire—his term, in part, for the lack in Being that results from our status as subjects of the unconscious and of language. This may be very close to what it means, in Dostoevsky, to be a creature of grace; to Lacan, desire, as it encodes unconscious truth and as it figures the possibility of a kind of subjective grace, is what an analysis allows us to pursue. In asking Raskolnikov to speak the pawnbroker's name, the novel is demanding that he rectify his fault not so much by suturing his split but by registering that he is not alone in this state: he must register the subjectivity of the other precisely by recognizing her own split existence within language—that is, by recognizing that she too is a creature of desire and grace. When Raskolnikov's confession does appear ("*It was I who killed the old civil servant's widow and her sister Lizaveta with an axe and robbed them*" '*Это я убил тогда старуху-чиновницу и сестру ее Лизавету топором и ограбил*'), it is in italics to underscore its significance as an act of speech, beyond its juridical efficacy; that he does not finally speak Alyona Ivanovna's name indicates how far he still has to go (Dostoevsky, *Crime* [2018] 584; *Prestuplenie* 410).

One might indeed think of Porfiry Petrovich as taking on a kind of analytic stance with respect to Raskolnikov. In class, when we come to the scenes that feature Porfiry Petrovich, students are very quick to see that he is hardly a typical policeman. He does not track anyone down; he does not seem terribly interested in collecting evidence; he waits for Raskolnikov to come to him; he then says bizarre things to him. Like *The Brothers Karamazov*, *Crime and Punishment* features practitioners of civil authority who end up serving divine ends: their interventions work more in the direction of spiritual confession than of juridical efficacy. At the same time, it seems to me that especially in *Crime and Punishment*, the policeman is also a psychoanalyst. A proper detective and a proper confessor may want the speech of the subject in question, but the ends they seek are clear: a detective wants to lock you up, and a confessor wants to save your soul. By contrast, an analysis runs on the motor of what Lacan calls the "desire of the analyst" precisely because that desire is enigmatic: the analyst wants your speech, but it is perfectly unclear why, or what its effects will be. This, I believe, is the position that Porfiry Petrovich takes on vis-à-vis Raskolnikov in the novel. By positioning himself enigmatically and somewhat askew of Raskolnikov's expectations of him, he manages to provoke the act of speech that is necessary to allow Raskolnikov to live.

It is not coincidental that Freud began his psychoanalytic investigations with his *Studies in Hysteria*. Hysteria as a diagnostic category, discursive position, and cultural idea has a complicated history, equally reviled and romanticized. For our purposes, we might keep in mind its association with femininity and its proximity to unconscious desire. Freud invented psychoanalysis by listening to the hysterical women of his day—women with unexplained somatic symptoms that, when one listened carefully to their speech, seemed to be expressions of wishes and conflicts that could not be consciously acknowledged. Unconscious desire was clamoring to be heard in bodily symptoms until it could be articulated in speech. Thus, as much as hysteria may be considered a neurotic condition by which one is inhibited, it also contains liberatory potential—the hysteric's symptoms mean that she is never able entirely to ignore her desire. Lacan further viewed the discourse or subjective position of hysteria as one turn of the screw away from those of the analyst. As much as the analyst returns to the hysteric her words askew in order to introduce the dimension of cure as it lies in the direction of unconscious desire, the hysteric is already nearly there herself.

This is why the first step of an analysis, to Lacan, involves the hystericization of the patient: the patient must become a hysteric, if she isn't already. She must be moved away from the intellectualizations, rationalizations, and other defenses that are so close to conscious processing (which both Freud and Lacan associate with obsessionality, the other major neurotic diagnosis that is often in psychoanalysis coded masculine, as much as psychoanalysis troubles the status of sexuated and gendered positions), toward the truth of the unconscious—and it is in part the analyst's elliptical, mysterious positioning that provokes the patient to come into contact with unconscious desire. One of the functions of much of the ideological content of *Crime and Punishment*—its utilitarian and other materialist ideologies—is to serve as intellectualizations: not only for Raskolnikov himself in committing the murder, but for anyone in the novelistic milieu who applies them to justify actions in the social. They may sound good as explanations, but they don't speak to what Raskolnikov or anyone else really wants. (It is also not unimportant that these ideologies are Western imports to Russia, to the extent that, as in many of Dostoevsky's works, the novel positions the Russian cultural epistemology—its mysticism and its Eastern Orthodox influences as they are bound up in a privileging of femininity—as indigenously hysterical, especially in comparison to rationalist Western principles. In fact, in many ways

I think that Dostoevsky was out to hystericize the novel genre, and especially the detective novel, itself a Western importation.) It is these defensive formulations that must be shorn away at the beginning of an analysis, and, broadly speaking, I believe that this is what *Crime and Punishment* attempts to achieve for both its protagonist and its readers. If we have read well, we, like Raskolnikov, walk away from *Crime and Punishment* as good hysterics, ready to undertake the work of figuring out how to live better, in our desire, as ourselves.

NOTES

1. Various scholars have written on Dostoevsky's relationship to or prediction of psychoanalysis. Of especial note is Michael Holquist's discussion of *The Brothers Karamazov* in relation to Freud's myth of the primal horde in *Dostoevsky and the Novel.* See also Louis Breger's *Dostoevsky: The Author as Psychoanalyst* and James L. Rice's *Dostoevsky and the Healing Art.*

2. Since the 1970s, scholars such as Joseph Frank (*Dostoevsky: A Writer in His Time*), John Bayley, Geir Kjetsaa (*Fyodor Dostoevsky*), and Jacques Catteau have challenged Freud's essay, and specifically his interpretation of Dostoevsky's epilepsy as a hysterical or Oedipal symptom, often disputing the biographical details on which Freud based his theories (Freud was mistaken, for example, in his claim that Dostoevsky's father was murdered) and bolstered by medical opinions on the nature of epilepsy. Whatever the evidence at issue, it seems to me that to read Freud literally—as much as he often invites such readings—is to sacrifice the possibility of reading him literarily. That is, such a reading, however valid, runs the risk of missing the import of Freud's ideas about the symbolic productions of the human subject—which is where psychoanalysis and literature can most productively be put in conversation. (In other words, to Freud, in a sense, a dead father may be considered a victim of psychic murder no matter the cause of death.)

Digital Media Projects in the Dostoevsky Classroom

Katherine Bowers

What benefit can digital media projects bring to the Dostoevsky classroom? In the past decade advances in media and technology have transformed the reading experience and the ways readers relate to texts. Students' daily reading material is primarily digital: social media, online news media, and, in the case of the literary text, the ebook. Dostoevsky's novels are particularly challenging for students who are more used to reading short bursts of text. Indeed, Robin Feuer Miller calls *Crime and Punishment* in the classroom "the elephant in the garden" precisely because we teach this "large, unwieldy, and difficult novel" to students who may not usually read literary texts (47). Although Dostoevsky's nineteenth-century texts seem removed from the digital world, digital technologies also make new ways of approaching the text of *Crime and Punishment* and Dostoevsky's historical context possible. Digital media projects can be a powerful classroom tool, both for engaging with the text and for helping students develop technology skills in addition to the classic learning outcomes of the literature class: critical thinking and academic writing.

This essay will give an overview of several different projects grounded in digital media approaches or digital humanities methodologies that work well in the Dostoevsky classroom: a collaborative digital research project, a digital mapping project, and digital text analysis. I will outline the benefits of each type of project, the nuts and bolts of constructing these kinds of assignments, helpful resources, and new ways of looking at the novel revealed through digital media approaches. Finally, I will conclude with a section on best practices that will address assessment of these projects as well as the level of support students will need as they engage in them. As we all know, technology changes rapidly. In five years some of my specific recommendations may no longer be functional or feasible, but the description of best practices and of the benefits related to bringing these kinds of projects into the classroom will hopefully remain a helpful resource. The examples I give here are specific to *Crime and Punishment*, but the methods could be applied to any literary work that the particular digital project will suit.

Digital Research: Dostoevsky's Life and Context

Crime and Punishment invariably prompts student questions about history and context. Russia in the 1860s is far removed from student experience, and the minutiae of daily life described in the text fascinate, from the significance of Sonya's yellow ticket and the ways her occupation as a prostitute might impact her family's social status to what student life was like in mid-nineteenth-century Russia, from the meaning of the Lazarus text to what Svidrigailov means when he says he is "going to America" just before committing suicide. Students are also curious about Dostoevsky's life in the context of the novel: his student days in St. Petersburg, involvement in the Petrashevsky circle, mock execution and imprisonment in Siberia, and religious awakening. Giving students the opportunity to do a collaborative research project can be a motivating way of harnessing their natural curiosity and using it both to explore other facets of the novel and to meet learning outcomes for the course.

In a collaborative digital research project, each individual or pair of students has an assigned topic to research; students then compile their individual research articles into a collective resource. Some examples of these projects include online exhibits, wikis (see "Wiki"), or electronic anthologies. For an online exhibit, each student is assigned an object to caption; the final product is a collective overview of a topic intended to engage public interest. For a wiki project—either a wiki compiled by the class or a *Wikipedia* editing assignment[1]—students each choose a topic and write a short research-led article with a presumed audience of classmates or members of the public. An electronic anthology in which each student writes a brief research note about an extract, theme, or character from *Crime and Punishment* could be assembled and distributed within the class as a PDF or could take the form of a class blog or website.

Each project requires students to conduct original research, to produce a text to a specific standard, and to consider the purpose of their writing and their audience. Writing an exhibition caption, for example, is different from writing a wiki entry, although both forms require similar research skills. Creating a public-facing project like this can additionally be empowering for student researchers. Rather than writing a paper that will be read only by their instructor or by a small group of peers, a digital collaborative research project creates a sense of collective purpose and also excitement about and pride in the finished product. In 2016 my Dostoevsky students created a library exhibit celebrating 150 years since the publication of *Crime and Punishment* (Crime and Punishment *at 150*). Afterward several students commented that the experience of researching the exhibit captions made them feel like "detectives" and requested that future students have a similar opportunity. In order to create the experience for future classes, I created what I have termed the Dosto-wiki ("Course: RUSS412/Dostowiki"), a wiki comprised of student research articles that grows every year I teach my Dostoevsky class and serves as a perpetual first-stop research resource for my students.

Digital Mapping: The Petersburg Text

Crime and Punishment is closely engaged with its setting. Many students, however, are not familiar with St. Petersburg's geography or prepared to imagine the novel's locations in the city. A digital mapping project is a wonderful tool for enabling a deeper engagement with spatiality, geography, and narrative, particularly in understanding Dostoevsky's Petersburg, and can open new avenues to interpretation. My first experience with mapping in the classroom was an assignment in which students drew their own maps of St. Petersburg and plotted a certain number of points from Dostoevsky's novel on it. This kind of assignment is useful, but with the sheer amount of information available online, students can easily find the points in a matter of seconds. However, updating the assignment to incorporate a research component allows it to function as a rigorous tool in unlocking the text's layers of meaning.

I assign my students two different digital mapping projects to help them visualize Dostoevsky's St. Petersburg; one involves finding and plotting points of interest and the second plots movement across a map. In both cases, I ask students to submit an annotated map and a research document—a short analytical text that uses the map as the basis for making an interpretive claim about the text. The research document helps align the projects more closely with the research-focused learning objectives of my class. While both projects could be done on paper, incorporating digital mapping tools such as *Google Maps* speeds the mapmaking process and gives students more time to focus on the critical analysis of the connections between the literary text and the space of the city, for example the novel's locations (Raskolnikov's room, Sonya's room, the pawnbroker's apartment, the Haymarket Square, etc.) and their distance from or proximity to the ceremonial spaces of the city.

Requiring that students demonstrate movement in the mapping project opens up further possibilities for analysis. They might, for example, map Raskolnikov's murder route or chart and juxtapose his wanderings with those of Svidrigailov. Sarah J. Young and John Levin's excellent website *Mapping St Petersburg: Experiments in Literary Cartography* shows examples of digital maps showing movement, created with *Google Maps*.[2] There are several other digital tools well suited to this kind of project, however. The presentation application *Prezi*, for example, can be useful in building narrative maps and presenting them to the class.[3] In my class, students use *StoryMapJS* to create narrative maps.[4] *StoryMapJS* was specifically designed to connect narrative and space in journalism. The site uses the *Google Maps* database but also allows users to upload any image.

After constructing their narrative maps, my students write a brief analytical text that addresses the way spatiality functions in the literary text.[5] I assign this kind of analysis because it enables students to see the text in a new way and leads to a final research paper topic that engages with questions of space and the novel. Plotting the important locations of the story on the map, and conducting visual and historical research into these locales, helps students better understand the geography of St. Petersburg and the way the spatiality of *Crime and Punishment* significantly informs its subject.

Digital Text Analysis: Visualizing Narrative

Digital humanities (DH) is a field that specifically employs digital tools to conduct humanistic research and analysis. The digital narrative mapping project as described above is one DH approach to literary text analysis. In this section, I will speak more generally about incorporating DH text analysis methodologies into assignments. As literature scholars, one methodology upon which we often rely is close reading. Digital text analysis is an extension of close reading and can be particularly useful in helping students visualize the way narrative functions in the text and thus come to see the literary text in a new light. There are several different ways to facilitate digital text analysis in the classroom. One method is to break the text down at the level of narrative using digital media, such as a social media platform (like *Twitter* or *LiveJournal*). Another method is to use a digital tool to parse and visualize the words of the text.

Digital media platforms offer opportunities for students to pull the text apart at its seams and reconstruct it through their own analysis. Digital media projects might include creating a *Twitter* feed from one character's perspective (see, for example, Bowers, "@RodionTweets") or using other interactive media, such as *LiveJournal* or *Facebook*, to re-create segments of the novel. This type of assignment is popular with students but also requires a deep analytical reading and thinking at a narrative level that fosters a deeper understanding of Dostoevsky's craft.[6] Using digital tools such as *Voyant Tools* to break down narrative is also a possibility and does not require coding knowledge. *Voyant* is a suite of text visualization tools to which users can upload digital texts, like the public domain translation of *Crime and Punishment* from Project Gutenberg, by entering a web address or uploading a file. Applying specific tools to the raw text generates a series of visualizations of word frequency and position within the novel. Manipulating variables allows users to determine, for example, the frequency with which particular characters or particular words (like "crime" and "repent") appear in various parts of the novel. These results then prompt other questions.[7] For example, the name "Raskolnikov" appears most frequently in every part of the novel except book 5, when "Sonya" is mentioned more often than any other name. Students might ask what Sonya's role is in book 5 in particular, or what kinds of narrative tension her prominence in book 5 and lesser status in other parts of the novel create.

Digital approaches to text analysis can yield powerful results, but incorporating them into the classroom can be more confusing than valuable for students unless projects are integrated into the class's learning objectives. Just doing digital text analysis is not an end in itself. However, as a methodology used to explore larger narrative questions, digital humanities text analysis can encourage deeper analysis and interpretation of the novel. In encouraging students to use this kind of analysis or in assigning projects, it is useful to always keep the larger goal of the project in mind. Deborah A. Martinsen suggests organizing classroom discussion of *Crime and Punishment* around four big questions: "1) How do we read the novel?; 2) Do we want Raskolnikov to get away?; 3) Do we forget Lizaveta, and why does this matter?; and 4) Is the epilogue organic or tacked on?" (162). Keeping questions like this, which digital humanities methodologies can help answer, central to project assignments will keep digital text analysis closely aligned with class learning outcomes.

Best Practices: Tech Support, Student Privacy Concerns, and Assessment

While there are many benefits to assigning digital media projects, instructors should think through questions of tech support, student privacy, and assessment well in advance of including these assignments on a syllabus. In addition to the information on best practices below, I recommend that everyone assigning digital media projects explore the literature of teaching and learning and digital humanities pedagogy, which includes excellent resources for instructors.[8]

The first consideration in planning digital assignments is tech support. I recommend seeking out your institution's digital humanities center, learning technology center, or digital resource librarian to find out what kind of support is available on your campus for the kind of project you want to do. Include details about available support in the assignment overview your students receive. You should also plan to complete a sample project yourself before assigning a similar one; this exercise will help you anticipate the issues that will arise for your students. Always remember that, even if your students are digital natives, this does not mean that they understand how all technologies function; having to learn a new application or tech skill for a class project can be stressful. Be sure that students have ample time and the support resources they need, whether that is a link to instructions on wiki coding, a *YouTube* video about how to use *StoryMapJS*, or an in-class tutorial in *Voyant Tools*.

The second concern is one of student privacy. Many of the projects I have outlined above are public facing, and it is important to consider students' privacy in creating them. How will students be credited for their public-facing work, and is an anonymous option possible? Who can see students' work? I have found it helpful to touch base with the teaching and learning center at my university about student privacy concerns and how best to address them; I recommend that anyone embarking on public-facing student digital projects do the same. Also, considering that contemporary social media can be dangerous and toxic, if you plan to use social media in the classroom, it is important to consider student safety and provide alternative assignment structures for students who are uncomfortable or feel vulnerable on social media. In terms of privacy, the watchwords for instructors assigning digital media projects should be flexibility and vigilance: the flexibility to adapt as students require and vigilance for student safety.

The final question is how to assess digital media projects. The broader issue here is how the digital media project aligns with the learning objectives of the course. In weighting these projects, I keep in mind the specific tasks involved and the amount of time I expect they will take. In my Dostoevsky class I use the collaborative digital research project in lieu of a midterm paper. Although students are not writing many words, going to the library and conducting research, refining the text so that it is clean and the tone is appropriate for the audience, and learning how to use a new application take considerable time. When creating an assignment rubric, I consider what I want students to focus on in the project. In my rubric, for example, the research component and the analysis receive stronger weight than the visual aspects of the project, but students also receive points for exceptional creativity or design elements.

Digital media projects allow students to interact with Dostoevsky and *Crime and Punishment* beyond typical essay or exam assignments. They empower students to think outside the box when conducting research and to pursue creative approaches to the text. Conducting research without having to worry about the intimidating task of making an original argument about Dostoevsky helps students acclimate to good research practice, a useful precursor to a research paper assignment. These projects also enable a discussion about research best practice to occur organically. For most students conducting research, the Internet is the first destination; digital media projects prompt class conversations about the importance of reliable, scholarly sources, issues of copyright and plagiarism, and how to responsibly use Internet resources like *Wikipedia* in conducting research. In my experience, though, the best benefit is that digital media projects create a vibrant research culture in the classroom and give students ownership over their role as burgeoning literary scholars and researchers.

NOTES

1. If your university does not have its own wiki platform, a free wiki can be created on a site like Wiki.com. Wikipedia offers helpful guidelines for educators that should be consulted as you plan editing assignments to avoid common pitfalls ("Wikipedia: Student Assignments").

2. Young and Levin's site includes a number of maps addressing narrative questions in *Crime and Punishment* (see "Mapping Dostoevsky").

3. See Stilwell for an example of a *Prezi* map of *Crime and Punishment* characters. The presentation could be adapted for narrative mapping with the addition of a background image that includes a map of St. Petersburg.

4. An example of a *StoryMapJS* map of *Crime and Punishment* locations submitted by my student, Olga Kim, and shared with permission, can be found at uploads.knightlab.com/storymapjs/609619096e98e9b0458fdf4280d3e6c3/raskolnikovs-map-1/index.html.

5. On the possibility inherent in these kinds of research questions, see Levin and Young.

6. See Kate Holland's chapter in the present volume or my blog post "Twitterature in the Dostoevsky Classroom."

7. I have written a colloquial guide to doing text analysis with *Voyant Tools* that may be helpful to those who have never used this tool before ("DSC #6").

8. A good starting point is the MLA Commons resource *Digital Pedagogy in the Humanities*, which is a curated site of open access tools, artifacts, and texts (digitalpedagogy.hcommons.org/).

From @RodionTweets to #Napoleoncomplex: A *Twitter* Assignment

Kate Holland

One of the biggest challenges in teaching *Crime and Punishment* in twenty-first-century classrooms is enabling students to experience the novel as its original readers might have done, as a work that engages maximally with the world beyond the text but does so in its own particular language and with its own particular tools. It can be difficult to find a balance between emphasizing the novel's universality and relevance and reminding students of its context within a particular society at a particular moment in its history. The work's status as high literature can prevent students from seeing its rootedness in real, urgent social, political, and moral issues and in specific forms of contemporary discourse. In its original serial form, published over twelve months in 1866 in the monthly periodical *The Russian Messenger*, *Crime and Punishment* shared column space with articles on economics, literary criticism, politics, theater, and state affairs; its novelistic universe reflects connections to all these realms. Konstantine Klioutchkine has shown how Dostoevsky's novel emerged out of the new discursive environment of 1860s Russia, with its wealth of new publications and the proliferation of new voices made possible by the *glasnost'* of the reform era. He argues that *Crime and Punishment* is a product of this new media landscape that at the same time offers a guide through it (88).

One recent attempt to recuperate something of the original reading experience as well as to translate the novel's engagement with media into a new context was the *Twitter* project @RodionTweets. Six Dostoevsky scholars tweeted *Crime and Punishment* in real time from Raskolnikov's perspective between 1 May 2016 and 24 April 2018 to mark the 150th anniversary of the novel's first publication (Bowers, "@RodionTweets," "Introducing @RodionTweets"). The idea was to imagine how Rodion Raskolnikov's voice might have sounded on *Twitter*, had *Twitter* existed in 1860s Russia. Limiting ourselves to the 140 characters of the original *Twitter* form, the participants "mined" tweets from the translation by Oliver Ready in a combination of direct quotation, transposition of the text from third to first person, and creative manipulation of the story by the addition of thoughts that might conceivably be ascribed to Raskolnikov. The narrative unfolding of the events of the novel in real time, the exclusive focus on the perspective of Raskolnikov, and the renewed focus on the novel's peculiar shifts in narrative perspective provided a new outlook on a novel the participants mostly teach on a yearly basis and allowed those following to experience the novel a little as original readers might have done, with other historical events unfolding simultaneously and intervening in the reading experience. It also provided a new pedagogical resource from which to mine our own future assignment ideas.

As one of those scholars and as someone who teaches *Crime and Punishment* every year in a number of different university classroom settings, I regularly use the @RodionTweets project as well as the scholars' blogged reflections on the project as the background for an assignment that asks students to write their own *Twitter*-style accounts of the events of the novel from the perspective of any of its other characters. Here I briefly provide some background on the @RodionTweets project as a scholarly resource and then explain how it works alongside a reading of the novel to help readers experience *Crime and Punishment* in a different way from that provided by a traditional class reading. I show how experiencing the novel in this way helps break down the boundaries between the text and the world beyond it but at the same time helps readers to understand how the text is structured. I then provide an account of how my *Crime and Punishment Twitter* assignment works and how it encourages students to think more broadly about the challenges of reading a novel in translation.

@RodionTweets

The idea for tweeting *Crime and Punishment* originated in a project to tweet Dostoevsky's early novella *The Double* from the perspective of its protagonist, Yakov Golyadkin, over four days in November 2015 (Bowers and McGuirk; Bowers, "Twitterature"; Armstrong, "On Golyadkin"). The project imagines Golyadkin tweeting his thoughts and responses to the events of the plot. *The Double* has caused confusion among critics and readers since its first publication; Dostoevsky himself rewrote it several times (Frank, *Dostoevsky: The Seeds of Revolt* 309–12). The project's goals were to increase student and readerly engagement with the novella by transposing it to a medium more immediately accessible to many contemporary readers. This *Twitter* project focuses solely on Golyadkin's perspective, combining direct transmission of his thoughts and utterances with improvisation that remains broadly in character while diverging from the novel as written. As Katherine Bowers explains, for some students and readers of the project, this has the effect of "cleaning up" one of Dostoevsky's most confusing novels, providing new possibilities for sympathizing with Dostoevsky's baffling protagonist and making a clear difference between the character of Golyadkin and the voice of the narrator ("Twitterature"). While the simple goal made the stakes of this project fairly low, the question of how to categorize a project like @YakovGolyadkin remains an interesting one. Should it be seen as a kind of creative criticism of Dostoevsky's novella or as a kind of loose translation or adaptation, albeit one that takes more liberties than the translations we normally use in our teaching? This question became even more pertinent for the next iteration of the Dostoevsky "Twitterature" project, @RodionTweets.

A much longer and far better-known work, *Crime and Punishment* presented at once greater potential and more significant challenges as source material for

Twitter. With a protagonist like Raskolnikov (a quintessential "media man" in Klioutchkine's sense), who dominates the novel, who seems a more convincing user of *Twitter* than Golyadkin, and who spends much of the novel talking to himself while walking the streets of St. Petersburg, the novel offered unparalleled opportunities for adaptation to the *Twitter* form. Its scale, though, required participation of more "twitterati": six scholars who would each mine one of the six parts of the novel for tweets, and an editor to provide consistency between the sections. It therefore became necessary to come up with some basic guidelines for the project. And as literary scholars normally bound by certain norms and limits of interpretation, we found ourselves outside our normal comfort zone, imagining Raskolnikov as a real person instead of the verbal construct of Dostoevsky. In this sense we also found ourselves approaching the interpretative positions of some of our students, positions we normally try to resist in the academic space of a classroom. A central question we found ourselves asking was under what circumstances Raskolnikov might tweet (Hudspith; Young, "On Tweeting"). We mostly agreed that he would not be able to tweet as he was conversing with other characters, but the temptation to have him live-tweet the murder of Alyona Ivanovna was too much to resist.

In its original location on *Twitter*, @RodionTweets unfolded in real time, beginning in the prehistory of the novel's fictional timeline, on 16 May 2016, with a tweet expressing Rakolnikov's frustration at not having heard back from the journal about his article "On Crime" (Bowers et al., "@RodionTweets: Prologue + Parts 1–3"). The novel's main plot commenced on 7 July, when Raskolnikov tweeted darkly about his plan "to do a thing like #that" and continued through his confession at the police station on 21 July ("@RodionTweets: Parts 4–6 + Epilogues"). The occasional tweets of the epilogue began in late July 2016 and continued all the way to Raskolnikov's final resurrection in Siberia and the hopes for a new life expressed in his very last tweet on 25 April 2018. As *Twitter* users retweeted and responded to Raskolnikov's tweets, real-world events taking place at the same time, such as the aftermath of the United Kingdom's referendum to leave the European Union (Young, "On Tweeting"), found their way into some of these responses. In this way, *Crime and Punishment*, or at least a translation or transposition of the novel, was newly set within a pulsing media environment similar to, and yet different from, the one that had originally given birth to the novel.

This *Twitter* project required three different modes of translation from the text: the most straightforward was direct transcription of Raskolnikov's thoughts as conveyed by Dostoevsky and translated by Oliver Ready; the second mode was transposition of the text from the third to the first person in order to convey Raskolnikov's thoughts as the context required; and the third was creative manipulation of the story by the addition of thoughts that might be conceivably ascribed to Raskolnikov (Holland). With so much access to the inner thoughts of Raskolnikov, the process of direct transcription was simple, allowing tweets such as, "So what is to be done? Kill her and take the money, so as to devote yourself afterwards to the service of all humanity and the common cause." Transposition was also fairly straightforward, allowing for the possibility of articulating our own internal commentary on the novel with the use of hashtags, a Twitter currency that had not been used in the Golyadkin project: an example of this mode early in @RodionTweets is Sarah Hudspith's tweet: "I don't want their #sacrifice! Over my #deadbody! I don't accept it! I won't accept it!" ("@Rodiontweets: Prologue + Parts 1–3"; Hudspith). Hashtags allow for emphasis on a particular word or phrase that seems to encapsulate a character or situation, such as #Napoleoncomplex, which brings together a central idea of the novel and a trope of its interpretation within the broader culture. The most challenging task was adaptation, or "filling in" gaps that the text intentionally leaves opaque, a process that at times could become fraught as participants brought their own readings of the novel to the table (Wilson; Bowers, "Raskolnikov"). Cognizant of the fact that this novel contains many passages that can be seen as stream of consciousness *avant la lettre*, participants nonetheless learned to be mindful of the great gap between stream of consciousness, where thoughts are conveyed in as unfiltered a way as possible, and tweeting, which involves a constant filter, an imaginary reader to whom every tweet is addressed, akin to the imagined listener to whom Dostoevsky's protagonists such as Raskolnikov and the underground man address their monologues (Bakhtin 52–54).

The combination of the three modes of *Twitter* translation redirects the reader's attention back to the extraordinary complexity of *Crime and Punishment*'s narrative structure (Holland). The process revealed how much gets lost if we translate the novel entirely into Raskolnikov's point of view and suggests some of the reasons why Dostoevsky might have rejected his original idea for first-person narration in favor of a third-person narrator. Here we lose Razumikhin as a moral counterweight to Raskolnikov, never guess at Razumikhin's burgeoning feelings for Dunya, and bypass Dunya and Pulkheriya Alexandrovna's response to their sudden meeting with Sonya. We are trapped instead in Raskolnikov's monomania. While we trace the vacillations of his self-deception and self-revelation, those psychological developments are never embedded into a broader moral or social context. Followers of @RodionTweets will find themselves trapped in Raskolnikov's perspective with no narrative respite. Moving beyond this vision of the novel requires a reorientation toward other characters and perspectives, which is what I seek to do with the project I assign based on @RodionTweets in my undergraduate Dostoevsky lecture course.

Twitter *Assignment*

I use @RodionTweets as the basis for a low-stakes creative micro-project (worth only five percent of the course grade) that takes place during our reading of *Crime and Punishment*, preceding both course papers and tests. I ask students to first read the full text of @RodionTweets and the participants' blog posts, which explain the guidelines and general practices of the group. I then ask them to choose another character from the novel, familiarize themselves with the genre constraints of *Twitter*, and write six tweets (in the old 140-character *Twitter* format) from the perspective of that character. The goals of the assignment are to encourage students to read the novel not as a work of high literature sealed off from the outside world but as a text that engages with the world beyond it; to motivate them to think about the novel's original publication context, serialization in a thick journal surrounded by other kinds of discourses; and to draw attention to the status of the text we read in class as a translation by undertaking their own small-scale act of translation or transposition. Marmeladov, Sonya, Razumikhin, Dunya, and Porfiry Petrovich have been particularly popular choices of characters to tweet. I have asked students to do this assignment in pairs or small groups during class time, which allows for more extensive discussion and analysis, or to do it individually in their own time, which allows for more creativity of presentation, and sometimes results in students opening *Twitter* accounts under that character's name. I do not require that the tweets be posted on *Twitter*, since having students work in forward-facing media creates privacy concerns, as Bowers discusses, and the goal of the assignment is for the student to show their engagement with the character's perspective and the novel and to prepare for the more substantive essay to be written on the novel a couple of weeks later (see the essay by Bowers in this volume).

How does the *Twitter* project allow students to engage with the novel in new ways? While the original readers of @RodionTweets were able to follow the events of the novel in real time, subsequent readers, including my students, read them in one or two sittings, thus more closely approximating their reading of the novel itself. However, seeing the events and the voices of the novel presented in a social media format that they do not associate with high literature frees them from some of their preconceptions about the novel's perceived inaccessibility and breaks down the barriers between the novel they are reading and the world in which they are reading it. Thinking about characters tweeting brings those characters into contact with the students' online lives in unexpected ways: one student reframed Pulkheriya Alexandrovna as a "proud mom blogger." Hashtags prove to be an unexpectedly rich mode for reframing aspects of the novel to enable a rediscovery of Dostoevsky's contemporaneity: one student tweeting Marmeladov's thoughts used the hashtag #TavernConfessional in the context of the drunkard's first meeting with Raskolnikov, finding a contemporary relevance in a quintessentially Dostoevskian mode, while another ascribed to Razumikhin the hashtag #drunktweets. They also provide the possibility of filtering the essence of a character or situation, as the student did who applied to Porfiry Petrovich the hashtag #mindgames. Writing within the constraints of only six 140-character tweets forces students to think about the most essential traits of the character they've chosen to voice. The assignment also serves as a simulation of the act of translation, reminding students that we are reading a translation and allowing those who do not know Russian to read and consider what

Dostoevsky might have meant by a particular turn of phrase and think about how such a phrase might be rendered or redefined in the context of their own times. We also discuss broader questions of cultural translation and how we might translate the historical specificity of Dostoevsky's novel to our own historical moment.

The assignment helps students build their knowledge of the novel from the ground up in preparation for a more traditional essay that tests their engagement with the central ideological, literary, and philosophical questions that *Crime and Punishment* poses. If @RodionTweets revealed how much of the novel is lost by focusing on Raskolnikov alone, these microprojects reveal how the novel's overall dynamics are uncovered through characters who seem at times peripheral to the novel's central ideological and philosophical message. In combination, @RodionTweets and students' own assignments cast light on how Dostoevsky balances the articulation of Raskolnikov's perspective with his reflection in the ideas and choices of the other characters.

The project typically yields high marks because of the nature of grading creative work, and while I weight the *Twitter* project fairly low, I provide written feedback suggesting further directions to pursue or possible connections to the midterm paper on *Crime and Punishment* that students are preparing. I conceive of the *Twitter* project in grander terms than that of a graded assignment. Instead, it is an attempt to show students the ways in which Dostoevsky's novel, which is rooted in a new media landscape, which depicts a hero marked by the possibilities and limitations of new media, and which itself exploits some of the methods and techniques of that new media, can be opened up by the new media of our own historical moment. By placing characters and their thoughts into dialogue with the students' own online lives, the *Twitter* project helps place Dostoevsky's novel and its ideas back into the media flow that the students are themselves continually experiencing.

Mapping the Networks of *Crime and Punishment*

Chloë Kitzinger

Anyone who works on nineteenth-century literature has grappled with the question, How do we teach very long novels? The narrative structure of *Crime and Punishment* poses special difficulties. The novel is built as a spiral—a chain of near-repetitions that brings Raskolnikov ever closer to the discovery of his true motives and self. It can become more confounding the more slowly one reads it, especially when adopting the narrative's close focus on Raskolnikov's evolving perspective. This chapter lays out an approach to *Crime and Punishment* that encourages students to think beyond the central hero and beyond sequential reading by analyzing and creating "maps" of the novel's characters, images, ideas, or spaces. I start by discussing a comprehensive network graph of connections among the novel's characters, which I made using the free platform *Gephi* (0.9.2), downloadable at gephi.org.[1] I go on to describe an assignment that asks students to draw their own graphs or "maps," images that crystallize some aspect of the novel's narrative structure or fictional world. Occupying a middle ground between the methods of close and distant reading, the project of mapping *Crime and Punishment* invites students to discover their own paths through Dostoevsky's inexhaustible text.

Network analysis is one of the productive methods that literary and cultural studies have borrowed from the social and applied sciences under the large, often ungainly umbrella of the digital humanities. Almost anything can be represented abstractly as a network, defined for technical purposes as "a set of items" (*vertices* or *nodes*) "with connections between them, called *edges*" (Newman 168). From the mid-twentieth century on, scientists and mathematicians have used graph theory to analyze patterns of interpersonal communication, the spread of information and disease, railways and power grids, metabolic pathways, and more (168–80; Newman et al. 1–8). Interdisciplinary interest in the tools of network analysis has only grown with the explosion of the Internet, the World Wide Web, and online social media. In recent studies, humanities scholars have used these tools to explore developments in literary genres and institutions and to parse the "social networks" and formal configurations of fictional characters in works from *Hamlet* to *The Wire* (and beyond).[2]

Told as a series of collisions among characters thrown into proximity by the urban spaces of St. Petersburg, *Crime and Punishment* looks like a natural subject for network graphing—if not to discover new interpretations of the novel, then to put some of what readers sense about it into a compelling visual form. The graphs discussed here aim to offer a comprehensive view of the novel's fictional world, envisioned as connections among its characters: "everyone in *Crime and Punishment*," on the model of George Newlin's mammoth encyclopedia

Everyone in Dickens. Network graphing software like *Gephi* lets readers envision this "everyone" not in the form of a hefty three-volume index but rather in a Dostoevskian "suddenly" (*vdrug*), as a single image.

To generate graphs, *Gephi* uses force-directed placement algorithms to visualize the connections between nodes as if the network were a physical system. The comprehensive graph labeled "Fig. 1" uses *Gephi*'s default algorithm, ForceAtlas 2. The individual nodes of the graph repel each other like particles with similar electric charges. But if two nodes are connected, they attract one another instead, as if they were joined by a spring. The resulting graph represents an equilibrium between these repulsive and attractive forces (Jacomy 1–3). Here, the size of a character's node and name corresponds to their "degree," or connectedness to other characters in the network: Raskolnikov is for obvious reasons enormous, while a character like "Achilles," the night watchman who witnesses Svidrigailov's suicide, is very small.

To understand what this network graph represents, students also need to know how I defined "characters" and "connections" when making it. As "characters," I counted any person or group mentioned in the narrative who is real within (and only within) its story-world. So the graph does not include historical figures, like Napoleon, or dream figures, like the peasant Mikolka, or animals, like the horse Mikolka beats. It does include anonymous figures, like the drunkards Raskolnikov sees on his first walk to Alyona Ivanovna's apartment, and characters who are mentioned but never seen "onstage" in the novel, like Svidrigailov's wife, Marfa Petrovna. As "connections," I included any encounter, whether narrated omnisciently or by a character. My definition of an encounter is minimal: anything counts, from a dialogue or family relationship to co-location in the same room or street. I have not weighted the edges of the graph to reflect the number of encounters or recorded encounters' directionality (that is, for example, who speaks to whom). It goes without saying that this schema causes radical distortion. There is a single plane for pivotal one-time events (like Raskolnikov's murder of Alyona Ivanovna and her sister Lizaveta), pivotal repeated events (like Raskolnikov's conversations with Sonya), and completely transient exchanges of glances, words, or blows. A graph including only speaking characters, or only substantive personal connections, would be meaningful in a different way.[3] Mine aims to offer as comprehensive a vision as possible of *Crime and Punishment*'s populated fictional world.

So how can such an image be useful in the classroom if it leaves out everything on which first-time readers and class discussions generally focus, from the horror of Raskolnikov's crimes to the enigma of his conversion in the epilogue? The simplest answer is, *because* it will strike students as so unfamiliar. As one scholar writes of the apartment-painter Nikolai Dementiev, who picks up a pair of earrings Raskolnikov has dropped and gets pulled into the investigation: "Choose almost any action, coincidence, or item at random from the novel and it will offer a link to something else; the pattern on the kaleidoscope will change as will the perspective of the whole" (Miller 49). A network graph helps translate the novel into this underlying "kaleidoscopic" form. If students can get in the habit of looking past the focal (and focalizing) center so hugely dominated by Raskolnikov, whom and what else might they come to see? For instructors with time to devote an extra session to experimenting with network graphs of *Crime and Punishment*, let me offer some examples of where the discussion could lead.

Students are first likely to notice the network's most densely connected nodes: Raskolnikov himself, followed by Svidrigailov and Katerina Ivanovna, and then Sonya and Razumikhin. It is worth pointing out that the novel's central network is very tightly woven: almost all of its prominent, named characters encounter all the others, so the differences among characters' degrees has mostly to do with their connections *outside* this central network—city crowds, figures from elsewhere or the past, and so on.

To direct students' attention toward more minor characters in the graph, *Gephi* can be used to make an "ego network"—a graph that shows only one character's direct connections. (To make this kind of exercise possible, I have posted a set of instructions for using *Gephi*, as well as the original spreadsheets that I used to create the network graph, at dx.doi.org/10.17613/gbk1-pz13). In an ego network for Raskolnikov (node 1), less than half of the graph will disappear. But what if we try it with Raskolnikov's own first (missed) connection, his landlady, Praskovya Pavlovna Zarnitsyna (node 2)? Zarnitsyna's network includes many of the potential points of transformation in Raskolnikov's life: not only Razumikhin, Pulcheria Alexandrovna, and Dunya, but also Zarnitsyna's daughter Natalia Yegorovna (Raskolnikov's onetime fiancée), and the two children she says he saved from a fire. The crucial position of Zarnitsyna's maid Nastasya Petrovna (node 40) may also come as a surprise. Aside from Sonya and Raskolnikov, she is the only recurring named character connected to Raskolnikov's second victim, Lizaveta Ivanovna, and through Lizaveta to her sister Alyona, the pawnbroker. *Crime and Punishment*'s wide-ranging moral possibilities thus cluster on the lev l of Zarnitsyna and her apartment, an intermediate space that dissolves for most readers into the more sharply defined chronotopes of Raskolnikov's grave-like room and the St. Petersburg streets around it.

Experimenting with "ego networks" encourages an imagination of *Crime and Punishment* as built around multiple, if unequal, centers, each of which suggests a particular model of interaction in both story and discourse. For Katerina Ivanovna Marmeladova, the novel narrates a family group's dissolution. For Razumikhin, by contrast, the story is of an ever-tighter network's formation, cohering at last in his marriage to Dunya. Students may be able to begin thinking about the novel's characters in this way by zooming in on different areas of the comprehensive network graph, but they will get more out of playing actively in *Gephi* with their own variations.

Another kind of insight comes from looking more carefully at the types of connections narrated in this novel, and here we have to depart from the mechanical functions of *Gephi* to think more creatively as readers of *Crime and Punishment*.

It is clear from the comprehensive network graph (fig. 1) that the configurations of Raskolnikov's and Svidrigailov's networks resemble one another. Both are connected to an unusually high number of peripheral characters; that is, characters with weak connections to the network as a whole. But consider two graphs made from a new set of data (figs. 2 and 3). Figure 2 shows only onstage encounters, meetings that readers "see" thanks to the omniscient narrative. Figure 3 shows only offstage encounters, rumored, remembered, or summarized after the fact. From the "onstage" graph, there is no doubt that Raskolnikov dominates the novel's center—he encounters over four times more faces than anyone else in *Crime and Punishment.* But the "offstage" graph makes other characters emerge more prominently: the gregarious Razumikhin, the aforementioned apartment-painter Nikolai Dementiev, and, most of all, the enigmatic Svidrigailov. Indeed, these paired "onstage" and "offstage" graphs serve as an illustration for Carol Apollonio's provocative argument about the slander of Svidrigailov throughout the novel (*Dostoevsky's Secrets* 67–92). Svidrigailov is at the core not of *Crime and Punishment*'s encounters but of its rumors. His network rises only partway out of the most shadowy realm of the novel's story-world, the past that we imagine preceding its narrative. What Mikhail Bakhtin would call the "unfinalizability [*nezavershimost'*]" of his character (51) springs from reinterpreting this past, whose ghosts grip Svidrigailov up to the moment of his suicide.

Raskolnikov's narrative is different. If we imagine the network graph without him, what we would lose is the swarm of passersby who pursue him and whom he pursues—drunkards, singers, the fat German who shoves him as he confesses in the square and the woman who throws a rolling pin at her dog before his confession at the station. Graphing draws attention to this large tragic chorus of people who know the secret of the novel's *peripeteia* long before the hero himself does.[4] If students feel disappointed when confronted with the epilogue, an abstraction of the novel's networks may offer an intriguing new recognition. The novel ends just at the moment it would have had to do away with its hero, which is also the moment when novelistic narrative can no longer tell the story Dostoevsky wants us to hear: when Raskolnikov, stripped of the sense of exceptionality that has kept him from repenting of his crime, at last begins to discover that he is just like *everyone* in *Crime and Punishment.*

So far, I have focused on using network graphs to explore dimensions of the novel's character system that are hard to notice on a first-time reading. I want now to describe a more adaptable assignment in which students produce their own abstract "maps" of the novel, whether using digital tools or drawing by hand. This mapping assignment offers an alternative to the traditional analytical essay that will help students delve into the patterns that organize *Crime and Punishment.*

Maps representing Dostoevsky's St. Petersburg abound (see "Materials" in this volume for one example).[5] For this assignment, though, I ask students to interpret the term *map* more broadly: to make a schematic visual representation of some key aspect of the narrative or a thread they notice running through it.

Students can use any medium to create and present their maps, working either singly or in groups. Along with their maps, they hand in a written explanation of what the map represents, how they created it, and what it has helped them discover about the novel. The assignment works best when provided early, so that students can begin thinking about and tracing patterns as they read. I offer them a few initial examples of approaches they might take, such as the following:

> Choose a key word, idea, anecdote, or rumor that you notice repeating throughout *Crime and Punishment*. Make a map that shows how it travels. What characters repeat it, and whom do they hear it from? How has mapping the spread of this particular word, idea, or story changed your interpretation of the novel?
>
> Choose an event or image that recurs throughout *Crime and Punishment* (e.g., Raskolnikov's dreams; bridge-crossings; encounters with drunkards; the color green . . .). Make a map representing when in the narrative and under what circumstances this event or image recurs. What patterns do you find, and what do they illuminate?
>
> Choose a key scene and make a diagram that shows how it unfolds in space. How and why is the setting important to the scene? More generally, what does this scene suggest about how Dostoevsky uses space to shape interactions between his characters?

I have found that many students accept the invitation to branch out from this initial list, resulting in particularly original and attentive written work. "Maps" I have received include charts illustrating Raskolnikov's intake and expenditure of money or his consumption of food and drink, a timeline of the police investigation from the investigators' perspective rather than Raskolnikov's; and even a modified Meyer-Briggs personality classification system meant to reveal lines of affinity and opposition among the novel's characters.

This assignment broadens the logic behind digitally produced character network graphs. It encourages students to think of the novel as their field of investigation, to "notice and fondle details" (Nabokov, "Good Readers" 1) and work outward from those details toward an insight that changes the way they interpret the text, conveyed to fellow readers in the form of an image.

I will end this essay on a note of caution. A drawback to working with network graphs and maps is that both assignments ask students to hold at arm's length a novel they may be reading with visceral immediacy, and to shelve the "universal questions" that drive the narrative forward. The risk of draining the thrill of a first-time reading of *Crime and Punishment* is not to be taken lightly. So I offer these pedagogical ideas for two specific purposes: first, to encourage students to think more adventurously about the construction of Dostoevsky's narrative worlds, and second, to engage those who feel bewildered or alienated by the novel and may find their way better by venturing in to see how it works. The project of mapping *Crime and Punishment* is only one response to an abiding challenge: without compromising on the attention that long realist novels demand on their own terms, how do we translate them into the many native languages of present-day readers? Teachers of Dostoevsky have been answering this question for decades, but continual changes to our analytical tools—and to our students—make now a rich moment to confront it again.

NOTES

1. The figures that accompany this chapter are posted at dx.doi.org/10.17613/krqz-db54.
2. For a few prominent examples, see Moretti, *Distant Reading* 211–40 and "Network Theory"; Levine 112–31; and Jagoda.
3. Benamí Barros García demonstrates one alternative approach by graphing the "discursive interactions" in *Crime and Punishment*.
4. Viacheslav Ivanov initiated the interpretation of *Crime and Punishment* as a novel-tragedy. Boris Tikhomirov summarizes the literature on the novel's "popular chorus" (51–53); for an English translation of his commentary, see Apollonio, *New Russian Dostoevsky* 100.
5. For illuminating maps of the geographical space of *Crime and Punishment*, and a bibliography of primary and critical sources on Dostoevsky's Petersburg, see Sarah Young's web project *Mapping St Petersburg* (mappingpetersburg.org).

Teaching *Crime and Punishment* through Discussion-Based Learning

Benjamin Rifkin

Dostoevsky's *Crime and Punishment* is a classic text precisely because it offers diverse readers numerous—and often conflicting—insights they can find salient in their own cultural contexts temporally and geographically far removed from nineteenth-century St. Petersburg. In this essay I will describe several discussion activity frameworks or templates, with sample content relevant to *Crime and Punishment*, to facilitate instructors' implementation of discussion-based learning activities. Instructors can select any discussion activity framework described in this essay and fill it with different content from the novel (not just the examples correlated with that framework in this essay) as befits instructional need for that particular community of learners. These discussion-based learning activities will help students develop their interpretative and analytical skills as they work together to understand layers of meaning in Dostoevsky's novel and the novel's relevance to their own lives.

One of the most successful discussion frameworks, commonly referred to as "Think-Pair-Square-Share," gradually shifts the locus of reflection from the individual to the entire class. For instance, one might raise the question of Raskolnikov's character, asking students to consider if he is warm or cold, antisocial or compassionate, charitable or murderous, and telling students to present evidence from the novel for whatever assertion they choose to make. To implement this activity, ask students to spend two minutes reflecting silently as to how they would answer the question, taking notes on evidence from the text to support their proposed response. Next, students are assigned to work with a partner to share their individual reflections and evidence and consider whether, after sharing with one another, they would revise their findings in anticipation of the next stage of the activity. Student pairs are then combined into groups of four. Each group is asked to summarize the conclusions of the two pairs and in so doing to refine those conclusions to reflect as much as possible the opinions of all four members of the new group. In the final stage of the activity, the groups of four are asked to present their conclusions to the entire class. During each presentation, a student from another group takes notes on the presenting group's findings and the presenters are asked to confirm that the notes are accurate. When all the groups' conclusions have been collected and displayed, the entire class discusses the strengths and weaknesses of each suggested answer to the original question and the instructor guides the class to a summary of the interpretations, which learners can then connect with the novel in order to understand it more deeply.

Alternatively, as Frederick suggests, students can be assigned to generate one or at most two questions about the assigned reading in the individual reflection phase of this activity. In the pair work, students consider the two to four questions they have generated individually and choose two questions to discuss, narrowing their attention to just those two. When the pairs combine into squares, the groups of four students consider the four questions they bring together and choose two on which to focus. Finally, the groups of four present one of their questions—together with their answers or the other questions they have raised—to the class for further discussion.

One of the strengths of the "Think-Pair-Square-Share" activity framework is that it guides students through reflection to communication in increasingly greater circles of engagement (individual, pair, two pairs, whole class), thus reducing the stress of contributing to discussion in front of peers that can be debilitating for some learners. This attribute is present for many of the other frameworks described below.

Students can be assigned to debate a proposition—for instance, the premise that the thought of a crime is itself a crime is a critical philosophical underpinning of *Crime and Punishment*, the premise that Svidrigailov is a more dastardly criminal than Raskolnikov, or even the premise that the novel is realistic. For such a debate, instructors might assign students to each side of the argument, give the students assigned to each side a chance to work with one another to collect evidence from the novel to support their proposition (which could be a homework activity), and then structure the debate itself by giving each team a certain amount of time for each student to speak. The debate experience can also be flipped, requiring students to take the opposing side before the concluding phase of the debate. After the debate is completed, instructors may ask students to take a moment to reflect silently and in writing on what they have heard and then be prepared to share their own opinions about how they view the given question in the context of the analysis of the novel that has unfolded in the debate and, perhaps, in their understanding of the world beyond the novel.

A number of different discussion formats bear some similarities to one another based on the idea of limiting discussion contributions to those who have the floor at any one time. In a fishbowl format, for example, students sit in two concentric circles, one inside the other, and the students in the inner circle are asked to discuss a topic, such as the importance of crossing spaces or bridges or moral boundaries, while the students in the outer circle listen and take notes; at a certain point, the speaking privilege shifts to the outer circle, whose students must respond to and engage with the propositions raised by the students in the inner circle. Ultimately, the entire class engages in analysis of the contributions by both circles. In a chain discussion, students must respond to the comment made by the person who preceded them, taking up the notion of the loophole or the paradox in the novel, for example, but connecting to remarks made by students who preceded them in the discussion before passing the speaking privilege on to the next student in the sequence (who may or may not be seated in the adjacent seat in the classroom). This format might be used to discuss the theme of coincidence in the novel or the conflict between the expected and the unexpected.

In classroom communities in which some students tend to dominate discussion, the instructor can use "contribution coupons," which are distributed to students in equal number but must be surrendered each time a student wishes to contribute to the discussion. Soon those students who tend to dominate discussion will use up their contribution coupons and the students who tend to be more reserved will have the floor without fear of interruption. Alternatively, instructors could establish a ground rule that anyone who has contributed to discussion cannot contribute again until three (or four or five) other students have also contributed. For instance, this approach can be taken for the consideration of the nature of the delusions held by different characters or a close analysis of Raskolnikov's dream about the horse that asks whether those delusions or the dream are important for our understanding of the novel as a whole. This approach can also be taken for the discussion of the power of confession, asking, for example, how we might view Raskolnikov differently had Porfiry arrested him and had Raskolnikov insisted on his innocence.

Another approach to discussion helpful for the study of a novel as long as *Crime and Punishment* is a prediction activity. Students can be assigned to work in groups to consider a particular scene in a chapter they read for that day's class and then to develop a proposed extension of the given scene, arguing for the plausibility of their proposed extension on the basis of what they've read previously in the novel, or imagining a scene that could have but did not take place in the novel's imagined universe. For instance, students might be asked to work in groups to consider the scandal at the wake for Marmeladov in part 5 of the novel and to predict what might have happened next among those left behind at the wake after Katerina Ivanovna's (and Raskolnikov's) departure, on the basis of what they had read thus far in the novel. The hypotheses of what might happen next could be listed visually (on the blackboard, for example) with references to evidence in the text supporting each proposed alternative ending to the scene. Students could then discuss—either in groups or as a class—which proposed scene ending they find most satisfying as readers, which most faithful to Dostoevsky's vision of the novel, and why.

One activity format that is very helpful in energizing discussion involves a physical mingle in which students get up out of their seats and walk around the classroom space, talking with numerous classmates sequentially. For instance, after the students have read the entire novel, an instructor could ask the students to reflect silently on what they thought were the three most important turning points in the narrative (for example, the murder of Lizaveta and Alyona, Raskolnikov's meeting with Sonya Marmeladova, Raskolnikov's confession to Sonya, or some other event in the narrative). After the silent reflection phase, students are asked to rise and mingle with one another, exchanging answers to this important question and considering what their classmates have to say. During the mingle phase, students can be required to talk with some minimum number of classmates, say three or four, and to take notes on their classmates' opinions. After the mingle phase, students take their seats and spend a moment or two in silent reflection before the instructor opens up class-wide discussion, generating ideas to put on the board and asking for evidence to support each of the proposed turning points as critical to the novel.

The mingle activity can also be used before students have read the entire novel. For instance, students could be assigned to mingle with one another, each asking a question they have been assigned individually; one student could be polling classmates about the importance for the novel as a whole, based on their reading thus far, of a particular minor character, such as Lebezyatnikov or Nikolai/Mikolka, while another might be asking about the importance for the novel of a particular episode, such as Sonya's reading of the story of Lazarus or the (false) confession of Nikolai/Mikolka, while a third student might be asking about a thematic element in the novel, such as humor or suspense. After the students have mingled and gathered impressions from their classmates, they reflect and then individually give a short presentation to the class that generates more discussion—with presentations and discussions spread out over a few class sessions.

Another group-based discussion activity format involves the assignment of roles to individuals within each group and the setting of a discussion goal for each group of characters. For example, students could be divided into groups of four in which each student is assigned the role of a different minor character from the novel (e.g., Zosimov, Zametov, Dunya, Lebezyatnikov) and asked to compile a narrative of the novel's events from what their character would know at this stage of the reading, then to work with the other group members to create as comprehensive a view of the novel's narrative as possible by putting together their respective characters' experiences. The students could then be asked to identify what in their characters' lives has most influenced the way those characters view the events depicted in the novel. Each group could then make a presentation to the class on what they learned from the exercise about the different perspectives of these diverse characters. An alternative to these questions, for this very format, might focus on asking the students to describe, from their assigned characters' perspectives, a particular episode from the novel, creating a variety of narratives reflecting, again, the distinct voices and worldviews of Dostoevsky's characters. This conversation, in any of its variants, could then be linked to Bakhtin's argument about polyphony in Dostoevsky's poetics (6).

Indeed, the notion of role play can be very useful in discussion-based learning. A role play activity could take the format of a talk show, a trial, a publicity campaign, or a commercial, among others. In each format, students are assigned to play a particular role in a specific context with a given topic in a group or in a whole-class role play exercise. For instance, one student could take the role of a talk show host, prepared with questions to ask, another student the role of the show's producer, whose task it is to ensure that all the guests have an equal opportunity to speak. (The role of the producer might profitably be assigned to a student who tends to dominate discussion.) The guests on the talk show could be characters in the novel who must answer questions from the host about a variety of topics in ways that reflect their characters' actual life experiences, perspectives, and interests. For instance, the host and a group of guests such as Dunya, Sonya, and Katerina Ivanovna could discuss their personal experiences of spiritual transformation, and the guests would have to call upon their own biographies as described in the novel. Guests such as Svidrigailov, Razumikhin, and Raskolnikov might discuss with their host the question of "what is truly unforgivable," leading to what could be a spectacular scandal scene à la Dostoevsky. Students not appearing "on stage" could be asked to play audience members who pose additional questions for the guests.

Another role play activity well suited to *Crime and Punishment* is based on the format of a trial. For instance, one student could be assigned the role of a judge, others the roles of the defense and prosecuting attorneys, still others the roles of jury members, the defendant, witnesses, and members of the press. Such a format could be used to try not only Raskolnikov but also to Svidrigailov (before his suicide) as well as many other characters in the novel. For instance, Porfiry Petrovich could be put on trial for not having discharged his responsibility as a police officer to arrest Raskolnikov after he realized that Raskolnikov had murdered the two old women, or Nikolai/Mikolka could be put on trial for having made a false confession. In either of these cases, the judge could be Razumikhin, the defense attorney Pulkheriya Aleksandrovna, and the prosecutor Luzhin, and other characters from the novel could be assigned to the jury and the press. (The point is not to accurately depict nineteenth-century Russian imperial jurisprudence but to engage students in discussion that promotes their deeper understanding of the novel.) It is important to understand that the trial activity can revolve around a crime that was depicted in the novel or around one that wasn't (and may not have happened at all in the imagined world of the novel). For instance, a character could be put on trial for sexism based on evidence found in the novel, although there is of course no such crime in the legal code of the Russian Empire. In the trial role play, students contribute to the exercise by providing information based on the text, thereby exercising their knowledge of the text and increasing their understanding of the vibrancy of the novel and its characters. If the novel has been read in a course in which students are reading other works by Dostoevsky, some of the roles in the trial—for instance, one of the attorneys or a judge or a member of the jury—could be assigned to a character from one of Dostoevsky's other works, such as Father Zosima (*Brothers Karamazov*), Nastasya Filippovna (*The Idiot*), Yakov Golyadkin (*The Double*), or Liza (*Notes from Underground*). If the course includes works by other authors, characters from those works may be pressed into service in the classroom trial. This approach helps extend the discussion to embrace more of Dostoevsky's oeuvre, in comparison with others of his works or in comparison with works by other authors, which may serve well as a culminating exercise in such a course.

Role play activities can also be profitably assigned for work outside class. For instance, a group of students could be asked to create a "public service announcement" (PSA) designed to recruit candidates for the police academy with Porfiry Petrovich as an exemplary detective. This would involve writing a script and performing the PSA live or on a video shown in class. Similarly, students could produce a commercial encouraging viewers to visit places in the novel, with an emphasis on the connection between physical and psychological space in Raskolnikov's Petersburg.

For any role play framework, instructors should provide students with clear guidelines as to how their role play activity will be evaluated, with some points assigned to compelling evidence drawn from the novel. Whether the role play activity is conducted in class or as a homework assignment, this discussion framework has the advantage of assigning students a communicative purpose and ideological or cultural perspective that may be different from their own, as described by Penny Ur; for some students, having an assigned communicative purpose and perspective may be liberating.

Group activities that bring together discussion with collective writing can also be helpful learning exercises. If *Crime and Punishment* is assigned in a course in which students are reading works by other authors, a group discussion activity could focus on the analysis of the literary styles of the different authors. For this activity, students can read a one- to two-sentence description of a very nondescript event with minimal detail provided; for example, a patron in a café drops a fork and a staff person picks it up and replaces it with a clean one, or an employee arrives at work and is introduced to a new hire by the supervisor.

Each group of students is assigned a different author in whose style they must retell this nondescript event in a group writing exercise. For example, in a course on nineteenth-century Russian prose fiction, each group might be assigned one of these authors, each with a distinct prose style: Alexander Pushkin, Mikhail Lermontov, Nikolai Gogol, Ivan Turgenev, Karolina Pavlova, Nikolai Chernyshevsky, Leo Tolstoy, Avdotya Panaeva, Nikolai Leskov, Evgeniya Tur, or Anton Chekhov. Each group writes a one- to two-page story treatment of the nondescript event, with their treatment demonstrating as many characteristic stylistic traits of the assigned writer as possible. The groups' texts are then projected onto a screen, one at a time, for discussion by the whole class. First, the class tries to identify all the stylistic features and then guess which author's style the group was emulating. Next, the class tries to offer improvements to enhance the stylistic copy. (The same approach can be used in a course in which *Crime and Punishment* is read together with works by authors from other cultures.) The collective writing exercise can be a very productive culminating task at the end of a semester, helping students synthesize what they've learned about the writing styles of the different authors they've studied in the course.

The role play and collective writing activities described above are conducted at a level of creative and synthetic thinking, as per Bloom's taxonomy of learning tasks, challenging students to consider what they've learned from and about the novel at the highest order in that cognitive hierarchy (Anderson and Krathwohl).

Some readers might ask if one or another discussion framework described above is best suited for the discussion of *Crime and Punishment*, but in fact there is nothing inherent to this novel, or to any other work, that lends itself more to one framework or another. Instead, instructors should consider their own teaching style and preferences and the chemistry of the class they're teaching in making their selections. Furthermore, experience has shown that over an extended period of study, such as is likely for a work of the length and complexity of *Crime and Punishment*, students tend to prefer a variety of discussion frameworks and to lose interest if the same framework is used regularly. Some of the frameworks described in this essay might, however, be profitably revisited at various stages of the reading of the novel to engage students in reassessing their previously asserted hypotheses and interpretations, while others, such as a trial role play, might be best run as a summative exercise after the class has read the entire novel and can see it as an artistic whole from the perspective of the novel's end.

The discussion frameworks outlined in this essay have the potential for impact on student learning in the context of the study of *Crime and Punishment* because they all contribute to holding learners accountable for active engagement with this rich and challenging text. Engaging students with this novel and with one another in a shared journey of interpretation through discussion-based activities promotes students' growth in both intellectual and emotional intelligence as well as in the area of critical thinking and successful spoken communication.[1]

NOTE

1. For more information about the discussion activity frameworks described here, as well as others, I recommend Barkley et al., Brookfield and Presskill, Howard, and Herman and Nilson.

TRANSLATIONS AND ADAPTATIONS

Slow Reading: Performing Translation

Carol Apollonio

There have been at least twelve translations of *Crime and Punishment* into English. The mere existence of such a wealth of options suggests that each translation has something unique and different to offer. Naive readers naturally tend to assume that the different versions can be easily ranked from best to worst, and that the instructor has gone through them all and chosen the one that is indisputably the best. This is probably not the case; it is unlikely that anyone, even a specialist, has actually read and evaluated all the available translations. Let us admit this: other factors in addition to the translation's quality—however that might be defined—can contribute to the decision about which edition to use: personal taste, cost, availability, familiarity, and critical apparatus (notes, maps, critical articles, etc.). We might even recognize that a new translation is better for some purpose than the old one we have been using but prefer to keep the old one because we've written comments into its margins and indexed the page numbers of key passages in our class notes. Furthermore, standards for evaluating translations differ; readers, even uninformed ones, tend to pontificate on the matter, and monolingual critics and book publicists are prone to press their fingers on the scale. At the end of the day there is no obvious critical consensus as to the "best" translation. Caution is advised when using online versions, but most hard-copy translations put out by reputable publishers tend to be reliable; through word choice and syntactical variations they emphasize different nuances in the original text.

Translations tend to array themselves along a scale extending from the very literal to the very free. One reader may prefer a literal version that sticks closely to the original syntax; another would rather enjoy a relaxing and pleasurable reading experience—which is not always the case with a literal translation. Literalism can highlight important lexical features of the original, even at the cost of affecting the text's readability. For example, translating "чёрт" (*chort*) every time literally as "devil" (rather than using more fluent wording like "damn it all") can help convey the tangible presence of the devil in Dostoevsky's texts—as a sort of shadow character haunting the language. This is certainly the case in *Crime and Punishment*, though the Evil One never materializes, despite an alarming number of explicit verbal summons. Scholars tend to favor literal translations, but there are compelling reasons to choose free ones.

Regardless of which version is chosen, instructors should draw attention to the *fact* of translation. In my own practice, I encourage students to obtain whichever translation is most convenient, stipulating that the text must be unabridged and the translator needs to be named. Despite the occasional logistical difficulties (finding passages during class time, for example), it is usually worth the trouble to have a few translations in play. Used book stores tend to have a couple of versions of *Crime and Punishment* in stock. Libraries usually have several different translations—these can be put on reserve, or students can be encouraged to grab a copy off the shelf. The additional benefit of this strategy is that it sends students into the library, a place they are increasingly unfamiliar with. Beginning in the COVID-19 era, it is likely that many students will be using electronic versions of the text; instructors need to take the extra step of checking that these sources are acceptable. Focusing students' attention on the integrity of the text they are using teaches an important lesson in itself.

Let us assume that a typical course plan will devote one class session to each of the novel's six parts, with an additional day for the epilogue and summing up. One of these six days—let's say the first—could be devoted to considering issues of translation. Below I offer a lesson plan for teaching part I, chapter 7 of the novel based on a dramatic reading and comparison of several translations of a particular passage. This lesson works well whether or not anyone (students or instructor) knows any Russian; comparison of several translation texts can give an excellent idea of what is going on in the original. The Russian term for "close reading" is "slow reading" (медленное чтение). By slowing down the pace of reading so as to savor every word, this method draws attention to the materiality of language, reminding us all that a novel's power is rooted in meticulous word-for-word craft—the writer's as well as the translator's. By comparing translations, students come to understand not which translation is "better" but the power of the original text, and literature in general, to yield multiple and nuanced meanings. This particular lesson also nurtures active learning—student voices fill class time and there's minimal lecturing from the podium. At the same time, there's no sloppiness, given that these voices are channeling Dostoevsky's novel rather than sharing individuals' random and, as seasoned instructors know, occasionally idiosyncratic thoughts.

It is always better to show than tell. It is even better to act and experience.

Classroom Exercise: Unrehearsed Dramatic Reading

This exercise should take up an entire 75-minute class period.

Methodology, Learning Objectives, and Assessment

The methodology includes active learning, performance, and small group activity. The activity is designed to enable students to

- learn about translation
- develop critical thinking skills
- hone techniques for textual analysis
- nurture an appreciation for literary language
- understand Dostoevsky's poetics of polyphony and dramatic construction
- refine oral communication skills
- learn how to listen
- be entertained
- realize that big thoughts come from little words

This crowd-sourced interpretive exercise is entertaining and fun, helps break down the affective filter, and builds class community and spirit. Assessments are performed before and after the activity in the form of a content quiz at the beginning of class and short reflections assigned as homework.

Preparation

Before class, the students have read part 1 of *Crime and Punishment* in whatever translations they have acquired. This particular course plan is oriented to an in-person classroom, but it can be adjusted for a remote lesson. The instructor has prepared the following materials:

- A small handbell with a thin, tinny jingle.
- Two pairs of clean heavy work shoes, or any items at hand that can simulate the noise of footsteps on a stairway. Students may volunteer to use their own shoes.
- Index cards and spare pens or pencils. The number of cards depends on the number of students in the class. This exercise assumes that there are at least six students. For large classes, the roles can rotate. There are three categories of cards: Four (or multiples of four, depending on class size) cards are inscribed with the names of characters in the text (in the case of this excerpt, Raskolnikov, Koch, the Student, the Narrator). Additional cards can be provided with interjections, which

students can introduce as interruptions into the performance, such as "No kidding!" "The Devil!" "Oh God! "Hell!" "Good question!" "Good suggestion!" and "Why all the noise?" Finally, each student is provided with three blank cards for jotting down notes and observations.
- Scripts: multiple translations of the excerpt under study, taken from the part of the novel that has been assigned for homework (one script of one translation per student). These are not to be provided in advance, so that students do not feel pressure to prepare beyond doing the assigned reading; the value of the exercise emerges from its spontaneity and spirit of discovery.
- Content quiz (optional): I give a very short quiz at the beginning of every class to ensure that students have done the reading and come prepared.
- Film clip (optional): I recommend Lev Kulidzhanov's 1969 classic.

The instructor may choose a favorite excerpt; the example provided here is from the "Koch and Raskolnikov with the door between" passage in part 1, chapter 7. The text begins with Koch's arrival at the pawnbroker's door and ends just over two pages later, when the painter shouts "Mitka! Mitka! Mitka! Mitka! Mitka!" and delivers an imprecation whose wording will vary with each version of the script.

Assembly of the scripts takes up the bulk of preparation time. Though in theory there could be twelve different scripts, in practice the exercise can work very well with just three. Each student will have their own hard copy of the novel, plus one version of the script. Scripts should ideally be provided in hard copy; if instead they will be posted on the course website or sent by e-mail, students must be told beforehand to bring devices where they can access the text. If there are students in the class proficient in Russian, their scripts should or could include the Russian text; if this is not possible, they can be asked to access an online version (e.g., ilibrary.ru/text/69/p.7/index.html). For one class period, the script can be divided up into three parts, which can be performed like short theatrical acts, with discussion or reassignment of roles in between, as the spirit prompts.

Class Plan

Preliminaries

Just before class, cue up the film clip (optional); students can watch while you take care of preliminaries. *Be sure the film is on audio mute.* Stop the film at any moment if it is distracting.

Administer the quiz (optional; 8 minutes). During the quiz, hand out scripts: ensure that as many different versions are in play as possible. Hand out props and index cards. Assign roles randomly (e.g., by dealing the cards to students face-down). "Sound effects" students are given the shoes or blocks and handbell. "Interjection" cards are handed out randomly (to students who are not given speaking roles). Roles can rotate between excerpts.

Provide instructions, as follows: Students are to perform their assigned part, each reading from their particular version of the script. They are to read slowly, with expression, and be aware that the exercise is not a race. Listeners follow along using their own versions of the script. Readers pause at logical breaks—after each sentence or short paragraph. During the pauses, the other students, who are following along, may read out loud the equivalent wording from their own translation, if they feel that there are significant differences. (It is possible to structure this exercise with *every* version to be read out loud, line by line; in this case each paragraph repeats in several versions, creating a *mise en abyme* effect—but monitor students for boredom as the reading progresses.). All students need to be ready to provide or respond to sound effects at the appropriate moments (shoes, bell, crowd noise, laughter, etc.). Students who are not performing a role follow along and provide commentary (using "interjection" phrases from the cards). Beyond scripted interjections and readings of phrasing from other translations the reading should not be interrupted, for the focus of the exercise, despite all the activity going on, is on the original text.

The Exercise (50 Minutes, in Three Parts)

Students perform the excerpt, reading from their scripts. The instructor remains silent and fulfills a minimal managerial role—for example, determining how many of the alternative translations should be read for each chunk of text and when and whether to encourage a free discussion. The instructor can also be a cheerleader or stage director, calling for more expression or emotion at key moments (despite Raskolnikov's silence, this scene is quite noisy). Russian students or students of Russian may be prompted to read phrases from the original, as appropriate. This is always worth doing—everyone loves it.

During the readings, or during the breaks between the readings, students can jot down impressions anonymously on their blank cards. Cards can be exchanged, and students can take turns reading out loud the cards they have received—a practice that allows students to channel one another's voices (not knowing whose card they are reading) as they have channeled the voices in the novel, building community and lowering everyone's stress level. If something interesting is going on at this point, a back-and-forth discussion can ensue. If not, the next chunk of text can be performed (with switching of roles as appropriate).

Below is a sample transcript of part of a class as it would unfold in the extremely unlikely circumstance that all possible translations were in play. This is not a script (it would take up too much space to provide a script of even one translation here). The purpose is to give a glimpse into the wide variety of English equivalents possible for any given segment of text as well as to spark ideas as to how instructors might modify the exercise to meet their own goals. Of necessity the excerpt is extremely short, and since it includes all the translations available to me, it is unlikely to be a realistic transcript of any given class. Here, the translations are ordered alphabetically by translator name and labeled with each translator's initials.[1]

Discussion of this particular excerpt may focus attention on the language of damnation and the translator's decisions related to who or what is "thrice confounded" (e.g., *it*, *them*, *you*). Students may notice that all this noise is being processed through Raskolnikov's ears and that people are summoning the devil (and, elsewhere in the text, God).

[Original text]

— Да что они там, дрыхнут или передушил их кто? Трррeклятые! — заревел он как из бочки. — Эй, Алена Ивановна, старая ведьма! Лизавета Ивановна, красота неописанная! Отворяйте! У, треклятые, спят они, что ли? (Dostoevsky, *Prestuplenie* 67)

[Speech]

KOCH. Are they fast asleep in there, or dead, or what, confound them? (JC; *Crime* [1975] 70)

What's up? Are they asleep or murdered? D-damn them! (CG; *Crime* [1994] 84)

What the hell are they doing in there? Are they dead to the world or did someone strangle them? Goddamn them! (MK; *Crime* [2018] 91)

Are they all asleep in there, or strangled by somebody, the thrice-confounded old crones . . . (JK; *Crime* [1989] 101)

Are they both asleep, or has someone strangled them? (AK; *Crime* [1953] 68)

What's the matter with them? Are they asleep or has someone strangled them? (DM; *Crime* [1951] 102)

What's wrong with them in there, are they asleep or has somebody strangled them? The cursed wr-r-etches! (DMc; *Crime* [1991] 120)

What the he-e-ell's going on here! They snoring away, or somebody strangle them? (SM; *Crime* [1968] 89)

What's up there, are they snoring, or has somebody wrung their necks? Cur-r-se it! (PV; *Crime* [1993] 82)

What are they doing in there—dozing? Or has someone done them in? Damned women! (OR; *Crime* [2015] 77)

What are they all up to in there, fast asleep—or has someone strangled them all? Damn you all! (NPS: *Crime* [2017] 75)

Are they both asleep, or has some one strangled them? The thrice-confounded creatures! (FW; *Crime* [1911] 74)

[Improvisation]

INTERJECTORS. Good question! The Devil! (*etc.*)

[Narration]

NARRATOR. The visitor boomed in a resounding voice. (JC; *Crime* [1975] 70)
He bawled in a thick voice. (CG; *Crime* [1994] 84)
He bellowed as if from a barrel. (MK; *Crime* [2018] 91)
The caller boomed. (JK; *Crime* [1989] 101)
Growled the visitor in a guttural voice. (AK; *Crime* [1953] 68)
He roared suddenly, as though from the bottom of a cask. (DM; *Crime* [1951] 102)
He roared, in a voice that seemed to come from a barrel. (DMc; *Crime* [1991] 120)
He roared in a booming voice. (SM; *Crime* [1968] 89)
He bellowed, as if from a barrel. (PV; *Crime* [1993] 82)
He roared, as if from a barrel. (OR: *Crime* [2015] 77)
The visitor roared in a booming voice. (NPS; *Crime* [2017] 75)
Growled the visitor in a guttural voice. (FW; *Crime* [1911] 74)

[Improvisation]

INTERJECTORS. Why all the noise?

[Speech]

KOCH. Hey! Alyona Ivanovna, you old witch! Lizaveta Ivanovna, my peerless beauty! Open the door! Oh, confound it all, they must be asleep or something! (JC; *Crime* [1975] 70)
Hey, Alyona Ivanovna, old witch! Lizaveta Ivanovna, hey, my beauty! Open the door! Oh, damn them! Are they asleep, or what? (CG; *Crime* [1994] 84)
Hey, Alyona Ivanovna, you old witch! Lizaveta Ivanovna, you indescribable beauty! Open up! Hey, goddammit, are you asleep or what? (MK; *Crime* [2018] 91)
Hi, you there, Alyona Ivanovna, you old hag! And you, Lizaveta Ivanovna, you pearl of beauty! Open the door. Oh, confound it all, can they be asleep? (JK; *Crime* [1989] 101)
Hi! You old witch! Elizabeth, you gorgeous creature!—open the door! (AK; *Crime* [1953] 68)
Hi, there, Alyona Ivanovna, you old witch! And you, too, Lisaveta Ivanovna, my beauty! Open up, damn you! Are they asleep, or what? (DM; *Crime* [1951] 102)

Hey, Alyona Ivanovna, you old witch! Lizaveta Ivanovna, my fabled beauty! Open up! Ach, the cursed wretches, are they sleeping or what? (DMc; *Crime* [1991] 120)

Hey, Alyona Ivanovna, you old witch! Lizaveta, you fabulous beauty! Open up! Oof, hell! They asleep, or what? (SM; *Crime* [1968] 89)

Hey, Alyona Ivanovna, you old witch! Lizaveta Ivanovna, you indescribable beauty! Open up! Ohh, curse it all! Are they asleep, or what? (PV; *Crime* [1993] 82)

Oi! Alyona Ivanovna, my old witch! Lizaveta Ivanovna, my beauty! Open up! Fast asleep, are they? (OR; *Crime* [2015] 77)

Hey, Alyona Ivanovna, you old witch! Lizaveta Ivanovna, my raving beauty! Open up! Ooh, damn you both, are they asleep or what? (NPS; *Crime* [2017] 75)

Hi! Alyona Ivanovna, you old sorceress! Elizabeth Ivanovna, you indescribable beauty!—open! Oh! the witches! can they be asleep? (FW; *Crime* [1911] 74)

[Narration]

NARRATOR: In his rage, he again tugged at the bell-pull with might and main some ten times in a row. (JK; *Crime* [1989] 101)

In his exasperation he rang ten times running, and as loud as he possibly could. (AK; *Crime* [1953] 68)

[etc.—reading other translations]

[Sound effects]

SOUND EFFECTS: bell

[Improvisation]

INTERJECTORS: *[can improvise here]*

Cooldown (Fifteen Minutes)

Every student writes overall impressions anonymously on a blank card. Collect and exchange cards. Students read aloud from the other students' cards they receive (choose students to read who did not "perform").

Homework and Self-Assessment

Students can be asked to take home the cards they received and to write a response to them. They can also be asked to share their impressions of the exercise; these can be turned in, posted to a class discussion board, or brought to class for additional exchange and reading.

What Students Learn

The benefits of this exercise extend well beyond the insights students gain about Dostoevsky's novel and about translation. Everyone has fun; the narrator's lines and the sound effects can be particularly funny. Slow, communal, scripted reading liberates students from performance anxiety that can interfere with learning. No one is graded on participation or on their brilliance or eloquence; the quieter students participate to an equal degree with the louder ones. The activity is low-stakes in terms of students' identity, as they are not voicing their own thoughts but channeling those of the novel's characters and narrator. The design of this exercise also bridges the gap between students and instructor, whose role is primarily to prepare and manage the reading, not to pontificate, promote a particular interpretation, or provide the last word.

This particular excerpt focuses students' attention on Raskolnikov's isolation at the scene of the crime. Dramatic reading of the passage, and of the episode that ensues, should draw attention to the drama taking place in the character's soul. The language of damnation (rendered by translators variously as "confound"; "hell"; "damn"; "goddammit," etc.) begins here. The murderer's isolation behind the door with his sin has generated a demon, whom the visitors to the apartment will soon invoke by name, as though summoning, or perhaps taunting, him. Since translations differ in the degree to which they translate "черт" or "леший" literally as "demon" or "devil," focusing on translation variants should allow this message to emerge naturally. At the key moment (which appears shortly after the excerpt above), Raskolnikov will appeal to "God" or "the Lord." By reading slowly, students will feel, word by word, the inner experience of a soul teetering on the brink of damnation.

For contrast to the intense interiority of this episode, a similar reading can be performed later of a distinctively Dostoevskian "scandal scene," with a mass of characters brought together around a melodramatic, ethically loaded action. My favorite part of the novel for this is part 5, chapter 3, where Dostoevsky gathers all the characters together at Marmeladov's funeral dinner to witness Luzhin's slander of Sonya. The advantage here is that there are many speaking parts and a lot of action. Props can include food, scarves or other clothing, and a hundred-ruble note that can be provided to the student reading Sonya's part.

Great literature creates a world that we can enter through attentive reading. All interpretations emerge from this experience. Dostoevsky's novels are constructed dramatically, emphasizing scene-setting, dialogue, and action, but they also feature a powerful narrative voice. Performing the text communicates this dynamic structure much more effectively than can be done through harangues from the podium. Students of Dostoevsky's work find it easy to get sidetracked by abstraction; communal slow reading anchors the class in the concrete details of the text and focuses their attention on its novelistic art. Raskolnikov's interiority and isolation emerge as students realize that most of his words are only thought, not spoken. By performing the text, students emerge from their own isolation and become involved and invested in the class community in ways that are in tune with the novel's theme of the dangers of individualism, ego, and pride.

Every word in a text is important. Before class, students are likely to be thinking about the murder scene or about the various thoughts and arguments warring in Raskolnikov's mind; focusing on parts of the text they may not have noticed—outside the protagonist's head—immerses them in the world of the novel. At the same time, by reading and comparing different translations, students discover multiple dimensions of that world that would not be accessible to them from only one translation. Along the way, they learn that translations differ not necessarily because one may be objectively better than the other, but because translators offer different interpretations of any given passage. The payoff to this approach is that arguably it may offer a broader and more multidimensional—yet still authentic—experience of reading than would be possible even to a reader fluent in the original Russian, who might not be paying such close attention.

NOTE

1. The translators cited are Jessie Coulson, Constance Garnett, Michael R. Katz, Julius Katzer, Alexandra Kropotkin, David Magarshack, David McDuff, Sidney Monas, Nicolas Pasternak Slater, Richard Pevear and Larissa Volokhonsky, Oliver Ready, and Frederick Whishaw.

Teaching *Crime and Punishment* through Its Different Translations

Cassio de Oliveira

Instructors of Russian literature in translation will likely face, at some point, the question of which version of *Crime and Punishment* to adopt in the classroom. The choice often hinges on factors such as price, availability, ancillary resources (such as annotations or supplementary texts), and the type of course in which the text will be taught (e.g., a world literature survey or a seminar for Russian majors). The decision also depends on the evaluation of such elusive and subjective concepts as "faithfulness" to the original and "readability" in English. Translation scholar Carol Maier's most important recommendation to instructors when selecting a translation is, "*Choose one, use many (if not all)*." Whereas instructors should choose only one translation, Maier writes, they should readily explain their rationale to students; furthermore, they should not shy away from bringing other translations into the classroom. With the plethora of excellent translations of *Crime and Punishment* currently available, instructors may find great pedagogical benefits in introducing students to different versions of the novel beyond their own selection for the course. To "limit oneself to one version" when multiple translations are available, Maier argues, "is to deprive oneself (or one's students) of the pleasure of awakening to the strangeness of language that is often revealed strikingly by variations, even small ones, among multiple versions of a given text." (16). In this essay, I present some activities aimed at stimulating a fruitful discussion of different translations of Fyodor Dostoevsky's novel. I also suggest a framework, drawn from a Russian literature and culture seminar I teach at my institution's Honors College, that takes further Maier's exhortation: building on her caveat that "No choice should be considered final" (17), I contend that there is no need to choose only one translation of *Crime and Punishment*. Instead, I recommend providing multiple translations and assigning each one to a different group of students. The contrast between translations, and the discussion of the different interpretive implications and strategies that they elicit, can help students focus on the novel's formal devices and traits. Comparative work on the translations thus equips students with useful tools for developing close readings that integrate the analysis of formal traits and dominant themes in *Crime and Punishment*.

While this approach is certain to enrich a discussion of any text in translation (or the comparison between original and translation, when appropriate), *Crime and Punishment* lends itself particularly well to such an analysis. For starters, the instructor could draw attention to the various acts of, or references to, reading and translation contained in the novel: in part 2, chapter 2, for instance, Razumikhin informs Raskolnikov that he makes ends meet by translating German philosophical and sociological treatises into Russian; he tries to help Raskolnikov by arranging for him to do such translations too. Raskolnikov promptly refuses, blurting out that he doesn't want [to work on] translations ("Не надо . . . переводов"; Dostoevsky, *Prestuplenie* 89), an assertion that also hints at his attempts at uttering a "*new word*" '*новое слово*' (200) that lead him to commit murder and to reject the Christian faith.[1] To Brian Baer, translation here "serves as a metonym for the corrupting influence of contemporary Western culture . . . which, Dostoevsky suggests, should not be carried over into Russia" (55). In part 2, chapter 6, furthermore, Razumikhin calls Raskolnikov "перевод с иностранного," adding that "Ни признака жизни в вас самостоятельной!" (Dostoevsky, *Prestuplenie* 130)—rendered by Richard Pevear and Larissa Volokhonsky as "a foreign translation" without "a sign of independent life" (*Crime* [1993] 167) and by Oliver Ready as "a walking translation" with "not a spark of independent life" (*Crime* [2015] 156). I ask students which negative qualities are associated with translation in this insult. They typically list such items as derivativeness, lack of originality, or lack of freedom. My goal is to make students aware of such stereotypes so that they may challenge them as they continue to read the novel and realize the multiplicity of meanings that translations afford the written text.

Attention to translation also provides an important frame for discussing the contrast between Russia and the West prevalent in the novel, which relies on the circulation of ideas, many of them broadcast through translation (such as Razumikhin's hackwork).[2] Whereas most of those ideas are imported or reinterpreted from Western paradigms, translation is present in an exemplary instance of Russian "meekness" in the novel—namely, the episode in part 4, chapter 4, in which Sonya Marmeladova reads to Raskolnikov Lazarus's resurrection from the Gospel of John. Sonya reads from a copy of the Bible "в русском переводе" (*Prestuplenie* 248)—"in Russian translation" per Pevear and Volokhonsky (*Crime* [1993] 324) and Ready (*Crime* [2015] 303)—rather than in Church Slavonic, a fact glossed in the endnotes for many current English-language editions. This episode contradicts the negative view of translation displayed elsewhere in the novel; instead, the fact that the Bible is available in Russian allows the meaning of the biblical text to be conveyed in unmediated form to Sonya and Raskolnikov (i.e., without the barrier that a sacred language imposes). By highlighting the ways in which the practice of translation is contained in the plot of *Crime and Punishment*, the question of translation in Raskolnikov's meetings with Razumikhin and Sonya prepares students for a more thorough engagement with the different versions of the novel.

Comparing Translations

The main activity related to translation consists of the very act of reading *Crime and Punishment* in translation. Since no single choice of translation *has* to be made, instead I give students two options of editions to read, with my only condition being that approximately half the class read one edition and the other half read the other. I privilege translations of the novel available in more affordable paperback editions, in this case the well-known translation by Pevear and Volokhonsky and the more recent translation by Ready. Other combinations are evidently possible. This arrangement aims to strike a balance between having to choose a translation at the expense of all others and providing so much freedom of choice as to make classroom discussion logistically difficult. In class, I explain in general terms what I understand the artistic principles supporting the two translations to be so that students may make an informed choice that still leaves room for discovery and for independent conclusions about the reading. Discussion of translation per se does not always take center stage. Instead, I explore three opportunities for in-depth work on the topic. For the remainder of classroom discussion, translation lies in the background, something hard to ignore but not necessarily the center of our attention: for instance, the class will notice differences every time I ask a student to read aloud a passage from the novel and they follow along in their own editions.

In the first sustained discussion of translation, I distribute a copy of the first paragraph or entire first page of the novel in a third version (e.g., Constance Garnett's) and ask the class to compare that to their respective editions.[3] Beginnings of novels are notoriously rich semantically, and the opening episode of *Crime and Punishment* is no exception: it describes Raskolnikov's furtive escape from his room, the room itself, and the atmosphere of St. Petersburg in summer. The reader is also introduced to the narrator, an ambiguous figure who is neither a neutral third-person narrator nor a fully personified and individualized speaker. The class can explore these elements by focusing, for instance, on the lexicon, repetitions, and phrasing adopted by the translators. Is the "каморка" that Raskolnikov rents a "garret," as in the Garnett and Ready translations, or a "closet," as in Pevear and Volokhonsky's? Does the fact that "Он был должен кругом хозяйке" mean that he was "hopelessly in debt," per Garnett, or "over his head in debt," per Pevear and Volokhonsky, or that he "owed his landlady a small fortune," per Ready?

My goal with this exercise is not to tell students which translation is "better" or "more faithful"[4] but rather to elicit an appreciation of the gamut of aesthetic and semantic effects that result from translators' artistic choices. A good example occurs in Raskolnikov's departure from his room at the end of the first paragraph:

> Raskolnikov "вышел из своей каморки . . . на улицу и медленно, как бы в нерешимости, отправился к К—ну мосту" (*Prestuplenie* 5);
>
> > he "came out of the garret" and "walked slowly, as though in hesitation, towards K. bridge" (*Crime* [1994] 3);
> >
> > he "left the closet" and "walked out to the street, and slowly, as if indecisively, headed for the K——n bridge" (*Crime* [1993] 3);

> he "left the garret . . . stepped outside, and slowly, as if in two minds, set off towards K——n bridge" (*Crime* [2015] 3).

Which translation conveys more tension in Raskolnikov's furtive departure? How does our understanding of the events change with the different translations? The instructor may wish to highlight, for instance, Ready's reference to "stepping outside," which evokes the sense of overstepping one's boundaries contained in the Russian verb *perestupat'* (переступать), thus hinting at *prestuplenie* (преступление), the word for "crime" in the title of the novel. Alone among the three translations discussed here, Ready grants an ominous criminal connotation to Raskolnikov's act of leaving his room, besides evoking the thresholds that are so prevalent in the novel and in Dostoevsky's poetics in general.[5] Instructors may also ask the class about the implications carried by each of the renditions of the phrase "kak by v nereshimosti" ("как бы в нерешимости"): "as though in hesitation," "as if indecisively," and "as if in two minds."

These probing, admittedly impressionistic questions encourage students to notice the formal traits of the text and to consider how they influence their interpretation of the novel. The instructor may wish to attempt a more sustained analysis of the translations, for instance by tracking the usage of a group of words related to a specific concept, or by engaging in a close reading of a specific passage or description. For example, later in part 1, chapter 1, Alyona Ivanovna, the pawnbroker, is said to have "с . . . злыми глазами" (*Prestuplenie* 8)—eyes described in English as "spiteful" (*Crime* [1993] 6), "evil" (*Crime* [2015] 6), or "sharp" and "malignant" (*Crime* [1994] 7). The Russian adjective *zloi* accommodates both meanings rendered by the English-language adjectives, but the English renditions emphasize distinct nuances of the Russian adjective: "spiteful" eyes imply a down-to-earth, almost banal attitude appropriate to a moneygrubbing pawnbroker; in contrast, "evil" eyes contain a sinister undertone, suggesting a negative moral or philosophical dimension to Alyona Ivanovna's character beyond materialistic, everyday concerns.

In the second in-depth engagement with translation, students "exchange" renditions of part 4, chapter 4 (in practice, I distribute that chapter in handout copies) and discuss the major differences that they identify. Since that chapter is a particularly meaningful episode that lends itself to detailed discussion without going into the question of translation, instructors may alternatively wish to choose a less overdetermined, climactic chapter.[6] At the same time, much of part 4, chapter 4 consists of the biblical episode of Lazarus (for which Pevear and Volokhonsky use the King James Version, while Ready uses the Revised Standard Version), allowing the instructor to focus on the interaction between the ostensibly univocal biblical text and Dostoevsky's own narrative, malleable and in multiple translations. To guide the discussion, the class focuses on linguistic registers (bookish and Biblical versus colloquial); paragraph and sentence structure; and metaphors and figures of speech, for instance, "Недели через три на седьмую версту, милости просим!" (*Prestuplenie* 249), translated as "About three weeks, and welcome to Bedlam!" (*Crime* [1993] 325) and "Another three weeks . . . and they'll be showing her round the asylum!" (*Crime* [2015] 304). Once again, the class does not focus on which translation is "better" but rather on how the translator's choices affect our interpretation of the text. These choices can be reflected in different chains of causation, implications of events, or nuances of style (such as the colloquial form "na sed'muiu verstu" in the quotation above, meaning "to commit someone to an insane asylum").

The topic of translation concludes with a discussion forum in the course's online learning management system preceding the last meeting devoted to the novel. I prompt students to post a reflection on the linguistic qualities of the translation they read by producing a quote from the novel and analyzing its language. I try to focus the discussion entirely on the edition that each student used in order to develop something akin to a close reading of the episode. Yet it is also possible to elicit a more detailed comparison. Students may read their colleagues' posts and respond to a post that focuses on the *other* translation, explaining how the same episode is rendered in the version with which they are more familiar. Such an assignment could form the backbone of a more thorough comparative analysis of the translations, whether in the form of a group discussion in class or a take-home writing assignment such as a short essay.

This set of assignments aims to cover a variety of formats, including informal and low-stakes writing, class discussion, and low-stakes oral presentation. Within the oft-used Bloom's Taxonomy of Educational Objectives, these activities primarily require students to describe the formal features of individual texts and their parts (under the broader umbrella of *Remember*); to interpret their own experience of reading the text in translation and the mediated nature of any literary text, and to summarize their findings on the importance of translation to the interpretation of foreign texts (*Understand*); to compare and contrast the translations (*Analyze*); and to appraise the formal qualities of the translations (*Evaluate*) (see Ambrose et al. 246). I aim to create the building blocks for the development of close readings of the text and not to discuss exclusively the question of translation. Other instructors may wish to add or substitute higher-stakes activities or to adapt the activities in order to focus on specific themes or topics, such as the status of biblical texts within the novel, the role of the narrator, or the critical evaluation of translations.

Although focusing on translation helps students develop close readings and attend to complex questions of form and language in Dostoevsky's novel, this approach may contain drawbacks. Since students are analyzing the formal traits of a translated text, they may not know whether they are overinterpreting what is simply a translator's turn of phrase rather than Dostoevsky's own; for example, they may be reluctant to interpret a word choice in English when they do not know how it was rendered in the original. While there is no ready-made solution to such a problem, one of the implicit goals of the engagement with translation is to liberate students from the obsession with the concept of the "original" as the end-all of literary analysis, including when it comes to such a canonical text as *Crime and Punishment.* This exercise aims to demonstrate that translations are worthy of appreciation as modalities of interpretation of the original as well as literary objects in their own right. For that reason, students should be encouraged to interpret translations as coherent, self-contained texts with the acknowledgment that they also represent a specific means of reading the original.

Translation as Education

This set of assignments helps students develop close readings that, while informed by the foci of the course, are equally mindful of the fact of translation itself. The activities rely on a mode of formal analysis that starts with the text in order to reach a broader insight into the wealth of meaning contained in language and communication. Alison Cook-Sather develops the metaphor of education as translation in response to what she identifies as the misguided belief, in higher education and elsewhere in American society, in the fixity of connections "between a word and an idea, within a mind or a heart, in a role or a relationship, through a formal process or an institution" (vii). Rather than "fixing meanings or forms," education should instead encourage the connection between seemingly disparate "words and worlds, ideas and actions, identities and interactions" (viii). In Cook-Sather's metaphor, the student acts as "both the translator and the thing being translated" (26), an active participant in a process of self-reinterpretation and transformation. The approach described in this essay aims to turn this metaphor on its head, suggesting that translation is a form of education and discovery in itself, insofar as it mediates the encounter between reader and text. Just as Raskolnikov's self-understanding changes as he meets and dialogues with different characters, the encounter with different translations of *Crime and Punishment* allows students to find new interpretations—and, in the process, to improve their understanding of their own process of learning and self-discovery.

NOTES

1. See pages 112–13 and 260 in the translation by Richard Pevear and Larissa Volokhonsky (Dostoevsky, *Crime* [1993]) and pages 107 and 312 in the translation by Oliver Ready (*Crime* [2015]), both of which I used in the course I taught.

2. See Baer 55n7 for a brief overview of Dostoevsky's ambivalent relationship with translation.

3. Russian speakers enrolled in the class may also read a handout with the first page in Russian.

4. However, students soon notice that Garnett tends to take more liberty with phrasing than more recent translations. On Garnett's translation activity in general and her Dostoevsky translations in particular, including a comparison of her translation of *The*

Brothers Karamazov with Pevear and Volokhonsky's, see May, chapter 1, especially pp. 27–42.

5. On the importance of thresholds in *Crime and Punishment*, see Bakhtin 170. Susan Bernofsky organizes a similar activity in her workshops: she distributes the beginning of *Crime and Punishment* in different translations (with the translators' identities and dates omitted) and asks participants to evaluate and try to date the versions in relation to one another.

6. Part 4, chapter 3, is an interesting counterpart: a summary and interpretation of the preceding scandal with intimations of events to come.

Teaching *Crime and Punishment* through Film Adaptation

Alexander Burry

There are nearly forty film adaptations of Dostoevsky's *Crime and Punishment*, far more than of any other Russian literary work. These works range from short feature films to lengthy televised serials; from extremely close, accurate versions to loose, partial transpositions of the novel; and from Russian and Soviet films to cinematic reworkings by directors of French, German, American, Indian, Filipino, Australian, and numerous other nationalities. The enormous amount of attention *Crime and Punishment* has drawn from filmmakers stems in part from its absorbing murder plot; but, since unlike in classic detective novels the identity of the killer is known from the beginning, there are surely other factors that make it an attractive object of transposition for directors.

The various films based on *Crime and Punishment* offer instructors myriad opportunities to supplement discussions by observing different strategies of screening the novel and exploring interpretations of it in diverse time periods, cultures, and political contexts. It has long been common practice for instructors to show films based on *Crime and Punishment* and other classic literary texts. Often, this is done simply with the worthwhile goal of providing a change of pace in the midst of the grueling, time-consuming experience of reading and teaching a lengthy and difficult novel. But adaptations can be used more directly as productive teaching tools as well, and I will discuss ways in which they can open up fruitful discussions in high school, undergraduate, and graduate classrooms. Ideally, films of this text, whether shown in full or excerpted, can fulfill the dual goal of illuminating the director's interpretation of *Crime and Punishment* and in turn shedding light back on the novel itself.

As with adaptations in general, films of *Crime and Punishment* often elicit strong initial reactions concerning the degree of accuracy with which the source text is conveyed. Although fidelity criticism (the evaluation of adaptations based on the extent to which they replicate works) has long been disparaged as a methodology, it is a stubbornly persistent and perhaps instinctual approach to adaptations of classic works. The statement, "I liked the book better" (or, in rarer cases, the reverse) is likely to be heard as long as these films continue to be produced. In the past few decades, however, a host of adaptation scholars—including Robert Stam, Linda Hutcheon, and many others—have offered fruitful alternatives to fidelity criticism. Stam, for instance, takes a Bakhtinian approach, positing a dialogic relationship of literature to film in which adaptations, like novels that draw on other literary works, consist of an intertextual engagement with their source texts. This method seems particularly appropriate for Dostoevsky, who himself employs such a densely intertextual array of references to other literature, religious texts, journalistic reports of current events, his own biography, and many other sources. As an instructor who regularly teaches *Crime and Punishment* to undergraduates, I take such theoretical perspectives as a starting point for showing students the wide range of interpretations adaptations can draw from the novel and for encouraging them to use these films to reflect back on the source text.

In what follows, I will explore three series of *Crime and Punishment* adaptations—grouped by directors' nationality or stylistic interrelation—as dialogues with the novel and, in some cases, with each other. As we will see, each film offers a complex series of intertextual relations that instructors and students can discuss. This discussion does not claim to be a survey of the most important films based on *Crime and Punishment* but rather a series of examples of how such films can be interrogated. Each adaptation raises key issues on its relationship with the novel, and I will focus on such topics as: the length and format of the film; other film genres or literary texts that the filmmaker may incorporate or allude to; the director's reconceptualization or omission of Dostoevsky's religious or political material, especially in the light of the given director's beliefs (or lack thereof); and the controversial epilogue, which some critics have found necessary and others argue should have been omitted. Needless to say, these are only a few of the many topics instructors may profitably pursue, but they arise frequently in these films.

I will begin with Russian cinematic transpositions of *Crime and Punishment.* The earliest extant Russian version (five adaptations released early in the twentieth century are no longer available) is Lev Kulidzhanov's 1970 *Crime and Punishment.* For some viewers, this is the classic adaptation of the novel. Like most Soviet adaptations, it aims to reproduce the novel as closely as possible by including all essential plot events and dialogue. While it mostly relies on the naturalistic, theatrical mode of adaptation that typified Soviet adaptations (Lary 187), the opening features a mesmerizing dream sequence in which Kulidzhanov cuts between Raskolnikov's nightmare of committing the murder and being chased by police and the events of part 1 of the novel. As Nikita Lary remarks, however, the set scenes that follow this opening work less well, as Raskolnikov's character lacks depth: "We do not see his active and instinctive compassion, his liking of humble things, and his grand dreams of a better world" (185). And for all Kulidzhanov's close replication of Dostoevsky's basic narrative, a key part is missing: the epilogue, which the director chooses to omit, most likely at least in part for ideological reasons, since it introduces the possibility of Raskolnikov's eventual conversion to Christianity. This omission in itself provides instructors with a fruitful discussion question. Mikhail Bahktin, in *Problems of Dostoevsky's Poetics*, famously critiques the epilogue as a "conventionally monologic ending" (39) that ties together the novel's competing ideas; numerous other critics have also found this part of the novel artificial or unconvincing. Would students, the instructor may ask, prefer the novel to have ended with Raskolnikov's italicized confession at the end of part 6? Or was the director wrong to leave out the author's conclusion? Does watching a film with the epilogue omitted somehow negatively reinforce its importance?

Dmitry Svetozarov's serialized version of the novel (2007) represents a different approach to the act of both transposing and viewing *Crime and Punishment*. Like the films created during the 2000s of Dostoevsky's other three major mature novels, it was shown serially; Svetozarov's adaptation breaks the novel's narrative into eight fifty-minute episodes. In this sense, it imitates Dostoevsky's own formula of releasing parts of the novel in thick journals, thus facilitating a discussion of how the expectations of today's viewers compare to those of Dostoevsky's readers. Unlike Kulidzhanov, Svetozarov includes Dostoevsky's epilogue, vividly portraying the critical scene in which Raskolnikov gazes on the panorama of Siberian huts and falls weeping at Sonya's feet. Svetozarov's final scene begins with Raskolnikov thinking about his fate and protesting his guilt, at first lying in bed, then gradually rising to his feet and looking out his window, and finally leaving his cell and joining Sonya to gaze on his vast surroundings. Without showing Raskolnikov begging the earth for forgiveness, or any conversion process that could occur if he ever adopted Sonya's beliefs, Svetozarov confidently conveys it here through his camera angles and shots. Raskolnikov, together with Sonya, becomes iconicized before the camera quickly widens to a deep shot that integrates the two characters into the Siberian vista. Students may consider Svetozarov's visualization of Raskolnikov's ascent, which seems to add the symbolism of resurrection to Dostoevsky's description. If Dostoevsky's vision of Raskolnikov's future path seems deliberately vague and incomplete, does Svetozarov reflect this irresolution, or does he "finalize" it in some way, to use a Bakhtinian term?

A second line of *Crime and Punishment* adaptations, beginning with the French auteur Robert Bresson's *Pickpocket* (1959), distinguishes itself as radically un-Dostoevskian. Bresson's compact, seventy-five-minute film could not differ more in its length and stylistics from Kulidzhanov's and Svetozarov's epic films and from the novel itself. The viewer of *Pickpocket* is struck first, perhaps, by Bresson's substitution of the crime of petty theft for murder. As the film proceeds, however, the viewer is also shocked by the relative lack of dialogue—and by the fact that what dialogue Bresson does transport from Dostoevsky's novel is delivered almost deadpan by nondescript, nonprofessional actors. As part of Bresson's attempt to remove literary trappings from film, and to reduce the medium to purely cinematic elements, he develops an idiom that foregrounds gestures and gazes, and we are forced to reenvision Raskolnikov in this manner. This allows students to explore the ways in which the director recasts the novel's central focus on the protagonist's alienation and lack of human contact in a very different aesthetic and cultural context. As many critics have shown, however, Bresson's very "un-Dostoevskian" approach allows him to recover the novel's primary thematic concern of Raskolnikov's isolation or estrangement from other human beings. And, as S. Ceilidh Orr argues, a key subtext of the film, Albert Camus's *The Stranger*, whose hero similarly commits a crime without really understanding why, brings existentialist themes directly into dialogue with Dostoevsky's novel, underscoring Stam's point that dialogism in adaptations is never confined to the source text but also includes intervening texts, artists, movements, and stylistics.

More than two decades later, the Finnish director Aki Kaurismäki, in his feature film *Rikos ja rangaistus* (*Crime and Punishment*, 1983), employs similar cinematic language to convey Raskolnikov's crime and its aftermath. Like Bresson, Kaurismäki—who frequently films working-class misfits—is known for minimalism; Jaakko Seppälä sums up his style as "stylistically straightforward and understated yet intense" (5). This film, like Bresson's, features emotionally subdued performances and dispassionate acting. However, Kaurismäki makes significant departures from both Bresson's and Dostoevsky's narratives. First, he complicates the problem of motivation, already so thorny in Raskolnikov's recounting of his various possible motives to Sonya in his part 5 explanation of the murders. The hero, Rahikainen, kills a businessman named Honkanen who had accidentally killed his fiancée in a hit-and-run accident three years earlier and had been acquitted in his trial for lack of evidence. This would seem to simplify the complex motivations of both Raskolnikov and Bresson's hero; however, Rahikainen states that this is not the reason for his murder. Confronted with an absurd situation in which there is an ostensible motive that is quickly undermined, the viewer has to do detective work to figure out what the true motive might be. In addition, in replicating Bresson's through-the-grille final shot, in which Michel expresses his love for Jeanne, Kaurismäki strips his hero, Rahikainen, of possible redemption: Rahikainen, in the final shot, tells Eeva (the film's stand-in for Sonya) not to visit him any more. Thus, Kaurismäki in effect enters into dialogue with both Dostoevsky and Bresson, questioning the possibility of the hero's regeneration.

In 2012, the Kazakh director Darezhan Omirbaev continued this line of creative adaptation in setting the novel in contemporary Kazakhstan. Omirbaev, like Bresson using nonprofessional actors who give deadpan, expressionless performances, freely acknowledges his debt to the French director. But by focusing on the gap between the rich and poor in today's Almaty, he also adds an economic critique that raises parallels between his Kazakh society and Dostoevsky's. By foregrounding post-Soviet Kazakh life in relation to nineteenth-century Russian culture, the Soviet Union, and increasingly dominant Western economic and cultural values, Omirbaev harks back to Dostoevsky's own East-West opposition depicted in the novel and his critique of capitalism, a Western import that he viewed as focusing, like socialism, on materialism to the exclusion of spiritual wholeness. Like Bresson and Kaurismäki, Omirbaev includes the epilogue, this time gesturing toward the hero's possible redemption through love in a manner that recalls his French predecessor.

What are students to make of these three transformations of Dostoevsky's psychological novel, in which events turn on Raskolnikov's tormenting dreams, excruciating interior monologue on the murder and its aftermath, and tense conversations with Sonya, Svidrigailov, Porfiry Petrovich, and other characters? The issue of fidelity becomes effectively moot here, because all three directors depart so blatantly from Dostoevsky's novel. However, here one may note that if these directors essentially remove the aforementioned integral elements of Dostoevsky's prose, they foreground the gaze and silence, which in fact also represent key elements of *Crime and Punishment*. The attentive reader observes that some of the most crucial communicative moments of the novel—including Raskolnikov's confession of his crimes to Sonya and his falling at her feet sobbing in the epilogue—take place nonverbally. Thus, perhaps even if the films "look" and "sound" radically different from the novel, they nevertheless compel us to pay attention to aspects of it that may not strike us at first reading but are nevertheless vital.

Finally, I will discuss three adaptations of the novel that consciously assimilate Raskolnikov's murder into American crime film genres. The first, Josef von Sternberg's 1935 *Crime and Punishment*, is a showcase for the Hungarian-born actor Peter Lorre, who had fled the Nazis two years earlier and settled in Hollywood. Lorre had already made a name for himself in Europe, starring as a serial killer who feels compelled against his will to kidnap and kill children in Fritz Lang's *M*. Here the question of genre comes into play: traces of *M* appear throughout the film, from Lang's use of chiaroscuro lighting (contrasting light and darkness for special effect) to illuminate faces to the frequent use of shadows preceding or following Lorre in staircases. But these aspects of the adaptation, rooted in German expressionism, merge with Hollywood elements such as the almost obligatory happy ending: when we see Lorre go to Porfiry Petrovich to confess, arm in arm with Sonya, with his head proudly held high, we realize that there is no doubt that he will be redeemed somehow. In this way, Dostoevsky's epilogue, with its prospects of a better future for Raskolnikov, merges with Hollywood conventions. Students who know *M*—or other films starring Lorre—might be asked how awareness of Lorre's acting history affects their sense of his performance of the Raskolnikov role. More generally, one could ask what the director might be saying about Raskolnikov's motivation by casting an actor known for his ability to portray a sense of compulsion to murder. Does this sense, emphasized in the film, that the murder is unavoidable make it easier to sympathize with the hero?

Crime and Punishment, U.S.A. (1959, directed by Denis Sanders), by contrast, features a retelling of Dostoevsky's novel for the Beat generation. Filmed in black and white, with tense, dramatic, jazz-inflected music, it resembles the film noir style, itself descended from German expressionism and employed in American film of the 1920s to 1950s by directors like Sternberg. Sanders's film, however, presents the young George Hamilton in his first starring role in a film, picking up on Dostoevsky's description of Raskolnikov as physically attractive: "remarkably handsome, with splendid dark eyes and dark brown hair; he was taller than average, slender, and well built" 'замечательно хорош собою, с прекрасными темными глазами, темно-рус, ростом выше среднего, тонок и строен'

(*Crime* 4; *Prestuplenie* 6).[1] And unlike Sternberg, whose sets are very much a product of the studio, Sanders grounds his film very clearly in American life of the 1950s: the film features the beaches, cars, and apartments typical of Southern California at the time. With his focus on a disaffected American youth on the cusp of an unstable age in American life, Sanders's film allows us to look back on the novel and ask questions about Raskolnikov's youth. What makes crime alluring to disaffected young men, both in Dostoevsky's Russia and in the United States?

In Rob Schmidt's *Crime and Punishment in Suburbia* (2000), by contrast, we see the director much more loosely merging selected parts of the novel's plot with the teen movie and slasher film genres. The film also enacts a gender reversal, in which the murderer becomes Roseanne Skolnick (Monica Keena), a teenage girl who conspires with her boyfriend to murder her stepfather (Michael Ironside) after the stepfather rapes her in a drunken rage. Her Sonya-like confessor figure is a loner classmate, Vincent (Vincent Kartheiser), who obsessively stalks and photographs her (in a possible nod to the teenage photographer Ricky in *American Beauty*, released the previous year). Vincent turns out to be a spiritual guide who, in encouraging Roseanne to make her own choices, indirectly leads her to confess her crime; he also visits her in prison, and drives her away on a motorcycle at the end of the film. In showing a young woman who challenges herself to take control of her life and to refuse to be a victim, the film reframes Raskolnikov's daring of himself to say a "new word" 'нового собственного слова' (Dostoevsky, *Crime* 4; *Prestuplenie* 6) in terms of gender. The film's relentlessly intertextual approach to Dostoevsky may even include an homage to Bresson at the end. Could Roseanne's last line, "What a strange path it took to find my heart," allude to Michel's last line in *Pickpocket*, spoken to Bresson's equivalent for Sonya, who visits him in prison: "What a strange trip I've taken to find you at last, Jeanne"?

Thus, watching the ways in which directors alter and reconceptualize the novel, combining it with other intertexts, provides various opportunities to reexamine *Crime and Punishment* in a new light, and to ask questions that may not have occurred while reading the text. Along the way, students will register emotions of shock, amusement, and delight as they experience what Linda Hutcheon, in describing adaptation, aptly calls "the comfort of ritual combined with the piquancy of surprise" (4).

NOTE

1. This essay cites the translation of *Crime and Punishment* by Michael Katz (2018).

The Sound of Silence: Performing Scenes from *Crime and Punishment*

José Vergara

In his *Lectures on Russian Literature*, Vladimir Nabokov pulls no punches when analyzing Dostoevsky's prose. Nabokov deems his predecessor a "mediocre" writer for his "lack of taste, his monotonous dealings with persons suffering with pre-Freudian complexes, [and] the way he has of wallowing in the tragic misadventures of human dignity" (98, 104). In fact, Nabokov suggests, something went wrong in the development of Russian literature, causing Dostoevsky to misunderstand his very calling:

> Dostoyevsky characterizes his people through situation, through ethical matters, their psychological reactions, their inside ripples. After describing the looks of a character, he uses the old-fashioned device of not referring to his specific physical appearance anymore in the scenes with him. . . . He seems to have been chosen by the destiny of Russian letters to become Russia's greatest playwright, but he took the wrong turning and wrote novels. (104)

Nabokov discerns in Dostoevsky's writings the depths of human tragedy, often expressed at a fever pitch. He argues that Dostoevsky is far less concerned with the bodies of his characters than he is with their emotions, words, and psychological states. Their minds become externalized, not through their corporeal realities, but in their existential dialogues. Put simply, they are dramatic vessels for Dostoevsky to express certain ideas.

Nabokov is not alone in detecting something theatrical about Dostoevsky's poetics. For example, when reviewing a 2008 adaptation of *The Brothers Karamazov*, *The Guardian's* theater critic, Michael Billington, wrote, "I can't think of any living dramatist who would dare to deal so nakedly with religious issues. But there is another quality in Dostoevsky that makes him ripe for adaptation: the fine frenzy and impulsive extremism that drives all his characters." The Symbolist critic Dmitry Merezhkovsky, too, named Dostoevsky the "seer of the soul" in opposition to Tolstoy, the "seer of the flesh," drawing a contrast that echoes Nabokov's statements cited above (443).

These characterizations of Dostoevsky's writing all share an overarching concern with how the author stages his books and, in particular, his characters' interactions. That is, they define how Dostoevsky's characters come into conflict and debate their ideologies through dialogue. To varying degrees, they imply that the Dostoevskian hero is embodied in word rather than in physicality or action. Students, I think, tend to express similar kinds of ideas, whether or not they are formulated quite as eloquently as Merezhkovsky's or as virulently as Nabokov's.

Dostoevsky's bizarre characters and the extreme ideas that they espouse draw them in, and quite often those are what they remember, not Razumikhin's ears or Dunya's hair.

But is all this, whether exaggerated or not, really so? Can the two—the bodily and the psychological—be neatly uncoupled? While Nabokov argues that Dostoevsky cares less about the physical presence of his characters than he does about their emotional states and their wordy exchanges, I try to show to my students how Dostoevsky plays with both bodily presence and silence—the very opposite of what Nabokov emphasizes as Dostoevsky's literary weaknesses—to great effect. In this essay, I offer one approach by which to teach a few related aspects of Dostoevsky's *Crime and Punishment* along these lines. In opposition to its word-rich density—not for nothing is it considered one of those "loose, baggy monsters" (James x)—I instead propose focusing squarely on what is *not said*, on those instances of pregnant silence that torment characters, and on the characters' inaction.

To do so, when we reach part 2 of the book, after the students acquire a basic sense of Dostoevsky's prose and the plot, I ask several pairs to act out scenes from Raskolnikov's conversation with Zametov in the Crystal Palace. In particular, they read aloud and simulate the moments when the characters remain silent, often with their faces close together and without any movement, for a relatively long while.

Here are two of those interactions from their tête-à-tête:

> "I was looking—and that is the reason I came here—for news about the murder of the official's old widow," he finally uttered, almost in a whisper, bringing his face extremely close to Zamyotov's face. Zamyotov looked straight at him, point-blank, without moving or drawing his face back from Raskolnikov's face. What seemed strangest afterwards to Zamyotov was that their silence lasted for exactly a full minute, and that for exactly a full minute they sat looking at each other that way.
>
> (Dostoevsky, *Crime* 161)[1]
>
> Разыскивал – и для того и зашел сюда, – об убийстве старухи чиновницы, – произнес он, наконец, почти шепотом, чрезвычайно приблизив свое лицо к лицу Заметова. Заметов смотрел на него прямо в упор, не шевелясь и не отодвигая своего лица от его лица. Страннее всего показалось потом Заметову, что ровно целую минуту длилось у них молчание и ровно целую минуту они так друг на друга глядели. (*Prestuplenie* 125)
>
> "You are a madman," Zamyotov spoke for some reason almost in a whisper, and for some reason suddenly drew back from Raskolnikov. Raskolnikov's eyes were flashing; he became terribly pale; his upper lip twitched and began to tremble. He leaned as close to Zamyotov as he could and

> began moving his lips without uttering anything; this went on for half a minute or so; he was aware of what he was doing, but could not stop himself. (*Crime* 165)

> Вы сумасшедший, – выговорил почему-то Заметов тоже чуть не шепотом и почему-то отодвинулся вдруг от Раскольникова. У того засверкали глаза; он ужасно побледнел; верхняя губа его дрогнула и запрыгала. Он склонился к Заметову как можно ближе и стал шевелить губами, ничего не произнося; так длилось с полминуты; он знал, что делал, но не мог сдержать себя. (*Prestuplenie* 128)

By this point in the class, we will have discussed Raskolnikov's motives as presented in part 1, his relationships, and his plan for and the reality of the titular crime. Thus, students are primed to wrestle with his behavior and decisions. However, what comes before this particular class session can vary; this activity should work equally well in any type of course: The Classic Russian Novel, Dostoevsky, Realism, thematic offerings, and so on. The activity featured here allows the instructor to highlight some of the peculiarities of Dostoevsky's writing, no matter how familiar the students are with his work and no matter how many of his texts they have read previously. It simply calls upon students to slow their pace, to keep their eyes open to such moments of defamiliarized reality and heightened emotion. I have found that in their reading students habitually fly past these lines, not stopping to notice the stage directions, as it were, of the Crystal Palace scene. Thus, when I pause to draw their attention to this unusual interaction, their surprise is genuine and, all the better for pedagogical purposes, fresh.

I first ask for two volunteers without describing what exactly they will do. Then, I have these students sit face to face, assign each a role, and explain that they must now act out a scene from the chapter. For greatest shock value, I usually begin with the selection from page 161, which requires them to not only sit in silence but to whisper and to stare into each other's eyes at an extremely close distance. Frequently, both the actors and the "audience" become nervous, but I hold them to the full times with a stopwatch so that they experience the literal meaning of Dostoevsky's words. Although giggling is almost inevitable, we must make it through to the end with as much silence as possible. Depending on the class size and time constraints, I have another pair or two complete the same scene for variety's sake. It helps emphasize the oddity of this interaction to see it performed multiple times with different actors, and the second set can try to improve upon the first.

Next, we move on to the argument on page 165, which, although shorter at thirty seconds "or so," is perhaps more dramatic with Raskolnikov's trembling lip. As this goes on, I either try to re-create the space of the tavern as much as possible through sounds and dimmed lights or keep the focus on the silence itself.[2] The former immerses the students in the setting, while the latter highlights even further the tension found in Zametov and Raskolnikov's conversation. The exchange becomes totally divorced from its context, allowing us to view it as a hyperstylized scene.

I then pose such questions as, What do you make of this conversation? Why does Raskolnikov behave this way? Why does Zametov respond the way he does? What might Dostoevsky have intended by having his characters interact in this manner? Is it a "believable" scene? What sort of "realism" is this? Why is Dostoevsky so precise with the timing of the silence, and what effect does that specificity have on our reading of the text? What do these silences signify? What power is there in silence? One should not, of course, pose so many questions at once, but this sampling represents the various conversations that the activity can produce.

From there, we are able to discuss the psychology of the heroes, the so-called dramatic qualities of Dostoevsky's style, the tension between acts and words in *Crime and Punishment*, and the nature of Dostoevsky's realism, among other things. I have found that students naturally come to fascinating discoveries without much prompting when they pause to examine what Dostoevsky might have intended by featuring such unexpected silent moments. Providing students a few minutes for some free writing in response to a question or two works well here.

Perhaps the most obvious, if still quite fruitful, path to take is the psychological one. Students will propose that these interactions speak to the intensity or instability of Raskolnikov's mindset in the aftermath of his crime. The silence, therefore, emblematizes his troubled mind as he tries to rationalize his actions. How the students characterize Raskolnikov's actions in this scene, then, reflects how they understand him as a person: tormented or tormentor, conflicted or manipulative.

Students will also intuitively bring up the concept of the dramatic in Dostoevsky's writing, linking what he does here with Raskolnikov and Zametov to the kinds of readings produced by the critics mentioned at the beginning of the present essay. Even as this trait of Dostoevskian prose rises and falls in their estimation, it opens up new ways of exploring the concept of verisimilitude in fiction. If a naive reader takes Dostoevsky's prose for pure "realism," then what is one to do with these moments that feel rather stylized and, put simply, *un*realistic when examined closely? Life is strange, to be sure, but do these moments signify something else?

This class therefore provides an opportunity for the instructor to introduce Dostoevsky's famous concept of realism "in a higher sense" 'в высшем смысле' (Diary entry) and to explore possible interpretations with students. After discussing the tavern scenes and the way silence is manipulated there, I present this term along with the letter to Nikolai Strakhov in which Dostoevsky writes, "I have my own peculiar view of reality (in art), and what most people call nearly fantastic and exceptional is sometimes for me the very essence of reality. Everyday phenomena and a conventional view of them, in my opinion, are not only not realism at all, but even contrary to them" 'У меня свой особенный взгляд на действительность (в искусстве), и то, что большинство называет почти фантастическим и исключительным, то для меня иногда составляет самую сущность действительного. Обыденность явлений и казенный взгляд на них, по-моему, не есть еще реализм, а даже напротив' (my trans.). Dostoevsky's remarks seem to rebuke Nabokov's complaint that he fails to dwell on the details that make up human experience. Dostoevsky affirms that his realism is concerned with what William J. Leatherbarrow calls an "aesthetics of uncertainty," rather than verisimilitude, "where the narrative point of view deliberately blurs the boundaries of dream and reality, of subjective and objective" (83). Without this background information, students will still quickly note the way Dostoevsky strays from ostensibly realistic norms in order to accentuate some emotional perspective or to give symbolic value to silence and setting alike. The silence that invades characters' conversations can therefore also be productively linked to other non-"realistic" elements and questions in *Crime and Punishment*, such as fate, coincidences, and dreams. The marked silences lead us in those directions, permitting a clearer view of what Dostoevsky may have been after when developing his prose: "They call me a psychologist. It's not true. I am simply a realist in the higher sense. That is, I depict all the depths of the human soul" 'Меня зовут психологом: неправда, я лишь реалист в высшем смысле, то есть изображаю все глубины души человеческой' (Diary entry; my trans.).

I particularly enjoy linking this activity with yet another issue: the way the characters, especially female ones, conceive of the difference between word and deed. Much of the novel, it seems to me, is built upon this tension. Pulkheriya Alexandrovna, for instance, writes in her letter to Raskolnikov about how Luzhin spoke insolently to her, and Dunya responded that "words are not deeds" 'слова еще не дело' (*Crime* 30; *Prestuplenie* 32). Later, after her husband's accident, Katerina Ivanovna Marmeladova, channeling Hamlet, proclaims, "Words, nothing but words! Forgive him! And what if he didn't get run over? He'd come home drunk, wearing his only shirt . . . and flop down and snore, and I'd be sloshing in the water till dawn . . . So what's all this talk about forgiveness! As if I hadn't forgiven him!" 'Слова да слова одни! Простить! Вот он пришел бы сегодн пьяный, как бы не раздавили-то, рубашка-то на нем одна . . . так он бы завалился дрыхнуть, а я бы до рассвета в воде полоскалась . . . Так чего уж тут про прощение говорить! И то простила!' (*Crime* 184; *Prestuplenie* 144). In a time that leaves them largely at the mercy of their male counterparts, these women feel compelled to question what it means to speak in one way and behave in another. Katerina Ivanovna in particular probes the necessity of talking about forgiveness when her whole experience with Marmeladov has been one of tacit absolution.[3] Contrasting these kinds of statements with Raskolnikov's more brooding silence engenders intriguing conversations as students examine power relations between Dostoevsky's characters and observe how words, silence, or actions establish assorted dynamics among them.

When we continue reading, we revisit and observe several other silences, allowing us to return to these questions and to make comparisons between the various people involved. As Benjamin Jens notes in his excellent study of silence in *The Brothers Karamazov*, "Behind one's silence lies a communicative strategy . . . Dostoevsky's fiction is largely concerned with the rhetoric of silence" (51–52).[4] Students may be asked to consider, for instance, Lizaveta's "*dead* silence [lasting] a minute or two" 'мертвая тишина, с минуту или с две' when she discovers her sister's corpse (Dostoevsky, *Crime* 79 [emphasis mine]; *Prestuplenie* 65); the minute of "tense silence" 'напряженное молчание' that follows Luzhin's appearance on the threshold of Raskolnikov's apartment (*Crime* 142–43; *Prestuplenie* 111); the ten(!) minutes of "total silence" 'совершенная тишина' upon Svidrigailov's entrance into the novel; the interspersed lengthy silences that punctuate Raskolnikov's confession to Sonya (*Crime* 410; *Prestuplenie* 214); the silence that lasts "strangely long, for about ten minutes" 'даже до странности долго, минут с десять' when Porfiry confronts Raskolnikov with his guilt (*Crime* 456; *Prestuplenie* 319); or the "two minutes" 'минуты две' that cast a gloom over a conversation between Raskolnikov and Dunya near the novel's end (*Crime* 517–18; *Prestuplenie* 399). Then there are the silences that strain believability in different ways. The painter Nikolai's (false) admission to the murders renders everyone in the room speechless: "The silence lasted for about ten seconds, as though everyone were simply stunned; even the guard recoiled and no longer tried to approach Nikolai, but retreated mechanically towards the door and stood there without moving" 'Секунд десять продолжалось молчание, точно столбняк нашел на всех; даже конвойный отшатнулся и уже не подходил к Николаю, а отретировался машинально к дверям и стал неподвижен' (*Crime* 351; *Prestuplenie* 271). Although the silence is not particularly long in this latter scene, the way all action stops and the guard becomes an automaton suggests something Gogolian, as everything is theatricalized. The silence personifies this rupture in normalcy. Something similar takes place when Luzhin, again falsely, accuses Sonya of stealing from him: "Complete silence fell over the room. Even the crying children became quiet" 'Совершенное молчание воцарилось в комнате. Даже плакавшие дети затихли' (*Crime* 392; *Prestuplenie* 301). What should be most striking is not so much that Dunya's estranged fiancé has denounced a kindhearted woman but rather that as a result the children also refrain from making noise. These silences are then not "realistic" in a traditional way but in the "higher" sense, one in which they symbolize the drama and tragedy of what is taking place. Any of these scenes and their respective silences may be performed by students; their results and their focal points vary, but they all highlight at least some of the most fascinating features of Dostoevsky's poetics as they demonstrate how a writer incredibly fascinated with the word still allowed his heroes to stew in quietude—made a point of it, actually.[5]

On the topic of the performance of silence, instructors may also note Dostoevsky's use of the two Russian words for silence: *tishina* (тишина) and *molchanie* (молчание). The linguist N. D. Arutiunova and the cultural critic Mikhail Epstein have both proposed that the two words signify quite different things. As Epstein writes, *tishina* "simply is" or exists on its own, while *molchanie* and *molchat'* presuppose that silence bears a subject (179). In other words, an instructor can show students how Dostoevsky's very diction encodes the idea of a performative silence. Asking students to stage these silence-filled scenes means asking them to find meaning in the absence of words—something with which they are not often tasked.

Anyone who teaches understands well the power of silence, whether intentional or not. After posing a question, sometimes letting the silence linger can feel disturbing. Other times it feels right. More often than not, it is a proper mix of the two. I find that performing the silence in *Crime and Punishment* allows students to take time with their thoughts, to hesitate and to ruminate on why exactly an author would so frequently and so clearly let his own characters pause in the same way. Acting out or witnessing these scenes grants students a different entry point into Dostoevsky's novel, one by which they can appreciate both its density and its omissions. In short, it serves as a useful tool to show how action and inaction, words and silence, all have much to say in his prose.

NOTES

1. All citations of *Crime and Punishment* refer to the 1993 translation by Richard Pevear and Larissa Volokhonsky.

2. Dostoevsky's narrator notes that the Crystal Palace is "a quite spacious and even orderly tavern with several rooms, all of them rather empty, however. Two or three customers were having tea, and in a farther room a group of some four men sat drinking champagne" 'весьма просторное и даже опрятное трактирное заведение о нескольких комнатах, впрочем довольно пустых. Два-три посетителя пили чай, да в одной дальней комнате сидела группа, человека в четыре, и пили шампанское' (*Crime* 159; *Prestuplenie* 123–124). One therefore need not find a lively track; rather, a quick search on *YouTube* produces several videos of quieter ambient bar or coffee shop noise.

3. Elizabeth Blake has studied the way Sonya's tale is told by three consecutive male figures before she takes on a voice of her own and narrates her own experience confidently.

4. For more on Dostoevsky and silence, see Holquist (148–64), Jones (139–46), and Williams. Consider also Taworski.

5. Other meaningful silences appear on pages 19, 24, 145, 152, 231, 253, 266, 272, 296, 341, 398, 459, 474, and 539 of the 1993 translation by Pevear and Volokhonsky.

NOTES ON CONTRIBUTORS

Carol Apollonio is professor of the practice of Slavic and Eurasian Studies at Duke University and author, editor, or translator of thirteen books, including *Dostoevsky's Secrets: Reading against the Grain* (2009), and some fifty articles about literature and translation. Her most recent book is *Simply Chekhov* (2020). She currently serves as president of the International Dostoevsky Society.

Brian Armstrong is associate professor of philosophy at Augusta University. He was the secretary and treasurer for the North American Dostoevsky Society from 2014 to 2019. His current project is an investigation of Dostoevsky's fiction as a critique of conceptions of human experience.

Katherine Bowers is associate professor of Slavic studies at the University of British Columbia. She has coedited several volumes, among them *A Dostoevskii Companion: Texts and Contexts* (2018) and *Dostoevsky at 200: The Novel in Modernity* (2021). Her monograph, *Writing Fear: Russian Realism and the Gothic*, is forthcoming in 2022 and, with Kate Holland, she is currently working on *Digital Dostoevsky*, a digital humanities project investigating Dostoevsky's corpus that is supported through a grant from the Social Sciences and Humanities Research Council of Canada. Bowers serves as the vice-president of the North American Dostoevsky Society.

Jamie Brummer serves as principal at Christian Brothers High School in Memphis, Tennessee, where he also teaches in the English department. In addition to conference presentations, he has contributed to *Callaloo, The Cormac McCarthy Journal, The Explicator, Gothic Studies*, the book *Bonds of Brotherhood in Sons of Anarchy: Essays on Masculinity in the FX Series* (2018), and the MLA volume *Approaches to Teaching the Works of Cormac McCarthy* (2021).

Alexander Burry is associate professor of Slavic and East European languages and cultures at Ohio State University. He is the author of *Multi-mediated Dostoevsky: Transposing Novels into Film, Opera, and Drama* (2011) and the coeditor, with Frederick H. White, of *Border Crossing: Russian Literature into Film* (2016). His current book project is on the Don Juan theme in Russian culture.

Yuri Corrigan is associate professor of Russian and comparative literature at Boston University. He studies the intersections of literature, philosophy, religion, and psychology in late imperial Russia with a special focus on Dostoevsky and Chekhov. He is the author of *Dostoevsky and the Riddle of the Self* (2017) and is working on a book that explores the significance of Dostoevsky's concept of personality for the contemporary world.

Cassio de Oliveira is assistant professor of Russian in the Department of World Languages and Literatures at Portland State University. He has published articles on Gogol, Daniil Kharms, and other Russian-language writers, as well as on the influence of Maupassant on Tolstoy, Babel, and Bunin. His work has appeared in *Russian Literature, Canadian Slavonic Papers, Slavonica, Tolstoy Studies Journal, Studies in Slavic Cultures, KinoKultura*, and other journals. He is currently writing a book entitled *Writing Rogues: The Soviet Picaresque and Identity Formation, 1921–1938*.

Caryl Emerson is A. Watson Armour III University Professor Emeritus of Slavic Languages and Literatures at Princeton University. She is a translator of Mikhail Bakhtin and author of *The Cambridge Introduction to Russian Literature* as well as works on Pushkin, Tolstoy, and Dostoevsky; on Russian music; and on the modernist writers Sigizmund Krzhizhanovsky and Vladimir Sharov.

Helena Goscilo is professor of Slavic at Ohio State University. She writes on gender, film, art, graphics, fashion, folklore, celebrity culture, and literature. The most recent of her thirty-plus published volumes include *Putin as Celebrity and Cultural Icon* (2013), *Fade from Red: The Cold War Ex-Enemy in Russian and American Film, 1990–2005* (2014), *Russian Aviation, Space Flight, and Visual Culture* (2017), and *Polish Cinema Today: A Bold New Era in Film* (2021). Her current projects are a multiauthored collection on the Slavic film musical and a coauthored book on the transmedia Anna Karenina.

Kate Holland is associate professor of Slavic languages and literatures at the University of Toronto. She is the author of *The Novel in the Age of Disintegration: Dostoevsky and the Problem of Genre in the 1870s* (2013), coeditor (with Katherine Bowers) of *Dostoevsky at 200: The Novel in Modernity* (2021), and has written articles on Dostoevsky, Tolstoy, Herzen, Saltykov-Shchedrin, and historical poetics. She is the president of the North American Dostoevsky Society.

Emily D. Johnson is professor of Russian language, literature, and culture at the University of Oklahoma. She is the author of *How St. Petersburg Learned to Study Itself: The Russian Idea of Kraevedenie* (2006), the editor and translator of Arsenii Formakov, *Gulag Letters* (2017), and, along with Julie Buckler, coeditor of *Rites of Place: Public Commemoration in Russia and Eastern Europe* (2013).

Michael R. Katz is C. V. Starr Professor Emeritus of Russian and East European Studies at Middlebury College. He is the author of two books, *The Literary Ballad in Early Nineteenth-Century Russian Literature* (1976) and *Dreams and the Unconscious in Nineteenth-Century Russian Fiction* (1984). He has translated over twenty Russian novels into English (including works by Herzen, Chernyshevsky, Turgenev, Dostoevsky, and Tolstoy) and is currently completing a new translation of Dostoevsky's *Brothers Karamazov*.

Chloë Kitzinger is assistant professor of Russian at Rutgers University. She has published work on writers including Tolstoy, Dostoevsky, Nabokov, and Bely. She is the author of *Mimetic Lives: Tolstoy, Dostoevsky, and Character in the Novel* (2021).

Ani Kokobobo is associate professor and chair of the Department of Slavic Languages and Literatures at the University of Kansas. She has written on Russian realist authors such as Tolstoy, Dostoevsky, and Goncharov, as well as on twentieth-century works by Vassily Grossman. She also studies Balkan literature and culture and has translated the Albanian writer Ismail Kadare.

Emma Lieber is a psychoanalyst in New York City as well as a part-time lecturer in literary studies at the New School. She is the author of *The Writing Cure* (2020) and the editor of *The Queerness of Childhood: Essays from the Other Side of the Looking Glass* (2021), coedited with Anna Fishzon. Her articles on psychoanalysis, literature, and culture have appeared in academic, psychoanalytic, and popular publications.

Susan McReynolds is associate professor in the Department of Slavic Languages and Literatures at Northwestern University. Her publications on Dostoevsky, philosophy, and religion include *Redemption and the Merchant God: Dostoevsky's Economy of Salvation and Antisemitism* (2008). She is also the editor of the Norton Critical Edition of *The Brothers Karamazov* (2011).

Olga Meerson is professor in the Department of Slavic Languages at Georgetown University. She was born in Moscow and emigrated to Israel. She subsequently moved to the United States. She has published books and articles on Old Testament exegesis, Russian Orthodox liturgical poetics and musicology, Ilya Zdanevich, Andrei Platonov, and contemporary Russian women writers.

Priscilla Meyer is professor of Russian emerita at Wesleyan University. She has published *Dostoevsky and Gogol: Texts and Criticism* (1979), two books on Vladimir Nabokov, and *How the Russians Read the French: Lermontov, Dostoevsky, Tolstoy* (2008), as well as articles on and translations of nineteenth- and twentieth-century Russian prose.

Robin Feuer Miller is Edytha Macy Gross Professor of Humanities and professor of Russian and comparative literature at Brandeis University. She is the author and editor of several books, among them *Dostoevsky and* The Idiot*: Author, Narrator and Reader* (1981), The Brothers Karamazov*: Worlds of the Novel* (2008), and *Dostoevsky's Unfinished Journey* (2014). She has also written on Tolstoy, Chekhov, Dickens, and Rousseau. Her current project is "Dostoevsky, Tolstoy and the Small of This World."

Gary Saul Morson is Lawrence B. Dumas Professor of the Arts and Humanities at Northwestern University and a member of the American Academy of Arts and Sciences. He is the author or editor of twenty books on Russian literature, the nature of time, and the role of quotations in culture. His most recent book, coauthored with Morton Schapiro, is *Minds Wide Shut: How the New Fundamentalisms Divide Us* (2021). His articles appear frequently in *The New York Review of Books*, *The Wall Street Journal*, and other national publications.

Benjamin Rifkin is professor of Russian at Hofstra University and the author of *Narrator's Discourse in Film and Prose Fiction* (1994), as well as over thirty articles in refereed journals on foreign language education, applied linguistics, and late–Soviet era Russian cinema. He is a coauthor of the intermediate-level Russian textbook *Panorama*.

Vadim Shneyder is assistant professor in the Department of Slavic, East European and Eurasian Languages and Cultures at the University of California, Los Angeles. He specializes in Russian literature of the second half of the nineteenth century and has published articles on Dostoevsky, Marxist literary theory, and Soviet postmodernist literature. He is the author of *Russia's Capitalist Realism: Tolstoy, Dostoevsky, and Chekhov* (2020).

Karen R. Smith is a member of the English faculty at the Alabama School of Mathematics and Sciences. Her essays on world literature have been published in several journals and collections, including *College English*, *Comparative Literature Studies*, and *Contemporary Literary Criticism*.

Rachel Stauffer is a project coordinator in the Russian, East European and Eurasian Center and Illinois Global Institute at the University of Illinois, Urbana, and conference manager for the American Association of Teachers of Slavic and East European Languages (AATSEEL). She has taught Spanish and Russian at the elementary, secondary, and post-secondary levels and conducts research in linguistics, multicultural education, and Russian literature and cinema.

José Vergara is assistant professor of Russian at Bryn Mawr College. He teaches courses on Russian language and all eras of culture, including a class on the nineteenth-century Russian novel conducted inside a correctional institution. He specializes in prose of the twentieth and twenty-first centuries with an emphasis on experimental works. His book, *All Future Plunges to the Past: James Joyce in Russian Literature* (2021), examines Russian literary responses to Joyce over the past century. He has also published several articles on authors including Vladimir Nabokov, Mikhail Shishkin, and Sasha Sokolov in journals such as the *Slavic and East European Journal*, the *Slavonic and East European Review*, and *The Russian Review*.

SURVEY RESPONDENTS

Brian Armstrong, *Augusta University*
Katherine Bowers, *University of British Columbia*
Daniel Brooks, *Rutgers University*
Jamie Brummer, *Christian Brothers High School*
Jeffrey Cass, *University of Houston*
Julian Connolly, *University of Virginia*
Wendy Crofts, *Newburyport High School*
Cassio de Oliveira, *Portland State University*
Rita Dirks, *Ambrose University*
Sibelan Forrester, *Swarthmore College*
Nathan Gilmour, *Emmanuel College*
Hilde Hoogenboom, *Arizona State University*
Emily D. Johnson, *University of Oklahoma*
Ritsuko Kidera, *Japan-Eurasia Society*
Chloë Kitzinger, *Rutgers University*
Shoshana Knapp, *Virginia Tech*
Elisa Kriza, *University of Bamburgh*
Anne Lounsbery, *New York University*
Andrew Macmillen, *University College London*
Priscilla Meyer, *Wesleyan University*
William Olmsted, *Valparaiso University*
Lynn Ellen Patyk, *Dartmouth College*
Zachary Rewinski, *University of Wisconsin*
Benjamin Rifkin, *Hofstra University*
Chip Rogers, *Middle Georgia State University*
George Scheper, *Johns Hopkins University*
Kristine Shmakov, *Portland Community College*
Vadim Shneyder, *University of California, Los Angeles*
Karen R. Smith, *Alabama School of Mathematics and Science*
Rachel Stauffer, *University of Illinois, Urbana*
Jon Stone, *Franklin and Marshall College*
José Vergara, *Swarthmore College*
Nancy Ann Watanabe, *University of Washington*

WORKS CITED

Works by Fyodor Dostoevsky

The Brothers Karamazov. Translated by Richard Pevear and Larissa Volokhonsky, Farrar, Straus, and Giroux, 1990.

Crime and Punishment. Translated by Michael R. Katz, Norton Critical Edition, 4th ed., W. W. Norton, 2019.

Crime and Punishment. Translated by Michael R. Katz, Liveright, 2018.

Crime and Punishment. Translated by Nicolas Pasternak Slater, Oxford UP, 2017.

Crime and Punishment. Translated by Oliver Ready, Penguin Books, 2015.

Crime and Punishment. Translated by Constance Garnett, Barnes and Noble Classics. 2007.

Crime and Punishment. Translated by Constance Garnett. *Project Gutenberg*, 2006, gutenberg.org/files/2554/2554-h/2554-h.htm.

Crime and Punishment Translated by Constance Garnett, Dover Publications, 2001.

Crime and Punishment. Translated by Constance Garnett, Modern Library, 1994.

Crime and Punishment. Translated by Richard Pevear and Larissa Volokhonsky, Vintage Books, 1993.

Crime and Punishment. Translated by David McDuff, Penguin Books, 1991.

Crime and Punishment. Translated by Julius Katzer, Raduga, 1989.

Crime and Punishment. Translated by Jessie Coulson, Norton Critical Edition, 3rd ed., W. W. Norton, 1975.

Crime and Punishment. Translated by Sidney Monas, Signet, 1968.

Crime and Punishment. Translated by Alexandra Kropotkin, The Literary Guild of America, 1953.

Crime and Punishment. Translated by David Magarshack, Penguin Books, 1951.

Crime and Punishment. Translated by Constance Garnett, Modern Library, 1950.

Crime and Punishment. Translated by Frederick Whishaw, Simpkin, Marshall and Co., 1911.

Diary entry. Jan. 1881. Dostoevsky, *Polnoe sobranie sochinenii*, vol. 27, p. 65.

Dostoevsky: The Notebooks for Crime and Punishment. Edited and translated by Edward Wasiolek, U of Chicago P, 1967.

The Idiot. Translated by Richard Pevear and Larissa Volokhonsky, Vintage Books, 2003.

Letter to Mikhail Mikhailovich Dostoevsky. 9 Aug. 1838. Dostoevsky, *Polnoe sobranie sochinenii*, vol. 27, pp. 49–51.

Letter to M. N. Katkov. Sept. 1865. Translated by Michael R. Katz. Dostoevsky, *Crime* [2019], p. 390.

Letter to Nikolai Strakhov. 26 February 1869. Dostoevsky, *Polnoe sobranie sochinenii*, vol. 29, bk. 1, p. 19.

Notes from the House of the Dead. Translated by Constance Garnett, Dover Publications, 2004.

Notes from Underground. Translated by Michael R. Katz, W. W. Norton, 2001.

Полное собрание сочинений в тридцати томах [*Polnoe sobranie sochinenii v tridtsati tomakh*]. Edited by V. G. Bazanov et al., Nauka, 1972–90. 30 vols.

Преступление и наказание [*Prestuplenie i nakazanie*]. Edited by L. D. Gromova and G. F. Kogan, Nauka, 1970.

Преступление и наказание [*Prestuplenie i nakazanie*]. Nauka, 1973. Vol. 6 of Dostoevsky, *Polnoe sobranie sochinenii*.

The Selected Letters of Fyodor Dostoevsky. Edited by Joseph Frank and David Goldstein, translated by Andrew MacAndrew, Rutgers UP, 1987.

"Three Tales of Edgar Poe." 1861. *Dostoevsky's Complete Works*, vol. 22, Bobbs–Merrill, 1974, p. 230.

A Writer's Diary. Translated by Kenneth Lantz, Northwestern UP, 1993.

Critical, Literary, and Pedagogical Sources

Ambrose, Susan A., et al. *How Learning Works: Seven Research-Based Principles for Smart Teaching*. Jossey-Bass, 2010.

Anderson, Lorin W., and David R. Krathwohl, editors. *A Taxonomy for Learning, Teaching, and Assessing: A Revision of Bloom's Taxonomy of Educational Objectives*. Pearson, 2014.

Antsiferov, N. P. Петербург Достоевского [*Peterburg Dostoevskogo*]. Непостижимый город . . . [*Nepostizhimyi gorod . . .*], by Antsiferov, Lenizdat, 1991, pp. 177–257.

Apollonio, Carol. *Dostoevsky's Secrets: Reading against the Grain*. Northwestern UP, 2011.

———, editor. *The New Russian Dostoevsky: Readings for the Twenty-First Century*. Slavica, 2010.

Armstrong, Brian. "On Golyadkin, Raskolnikov, and the Search for Empathy." *The Bloggers Karamazov*, North American Dostoevsky Society, July 15, 2016, bloggerskaramazov.com/2016/07/15/tweeting-part-four/.

Arutiunova, N. D. "Феномен молчания" ["Fenomen molchaniia"]. Язык о языке [*Iazyk o iazyke*], edited by Arutiunova, Litres, 2018, pp. 417–36.

Atwood, Margaret. *Alias Grace*. Random House, 1997.

Babitskaya, Varvara. "Life of Archpriest Avvakum." *Shelf*, 2018, polka.academy/articles/506.

Baer, Brian James. *Translation and the Making of Modern Russian Literature*. Bloomsbury, 2016.

Bakhtin, Mikhail. *Problems of Dostoevsky's Poetics*. 1929. Translated by Caryl Emerson, U of Minnesota P, 1984.

Balzac, Honoré de. *Père Goriot*. Translated by Marion Ayton Crawford, Penguin Books, 1981.

Barkley, Elizabeth F., et al. *Collaborative Learning Techniques*. Jossey-Bass, 2014.

Bayley, John. "Mr. Know-all." *The New York Review of Books*, 24 Nov. 1988.

Belinsky, V. G. "Взгляд на русскую литературу 1847 года" ["Vzgliad na russkuiu literaturu 1847 goda"]. *Современник* [*Sovremennik*], vol. 7, no. 1, sec. 3, 1847, pp. 1–39.

Belknap, Robert L. *Plots*. Columbia UP, 2016.

Bentham, Jeremy. *The Principles of Morals and Legislation*. Prometheus Books, 1988.

Berman, Anna A. *Siblings in Tolstoy and Dostoevsky. The Path to Universal Brotherhood*. Northwestern UP, 2015.

Bernofsky, Susan. "Workshop: An Introduction to Literary Translation." 19 Oct. 2018, Portland State U.

The Bible. New International Version, Biblica, 1973.

The Bible. New Revised Standard Version, National Council of Churches, 1989.

Библия. Книги Священного Писания Ветхого и Нового Завета в русском переводе с приложениями [*Bibliia. Knigi Sviashchennogo Pisaniia Vetkhogo i Novogo Zaveta v russkom perevode s prilozheniiami*]. 4th ed., Life with God, 1989.

Billington, Michael. "Dramatists Should Take a Leaf out of Dostoevsky's Book." *The Guardian*, 7 Nov. 2007, theguardian.com/stage/theatreblog/2008/nov/07/dostoevsky-delirium-theatre-adaptations.

Blake, Elizabeth. "Sonya, Silent No More: A Response to the Woman Question in Dostoevsky's *Crime and Punishment*." *The Slavic and East European Journal*, vol. 50, no. 2, 2006, pp. 252–71.

Bocharov, Sergey. "Conversations with Bakhtin." 1993. Translated by Vadim Liapunov, *PMLA*, vol. 109, no. 5, October 1994, pp. 1009–24.

Bowers, Katherine. "DSC #6: Voyant's Big Day." *The Data-Sitters Club*, 15 Sept. 2020, datasittersclub.github.io/site/dsc6.html.

———. "Introducing @RodionTweets: Translating Raskolnikov into 140 Characters or Less." *Bloggers Karamazov*, 5 July 2016, bloggerskaramazov.com/2016/07/05/rodiontweets-intro/.

———. "Raskolnikov in the Fog: Time and the *Crime and Punishment* End Game," *The Bloggers Karamazov*, North American Dostoevsky Society, 17 July 2016, bloggerskaramazov.com/2016/07/17/tweeting-part-six/.

———. "@RodionTweets." *Crime and Punishment at 150*, blogs.ubc.ca/cp150/digital-outreach/rodiontweets.

———. "Twitterature in the Dostoevsky Classroom." *Bloggers Karamazov*, 24 Apr. 2019, bloggerskaramazov.com/2019/04/24/twitterature-in-the-dostoevsky-classroom/.

Bowers, Katherine, and Kristina McGuirk, editors. "@YakovGolyadkin." By Fyodor Dostoevsky, translated by Brian Armstrong and Constance Garnett, *Humanities Commons*, 2015, https://doi.org/10.17613/M67S20.

Bowers, Katherine, et al., editors. *A Dostoevskii Companion: Texts and Contexts.* Academic Studies Press, 2018.

Bowers, Katherine, et al., editors. "@RodionTweets, Parts 4–6 + Epilogues." By Fyodor Dostoevsky, translated by Oliver Ready, *Humanities Commons*, 2018, https://doi.org/10.17613/M6VD6P45S.

———. "@RodionTweets, Prologue + Parts 1–3." By Fyodor Dostoevsky, translated by Oliver Ready, *Humanities Commons*, 2018, https://doi.org/10.17613/M6028PC8X.

Breger, Louis. *Dostoevsky: The Author as Psychoanalyst.* New York UP, 1989.

Bresson, Robert, director. *Pickpocket.* Criterion, 1959.

Brookfield, Stephen D., and Presskill, Stephen. *Discussion as a Way of Teaching: Tools and Techniques for Democratic Classrooms.* Jossey-Bass, 2005.

Brown, Archie, et al. *The Cambridge Encyclopedia of Russia and the Soviet Union.* Cambridge UP, 1981.

Burnett, Leon. "Fedor Dostoevskii." *The Encyclopedia of Literary Translation*, edited by Olive Classe, vol. 1, Routledge, 2000, pp. 365–71.

Camus, Albert. "Dostoïevski, prophete du XXe siècle." *Spectacles*, no 1, March 1958, p. 5.

———. *The Stranger.* Translated by Matthew Ward, Vintage Books, 1989.

Catteau, Jacques. *La création littéraire chez Dostoievski.* Institut d'études slaves, 1978.

Chapple, Richard. *A Dostoevsky Dictionary.* Ardis, 1983.

Cixous, Hélène, and Catherine Clément. *The Newly Born Woman.* Translated by Betsy Wing, U of Minnesota P, 1986. Theory and History of Literature 24.

Cook-Sather, Alison. *Education Is Translation: A Metaphor for Change in Learning and Teaching.* U of Pennsylvania P, 2006.

Corrigan, Yuri. *Dostoevsky and the Riddle of the Self.* Northwestern UP, 2017.

———. "Dostoevsky on Evil as Safe Haven and Anesthetic." *Slavic and East European Journal*, vol. 63, no. 2, summer 2019, pp. 226–43.

———. "Nihilism as Refuge: Rethinking the Philosophical Dostoevsky." ASEEES Annual Convention, Dec. 2018, Boston, MA.

"Course:RUSS412/Dostowiki." *University of British Columbia, 26 Aug. 2019, wiki.ubc.ca/Course:RUSS412/Dostowiki.*

Crime and Punishment at 150. University of Cambridge, 2016, exhibitions.lib.cam.ac.uk/crimeandpunishment/.

Dal, Vladimir. "Petersburg Yardkeeper." Nekrasov, *Petersburg*, pp. 57–70.

Damrosch, David. *What Is World Literature?* Princeton UP, 2003.

Dead to Me. Showtime, 2019.

Dexter. Showtime, 2006–13.

Dodd, W. J. *Kafka and Dostoevsky: The Shaping of Influence.* Palgrave, 1992.

Edgerton, Adam Kirk. "What's Wrong with Being from the South? Just Ask an Academic in the North." *The Chronicle of Higher Education*, 25 May 2018, chronicle.com/article/whats-wrong-with-being-from/243510.

Elets, Iu. L. "Биография Всеволода Владимировича Крестовского" ["Biografiia Vsevoloda Vladimirovicha Krestovskogo"]. Собрание сочинений Всеволода Владимировича Крестовского [*Sobranie sochinenii Vsevoloda Vladimirovicha Krestovskogo*], vol. 1, Obshchestvennaia pol'za, 1899–1900, pp. iii–lv.

Epstein, Mikhail. Слово и молчание: Метафизика русской литературы [*Slovo i molchanie: Metafizika russkoi literatury*]. Vysshaia shkola, 2006.

Felman, Shoshana. "To Open the Question." *Literature and Psychoanalysis: The Question of Reading: Otherwise*, edited by Felman, Johns Hopkins UP, 1982.

Frank, Joseph. *Dostoevsky: The Miraculous Years, 1865–1871*. Princeton UP, 1995.

———. *Dostoevsky: The Seeds of Revolt,* 1821–1849. Princeton UP, 1977.

———. *Dostoevsky: A Writer in His Time*. Princeton UP, 2012.

Frederick, Peter. "The Dreaded Discussion: Ten Ways to Start." *Classroom Communication: Collected Readings for Effective Discussion and Questioning*, edited by Rose Ann Neff and Maryellen Weimer, Magna Publishing, 1989, pp. 1–10.

Freire, Paulo. *Pedagogy of the Oppressed*. Continuum, 1970.

Frenzel, Fabian, et al., editors. *Slum Tourism: Poverty, Power, and Ethics*. Routledge, 2012.

Freud, Sigmund. "Dostoevsky and Parricide." *Writings on Art and Literature,* translated by James Strachey, Stanford UP, 1997.

———. "Some Character Types Met with in Psychoanalytic Work." *The Standard Edition of the Complete Psychological Works of Sigmund Freud*, vol. 14, Hogarth Press, 1914–16.

Frye, Northrop. *Fearful Symmetry*. Princeton UP, 1957.

García, Benamí Barros. "Las aportaciones de la visualización del texto al estudio del texto literario." *Tonos Digital*, no. 28, 2015, tonosdigital.es/ojs/index.php/tonos/article/view/1210/738.

Gilligan, Carol. *In a Different Voice*. Harvard UP, 1982.

Gogol, Nikolai. *The Overcoat and Other Tales of Good and Evil*. Translated by David Magarshak, W. W. Norton, 1965.

Goldrick-Rab, Sara. *Paying the Price: College Costs, Financial Aid, and the Betrayal of the American Dream*. U of Chicago P, 2016.

Goodwin, Renee D., et al. "Trends in Anxiety among Adults in the United States, 2008–2018: Rapid Increases among Young Adults." *Journal of Psychiatric Research*, vol. 130, 2020, pp. 441–46.

Gorski, Paul. "Equity Literacy for Educators: Definition and Abilities". *EdChange*, 26 Nov. 2017, edchange.org/handouts/Equity-Literacy-Introduction.pdf.

———. *Reaching and Teaching Students in Poverty*. Teachers College Press, 2018.

Gottlieb, Karla, and Gail Robinson, editors. *A Practical Guide for Integrating Civic Responsibility into the Curriculum*. 2nd ed., Community College Press, 2006.

Grigorovich, Dmitry. "The Petersburg Organ-Grinders." Nekrasov, *Petersburg*, pp. 71–100.

Grossman, Leonid. *Balzac and Dostoevsky*. Translated by Lena Karpov, Ardis, 1973.

Herman, Jennifer H., and Linda B. Nilson, editors. *Creating Engaging Discussions: Strategies for "Avoiding Crickets" in Any Size Classroom and Online*. Stylus Publishers, 2017.

Hingley, Ronald. *Russian Writers and Society 1825–1904*. U of Michigan P, 1967.

Holland, Kate. "Rethinking the Narrative Structure of *Crime and Punishment* through *Twitter*." *The Bloggers Karamazov*, North American Dostoevsky Society, 14 July 2016, bloggerskaramazov.com/2016/07/14/tweeting-part-three/.

Holquist, Michael. *Dostoevsky and the Novel*. Northwestern UP, 1986.

Howard, Jay. *Discussion in the College Classroom: Getting Your Students Engaged and Participating in Person and Online*. Wiley and Sons, 2015.

Hudspith, Sarah. "On Tweeting Part One of *Crime and Punishment*." *The Bloggers Karamazov*, North American Dostoevsky Society, 7 July 2016, bloggerskaramazov.com/2016/07/07/tweeting-part-one/.

Hunt, Joel. "Balzac and Dostoevsky: Ethics and Eschatology." *Slavic and East European Journal*, no. 26, 1958, pp. 307–24.

Hutcheon, Linda, with Siobhan O'Flynn. *A Theory of Adaptation*. Routledge, 2012.

Ivanov, V. I. "Достоевский и роман-трагедия" ["Dostoevskii i roman–tragediia"]. Собрание сочинений [*Sobranie sochinenii*], edited by D. V. Ivanov and O. Deshart, vol. 4, Foyer Oriental Chrétien, 1971, pp. 399–435.

Izmirlieva, Valentina. "Hosting the Divine Logos: Radical Hospitality and Dostoevsky's *Crime and Punishment*." *The Routledge Companion to Literature and Religion*, edited by Mark Knight, Routledge, 2016, pp. 277–88.

Jackson, Robert Louis. "Bakhtin's Poetics of Dostoevsky and 'Dostoevsky's Christian Declaration of Faith.'" *Close Encounters: Essays on Russian Literature*, Academic Studies Press, 2013, pp. 277–304.

Jacomy, M., et al. "ForceAtlas 2, a Continuous Graph Layout Algorithm for Handy Network Visualization Designed for the Gephi Software." *PLOS One*, vol. 9, no. 6, June 2014, pp. 1–12.

Jagoda, P. *Network Aesthetics*. U of Chicago P, 2016.

James, Henry. Preface. *The Tragic Muse*, by James, vol. 1, Macmillan, 1908, pp. v–xxii.

Jens, Benjamin. "Silence and Confession in *The Brothers Karamazov*." *The Russian Review*, vol. 75, no. 1, 2016, pp. 51–66.

Jensen, Eric. *Teaching with Poverty in Mind: What Being Poor Does to Kids' Brains and What Schools Can Do About It*. Association for Supervision and Curriculum Development, 2009.

Jones, Malcolm. *Dostoevsky and the Dynamics of Religious Experience*. Anthem Press, 2005.

Kafka, Franz. *The Trial*. Translated by Breon Mitchell, Schocken Books, 1998.

Kant, Immanuel. *Ethical Philosophy: The Complete Texts of Grounding for the Metaphysics of Morals, and Metaphysical Principles of Virtue, Part II of The Metaphysics of Morals, with On a Supposed Right to Lie Because of Philanthropic Concerns*. Hackett Publishing Company, 1983.

Katz, Michael R. *Dreams and the Unconscious in Nineteenth-Century Russian Fiction*. UP of New England, 1984.

Kaurismäki, Aki, director. *Rikos ja rangaistus*. Finnkino, 1983.

Kirillova, Irina. "Dostoevsky's Markings in the *Gospel According to St. John*." *Dostoevsky and the Christian Tradition*, edited by George Pattison and Dianne Oenning Thompson, Cambridge UP, 2001, pp. 41–50.

Kjetsaa, Geir. *Dostoevsky and His New Testament*. Solum Verlag, 1984.

———. *Fyodor Dostoevsky: A Writer's Life*. Viking Penguin, 1987.

Klioutchkine, Konstantine. "The Rise of *Crime and Punishment* from the Air of the Media." *Slavic Review*, vol. 61, no. 1, spring 2002, pp. 88–98.

Konechnyi, Al'bin. "Петербургские общедоступные увеселительные сады в XIX веке" ["Peterburgskie obshchedostupnye uveselitel'nye sady v XIX veke"]. *Europa Orientalis*, vol. 15, no. 1, pp. 37–50.

Konechnyi, A. M., and K. A. Kumpan. "Петербург в жизни и трудах Н.П. Анциферова" ["Peterburg v zhizni i trudakh N. P. Antsiferova"]. Antsiferov, pp. 5–23.

Koven, Seth. *Slumming: Sexual and Social Politics in Victorian London*. Princeton UP, 2004.

Kozhinov, Vadim. "The First Sentence in *Crime and Punishment*, the Word 'Crime,' and Other Matters." Translated by Robert Louis Jackson. Dostoevsky, *Crime* [2019], pp. 417–24.

Krestovsky, Vsevolod. Петербургские трущобы [*Peterburgskie trushchoby]. Художественная литература [Khudozhestvennaia literatura]*, 1993. 2 vols.

Kulidzhanov, Lev, director. Преступление и наказание [*Prestuplenie i nakazanie]*. Gorky Film Studio, 1969.

Kumpan, K. A., and A. M. Konechnyi. "Наблюдения над топографией «Преступление и наказание»" ["Nabliudeniia nad topografiei 'Prestuplenie i nakanzanie'"]. Известия Академии наук: Серия литературы и языка [*Izvestiia Akademii nauk: Seriia literatury i iazyka*], no. 2, 1976, pp. 180–90.

Lacan, Jacques. *Formations of the Unconscious: The Seminar of Jacques Lacan, Book V*. Edited by Jacques-Alain Miller, translated by Russell Grigg, Polity, 2017.

———. *The Seminar of Jacques Lacan, Book II: The Ego in Freud's Theory and in the Technique of Psychoanalysis*. Edited by Jacques-Alain Miller, translated by Sylvana Tomaselli, Cambridge UP, 1988.

———. *The Seminar of Jacques Lacan, Book XI: The Four Fundamental Concepts of Psychoanalysis*. Edited by Jacques-Alain Miller, translated by Alan Sheridan, W. W. Norton, 1977.

Lantz, K. A. *The Dostoevsky Encyclopedia*. Greenwood, 2004.

Lary, N. M. *Dostoevsky and Soviet Film: Visions of Demonic Realism*. Cornell UP, 1986.

Leatherbarrow, W. J. *Fyodor Dostoevsky:* The Brothers Karamazov. Cambridge UP, 1992.

Levin, John, and Sarah J. Young. "Mapping Machines: Transformations of the Petersburg Text." *Primerjalna književnost*, vol. 36, no. 2, 2013, pp. 151–61.

Levine, C. *Forms: Whole, Rhythm, Hierarchy, Network*. Princeton UP, 2015.

Lipton, Peter. *Inference to the Best Explanation*. Routledge, 1991.

Maier, Carol. "Choosing and Introducing a Translation." *Literature in Translation: Teaching Issues and Reading Practices*, edited by Carol Maier and Françoise Massardier-Kenney, Kent State UP, 2011, pp. 11–21.

Marrese, Michelle Lamarch. *A Woman's Kingdom: Noblewomen and the Control of Property in Russia, 1700–1861*. Cornell UP, 2002.

Martinsen, Deborah A. "Getting Away with Murder: Teaching *Crime and Punishment*." *Teaching Nineteenth-Century Russian Literature: Essays in Honor of Robert L. Belknap*, edited by Deborah Martinsen et al., Academic Studies Press, 2014, pp. 162–74.

Martinsen, Deborah A., and Olga Maiorova, editors. *Dostoevsky in Context*. Cambridge UP, 2015.

May, Rachel. *The Translator in the Text*. Northwestern UP, 1994.

Mearns, A. *The Bitter Cry of Outcast London: An Inquiry into the Condition of the Abject Poor*. James Clarke, 1883.

Meerson, Olga. "Библейские интертексты у Достоевского. Кощунство или богословие любви" ["Bibleiskie interteksty u Dostoevskogo. Koshchunstvo ili bogoslovie liubvi]." Достоевский и мировая культура [*Dostoevskii i mirovaia kul'tura*], vol. 12 1999, pp. 40–53.

———. "Библейские подтексты у Достоевского как арбитры при толковании спорных мест" ["Bibleiskie podteksty u Dostoevskogo kak arbitury pri tolkovanii spornykh mest"]. Достоевский и мировая культура [*Dostoevskii i mirovaia kul'tura*], 2019, no. 37, pp. 34–51k, dostmirkult.ru/images/DOST_2019-37-int-A-35-52.pdf.

———. *Dostoevsky's Taboos*. Dresden UP, 1998.

———. "Ivolgin and Holbein: Non-Christ Risen vs. Christ Non-Risen." *The Slavic and East European Journal*, vol. 39, no. 2, summer 1995, pp. 200–13.

———. Персонализм как поэтика. Литературный мир глазами его обитателей [*Personalizm kak poetika. Literaturnyi mir glazami ego obitatelei*]. Izdatel'stvo Pushkinskii dom, 2009.

———. "Raskolnikov and the Aqedah (Isaac's Binding)." *Dostoevsky beyond Dostoevsky*, edited by Svetlana Evdokimova and Vladimir Golstein, Academic Studies Press, 2016, pp. 379–93.

———. "Скелетом наружу: система интертекстов как структура произведения вне его. Мотив трагедии 'падшей' женщины в 'Идиоте'" ["Skeletom naruzhu: sistema intertekstov kak struktura proizvedeniia vne ego. Motiv tragedii 'padshei' zhenshchiny v 'Idiote'"]. Достоевский и мировая культура [*Dostoevskii i mirovaia kul'tura*], vol. 23, 2007, pp. 85–106.

Merezhkovsky, D. S. Л. Толстой и Достоевский [*L. Tolstoy i Dostoevsky*]. Nauka, 2000.

Meyer, Priscilla. *How the Russians Read the French: Lermontov, Dostoevsky, Tolstoy*. U of Wisconsin P, 2008.

Michelet, Jules. *L'amour*. Vol. 34 of *Oeuvres complètes, édition définitive*, Paris, 1893–99.

Miller, Robin Feuer. *Dostoevsky's Unfinished Journey*. Yale UP, 2007.

Mironov, Boris N. "The Development of Literacy in Russia and the USSR from the Tenth to the Twentieth Centuries." *History of Education Quarterly*, vol. 31, no. 2, summer 1991, pp. 229–52.

Mochulsky, Konstantin. *Dostoevsky: His Life and Work*. Princeton UP, 1967.

Moretti, F. *Distant Reading*. Verso, 2013.

———. "Network Theory, Plot Analysis." *Stanford Literary Lab*, litlab.stanford.edu/pamphlets/.

Morrison, Toni. *Beloved*. 1987. Vintage Books, 2004.

Mthethwa-Sommers, Shirley. "Pedagogical Possibilities: Lessons from Social Justice Educators." *Journal of Transformative Education*, vol. 10, no. 4, 2013, pp. 219–35.

Nabokov, Vladimir. "Fyodor Dostoevski." *Lectures on Russian Literature*, by Nabokov, Houghton Mifflin Harcourt, 1981, pp. 97–109.

———. "Good Readers and Good Writers." *Lectures on Literature*, by Nabokov, edited by F. Bowers, Harvest Books, 1980, pp. 1–6.

Nekrasov, Nikolai. Избранные произведения [*Izbrannye proizvedeniia*]. Khudlit., 1985.

———. "The Petersburg Corners." Nekrasov, *Petersburg*, pp. 131–57.

———, editor. *Petersburg: The Physiology of a City*. Translated and introduced by Thomas Gaiton Marullo, Northwestern UP, 2009.

Newlin, G. *Everyone in Dickens*. Greenwood Press, 1995.

Newman, M. "The Structure and Function of Complex Networks," *SIAM Review*, vol. 45, no. 2, 2003, pp. 167–256.

Newman, M., et al. *The Structure and Dynamics of Networks*. Princeton UP, 2006.

Nieto, Sonia, and Patricia Bode. *Affirming Diversity: The Sociopolitical Context of Multicultural Education*. 6th ed., Pearson, 2012.

Noddings, Nel. *Caring: A Feminist Approach to Ethics and Moral Education*. U of California P, 1984.

Omirbaev, Darezhan, director. Студент [*Stýdent*]. Global Lens, 2012.

Orr, S. Ceilidh. "Stealing the Scene: Crime as Confession in Robert Bresson's *Pickpocket*." *Border Crossing: Russian Literature into Film*, edited by Alexander Burry and Frederick H. White. Edinburgh UP, 2016. 85–101.

"Петербург Достоевского" ["Peterburg Dostoevskogo"]. Музей Достоевского [*Muzei Dostoevskogo*], md.spb.ru/dostoevskij/peterburg_dostoevskogo. Accessed 5 June 2021.

Pisarev, D. I. "Борьба за жизнь" ["Bor'ba za zhizn'"]. 1867. Lib.ru/Классика [*Libr.ru/Classica*], 2012, az.lib.ru/p/pisarew_d/text_0200.shtml.

———. "A Contemporary View: 1867." Crime and Punishment *and the Critics*, edited by Edward Wasiolek, Wadsworth, 1961, pp. 134–42.

Poe, Edgar Allan. "The Imp of the Perverse." Poe, *The Portable Edgar Allan Poe*, pp. 202–07.

———. *The Portable Edgar Allan Poe*. Edited by J. Gerald Kennedy, Penguin Books, 2006.

———. "The Tell-Tale Heart." Poe, *The Portable Edgar Allan Poe*, pp. 187–91.

Proudhon, Pierre-Joseph. *La justice*. Vol. 8 of *Oeuvres complètes*, edited by C. Bouglé, Paris, 1923–46.

Pushkin, Alexander. *The Bronze Horseman*. Rydel, pp. 151–55.

———. "The Queen of Spades." Rydel, pp. 311–25.

Rachels, James. *The Elements of Moral Philosophy*. McGraw Hill College, 2003.

Rahv, Philip. "Dostoevsky in *Crime and Punishment*." *Partisan Review*, vol. 27, no. 33, summer 1960, pp. 393–425.

Rice, James L. *Dostoevsky and the Healing Art*. Ardis, 1985.

Rimsky-Korsakov, Nikolai. *Russian Easter Festival Overture*. 1888. Leipzig, 1890.

Roberts, Peter. "Educative Suffering? Dostoevsky as Teacher." *Review of Education, Pedagogy, and Cultural Studies*, vol. 36, no. 5, 2014, pp. 372–85.

Rydel, Christine, editor. *The Ardis Anthology of Russian Romanticism*. Ardis, 1984.

Sanders, Denis, director. *Crime and Punishment, U.S.A.* Allied Artists, 1959.

Schmidt, Rob, director. *Crime and Punishment in Suburbia*. MGM, 2000.

Seppälä, Jaakko. "Doing a Lot with a Little: The Camera's Minimalist Point of View in the Films of Aki Kaurismäki." *Journal of Scandinavian Cinema*, vol. 6, no. 1, 2016, pp. 5–22.

Skorohodova, Elena, et al. "Reflection of Social Reality in the Context of the Legal Discourse of Russian Literature: Research Specificity and Objectives." *Mediterranean Journal of Social Sciences*, vol. 6, no. 2, Sept. 2015, pp. 290–94.

Stam, Robert. "Beyond Fidelity: The Dialogics of Film Adaptation." *Film Adaptation*, edited by James Naremore, Rutgers UP, 2000, pp. 54–76.

Stilwell, Katie. *Crime and Punishment Character Map*. *Prezi*, 20 Feb. 2018, prezi.com/p/is36ouv8gfbn/crime-and-punishment-character-map/.

Stites, Richard. "M. L. Mikhailov and the Emergence of the Woman Question in Russia." *Canadian Slavic Studies*, vol. 3, no. 2, summer 1969, pp. 178–99.

———. *The Women's Liberation Movement in Russia: Feminism, Nihilism, and Bolshevism, 1860–1930*. Princeton UP, 1978.

Straus, Nina Pelikan. *Dostoevsky and the Woman Question: Rereadings at the End of a Century*. Palgrave Macmillan, 1994.

Svetozarov, Dmitry, director. Преступление и наказание [*Prestuplenie i nakazanie*]. Maramant. 2007.

Taworski, Adam. *The Power of Silence: Social and Pragmatic Perspectives*. Sage Publications, 1993.

Terras, Victor. *Handbook of Russian Literature*. Yale UP, 1990.

Tikhomirov, B. «Лазарь! Гряди вон». Роман Ф.М. Достоевского «Преступление и наказание» в современном прочтении [*'Lazar'! Griadi von': Roman F.M. Dostoevskogo 'Prestuplenie i nakazanie' v sovremennom prochtenii*]. Serebrianyi vek, 2005.

Todd, William Mills, III. "Dostoevskii as a Professional Writer." *The Cambridge Companion to Dostoevskii*, edited by W. J. Leatherbarrow, Cambridge UP, 2002, pp. 66–92.

Tolstoy, Leo. "Why Do Men Stupefy Themselves?" *Recollections and Essays*, translated by Aylmer Maude, Oxford UP, 1961, pp. 67–89.

Toporov, V. N. "О структуре романа Достоевского в связи с архаичными схемами мифологического мышления" ["O strukture romana Dostoevskogo v sviazi s arkhaichnymi skhemami mifologicheskogo myshleniia]." *The Structure of Texts and Semiotics of Culture*, edited by Jan van der Eng, Mouton, 1973, pp. 255–302.

Tucker, Janet G. *Profane Challenge and Orthodox Response in Dostoevsky's* Crime and Punishment. Rodopi, 2008.

Ur, Penny. *Discussions That Work: Task-Centred Fluency Practice.* Cambridge UP, 1991.

Utechin, S. V. *Concise Encyclopedia of Russia.* Dutton, 1964.

von Sternberg, Josef, director. *Crime and Punishment.* Columbia Pictures, 1935.

"Wiki." *Wikipedia: The Free Encyclopedia*, Wikimedia Foundation, 18 May 2021, en.wikipedia.org/wiki/Wiki.

"Wikipedia: Student Assignments." *Wikipedia: The Free Encyclopedia*, Wikimedia Foundation, 18 May 2021, en.wikipedia.org/wiki/Wikipedia:Student_assignments.

Williams, Rowan. *Language, Faith, and Fiction: Dostoevsky.* Baylor UP, 2011.

Wilson, Jennifer. "Regarding the Pain of Others: Tweeting Part Five of *Crime and Punishment*." *The Bloggers Karamazov*, North American Dostoevsky Society, 16 July 16 2016, bloggerskaramazov.com/2016/07/16/tweeting-part-five/.

Woolf, Virginia. "The Russian Point of View." *The Essays of Virginia Woolf*, edited by Andrew McNellie, vol. 4, Hogarth Press, 1986–94, pp. 181–89.

Young, Sarah J. "On Tweeting Part Two of *Crime and Punishment*." *The Bloggers Karamazov*, North American Dostoevsky Society, 10 July 2016, bloggerskaramazov.com/2016/07/10/tweeting-part-two/.

Young, Sarah J., and John Levin. "Mapping Dostoevsky." *Mapping St Petersburg: Experiments in Literary Cartography*, 21 Jan. 2012, mappingpetersburg.org/site/?page_id=494.